Feelin'
Alright

Feelin' Alright

HOW THE MESSAGE IN THE MUSIC CAN MAKE HEALTHCARE HEALTHIER

Stephen K. Klasko, MD, MBA
with Ken Terry

ACHE Management Series

Library of Congress Cataloging-in-Publication Data is on file at the Library of Congress, Washington, DC.

ISBN: 978-1-64055-377-4

The paper used in this publication meets the minimum requirements of American National Standard for Information Sciences—Permanence of Paper for Printed Library Materials, ANSI Z39.48-1984. ∞ ™

Acquisitions editor: Molly Lowe; Manuscript editor: DeAnna Burghart; Cover designer: James Slate; Layout: PerfectType

Found an error or a typo? We want to know! Please e-mail it to hapbooks@ache.org, mentioning the book's title and putting "Book Error" in the subject line.

For photocopying and copyright information, please contact Copyright Clearance Center at www.copyright.com or at (978) 750-8400.

Health Administration Press
A division of the Foundation of the
   American College of Healthcare Executives
300 S. Riverside Plaza, Suite 1900
Chicago, IL 60606-6698
(312) 424-2800

To my patients . . .
Thank you for the honor of being part of
your families' new beginnings.

To my students . . .
Thank you for all that you have taught me.

To my mentees . . .
You often thank me for my time, but for me it is an
investment. The return is that you get it right and
continue to believe in doing the "impossible."

If you hit a wrong note, it's the next note that you play that determines if it's good or bad.

—Jazz legend Miles Davis

The problem in American medicine is not that we aim too high and fail. It's that we aim too low and exactly hit the mark.

—Loosely paraphrasing philosophy legend Aristotle

Contents

Detailed Contents

Foreword

In their previous book, *UnHealthcare: A Manifesto for Health Assurance*, Stephen Klasko and Hemant Taneja presented a convincing vision about the opportunity to reimagine a new model for healthcare delivery that expands beyond its current focus on sick care.

About 85 percent of our health spend in the United States is related to sick care. Yet it's estimated that 75 percent of sick care patients have high comorbidity conditions that could significantly improve if all consumers, both those who are ill and those who are generally healthy, adopted better daily health routines.

In *Feelin' Alright*, Steve Klasko shares insights from his extensive experience as a healthcare executive, shaped by his insatiable curiosity and relentless search for a better way to do things in healthcare.

In eight years, Steve Klasko built Jefferson Health from a three-hospital system to an 18-hospital health system that employs 35,000 full-time workers. He merged a health science university with a top-ten design university to reimagine the design of the human experience in healthcare, opened up new points of care in underserved neighborhoods through the collaborative for health equity, and radically collaborated to establish health hubs at retail locations. He built and ran Jefferson Health like he was building a Silicon Valley start-up while putting into practice many of the principles of health assurance described in this book. And he saw how the results changed lives as well as balance sheets. Along the way, he has advised some of the best high-tech entrepreneurs from Silicon Valley, helping them learn about the complexities of healthcare delivery while he learns about the incredible breakthroughs in digital data science, machine learning, and AI that will shape a new era in the industry.

This is a textbook example of transformational leadership.

My first encounter with transformational leadership was as president of PepsiCo. When I was first appointed head of marketing, Coca-Cola outsold Pepsi by about ten-to-one in most of the United States. We had a big idea then: If you can positively change the consumer *perception* of a company's or product's identity, you can change the *reality*—even the dominance of a much larger and more powerful competitor.

So we started a marketing campaign called the Pepsi Challenge that focused on Coca-Cola drinkers, most of whom had never even tasted a Pepsi. We set up taste-test tables in shopping centers, at community colleges, at sports events, and at county fairs, market by market, all across the United States. Many thousands of consumers across America sampled both colas from unmarked cups, because they were just plain curious. To their surprise, typically more than half of Coke drinkers chose Pepsi! We suspected that if we had used branded cups a very wide majority of these surprised consumers would probably have chosen Coke. That was the power of the Coca-Cola brand. Perception leads reality.

We wanted to make meaningful changes in how consumers perceived the Pepsi brand, so we focused first on price. In the 1970s, Coca-Cola was sold in small six-ounce returnable glass bottles. We developed a more modern Pepsi bottle—the first large-size plastic bottle for carbonated soft drinks—enabling us to offer a lower price per ounce. Consumers loved our "value pack," and Pepsi's market share grew rapidly. The Coca-Cola Company believed they were so much larger than PepsiCo that they took several years to effectively respond to this change. By the time they did, we had become a huge growth company, and in just a few years Pepsi passed Coke in the "cola wars" to become the largest selling consumer packaged good in America.

The perception of Pepsi's success became the new reality.

We adopted the same strategy when I became the CEO of Apple, focusing on changing perception first, and it worked beautifully.

Steve's unconventional leadership style and the culture he built at Jefferson Health have changed the perception that healthcare can't innovate its way out of its traditional high costs and focus on sick care. In *Feelin' Alright* he explains how the power to change perceptions works best when a leader focuses on the consumer's experience. He encourages more empathy to help consumers make behavioral changes and suggests new ways to pivot health professionals to using real-time personalized data captured by wearable sensors, ambient room sensors, even health sensors in automobiles. He uses creativity, flexibility, teamwork, innovation, and cooperation, not competition, as the engine for a perception transformation plan. Jefferson created the perception in Philadelphia of a health system as an innovative caregiver focused on healthy consumers as well as sick patients. It's a reimagination of healthcare delivery.

I have long been a fan of Sandy Pentland, PhD, who directs MIT's human dynamics laboratory. Dr. Pentland explains how machine learning and AI data are such powerful constructs that they will expand our concept of free market economics. Adam Smith correctly understood in 1776 that free enterprise markets and competition drive growth and innovation. Now Dr. Pentland has additional evidence that collaboration exchanges can be an even more powerful force than competition alone.

Our modern Internet of Things is composed of inexpensive sensors numbering in the millions, rapidly growing to billions, touching almost every aspect of our lives. In healthcare, these sensors can be designed to inexpensively track consumer health and health-related behavior. They can support remote patient monitoring for sick care and track routine indicators for healthy people, such as medication compliance, nutrition, weight, exercise, sleep, and stress and anxiety.

This data generation capability can lead to new first principles for a networked society, where privacy-assured individual health data secured by blockchain, together with anonymized population health data, can be interpreted with the aid of machine learning and AI.

Cooperating data exchange networks will become a building block for future health coaching and modernized, more efficient healthcare delivery systems. Markets used to be defined by geographical boundaries. In the digital health era, we can think of a market of one person that scales to millions of markets of one person—healthcare at any address.

Becoming a successful change agent isn't easy.

When I first met Steve Jobs in 1982, many engineers in Silicon Valley mocked him and what they considered his ridiculous vision for the Macintosh computer by saying he was living in a reality distortion field. He had never personally led the development of a new computer. Traditional computer engineers who had experience designing systems were confident the future would be cheaper, faster, better number crunching machines. Silicon Valley roundly rejected the idea of a huge market for a desktop publishing machine for consumers, most of whom had no previous experience owning or using a computer. Did I mention that the average age of the Macintosh design and engineering team was just 22? Several of them were entirely self-taught.

But Steve Jobs believed that personal computing should be a tool for the mind, and incredibly easy to use. So Jobs borrowed from the best ideas he could find. He personally oversaw every detail of the Macintosh design, which was inspired by the Sony Walkman's beautiful industrial design and attention to every hardware detail. In fact, many of the Mac's hardware components were designed by and sourced from Sony. The point, copy, click, and paste user interface technology was inspired by Xerox's famed Palo Alto Research Center. Conceptually, the Mac was all about empowering nontechnical users to exploit their own creativity to do tasks such as publishing and printing right from their own desktop. Jobs had no interest in building a number crunching machine.

Twenty years later, it was obvious to the entire world that his vision had been spot on.

Like Steve Jobs, Steve Klasko is a visionary—a health industry leader who believes in using smart teams, adaptable culture, flexibility, and creative problem-solving to shift perceptions in and of the industry. *Feelin' Alright* explains how healthcare leaders can help create a consumer-centric healthcare experience focused on health assurance, allowing more people to enjoy healthy lives as they age.

John Sculley

Foreword

IT'S TOUGH OUT there for hospital and health system leaders. The COVID adrenaline rush has ended. There's no more pandemic funding. Labor is in short supply. Supply chain and drug costs are skyrocketing. Red ink is everywhere. High-cost and often deteriorating facilities limit strategic flexibility. Worst of all, American consumers are losing faith. They fear paying medical bills more than contracting disease. How did it ever get this way? It's easy to give up and move on.

Into this dystopian mess marches Stephen Klasko with his remarkable new book, *Feelin' Alright*. Just because you're deadly serious about healthcare transformation doesn't mean you can't have some fun. In *Feelin' Alright*, Steve is a happy warrior who takes readers on a whirlwind tour of healthcare's complex and often incomprehensible landscape. Healthcare is complicated. Steve makes it accessible. He uses song lyrics from a massive playlist to explain healthcare's problems and inspire solutions. For Steve Klasko, life-long DJ, the music is the message.

The book itself is a memoir, manifesto, pep talk, policy primer, and how-to manual all rolled into a compelling and comprehensive narrative. Better yet, it lays out a cogent plan for reinventing US healthcare. Looking forward to 2035, Steve envisions universal "health assurance" through "healthcare at any address" that is "delivering kinder, smarter and affordable care for all."

The last quote is not from Steve's work; it's the subtitle of my 2019 book, *The Customer Revolution in Healthcare*. I share it to convey the philosophical and practical alignment that Steve and I bring to transforming America's bloated sick-care system. We're fellow healthcare revolutionaries. I'd jump the barricades with him anytime.

We met several years ago at a Health Management Academy conference. He was reinventing Jefferson Health System, and I was a former healthcare investment banker turned writer doing penance for my part in funding an overbuilt acute-care delivery system.

Our jujitsu idea exchange resulted in a coauthored and widely read commentary titled *A Second Coming: Medical Education's Desperate Need for Another Flexner Revolution*. I was blown away by Steve's dissection of the four biases that afflict medicine (see chapter 10 of that book) and the concrete steps he took to address them in the hiring and training of doctors at Jefferson.

The esteemed political commentator Thomas Sowell astutely observed, "When you want to help someone, you tell them the truth. When you want to help yourself, you tell them what they want to hear." In the best sense of the term, Steve Klasko is a truthteller intent on helping a dysfunctional industry help itself. But Steve does it with compassion, understanding, and encouragement. He knows and believes we can do better.

After dissecting the industry's dismal current state, *Feelin' Alright* briskly covers consumerism, AI, human-machine collaboration, population health, payment reform, performance ratings, social determinants of health, patient safety, and medical education and training. The range and breadth of the book's analysis are impressive.

While *Feelin' Alright* will resonate with all healthcare audiences, the book's title and content carry special significance for healthcare providers and administrators. These are Steve's people. He offers them not only sympathy and hope but also actionable strategies for navigating healthcare's troubled waters and building tomorrow's health system today.

Throughout, Steve is alert to the roles that disruption, private investment, technology, new competitors, breakthrough science, and proconsumer regulatory policies can and will play in transforming healthcare. In Steve's mind's eye, the industry will undergo more change in the next decade than it has in the last century. Unsustainable sick care will become affordable health care.

Steve's chapter on health inequity crackles with righteous intensity. It's my favorite. He has no tolerance for a system where people's health and well-being are more influenced by their zip codes than their genetic codes. He blames structural racism and he's right. Healthcare must work for all Americans. He amplifies these points through the lyrics of Curtis Mayfield's "Choice of Colors," which premiered in 1969:

> A better day is coming, for you and for me
> With just a little bit more education
> And love for our nation
> Would make a better society

Mayfield's words still resonate. Like healthcare today, the late 1960s was a time of massive social upheaval and change. If you catch Steve Klasko's vibe, a better healthcare day is coming for us all. I'll end with lyrics from *Get Ready* by the Temptations. They prep *Feelin' Alright's* readers for their full-on encounter with revolutionary healthcare.

> So tiddley-dee, tiddley-dum
> Look out baby, 'cause here I come
> And I'm bringing you a love that's true
> So get ready, so get ready.
> America's ready, Steve. Your country needs you.

David Johnson

Foreword

ALLOW ME TO introduce myself. My name is Jerry Blavat, born and raised in Philadelphia. I've had the good fortune in my lifetime to entertain people throughout the world with music that brings happiness to everyone regardless of race, color, creed, or orientation. I've written a book called *You Only Rock Once* that tells my life story and how my career began. Music and entertainment have always been a part of the human experience, bringing sunshine into everyone's life.

Here's something I've always known: music has healing powers.

Now, I would like to introduce my good friend, the former CEO of Jefferson Health, Steve Klasko. Our lives and work are intertwined. I make people happy by playing music and providing entertainment. Steve does the same thing through the world of medicine and healing. The passion he has shown throughout all his years in healthcare, developing new ways of saving lives through modern medicine and technology, is really no different than what I do.

We share the same passion: music for the soul that speaks where we've been, where we are, and where we should be going. You will read in this book that he shares the soul, the music, and the passion for making a change in people's lives. He does it from the healthcare side with a dash of music, and I do it from the music side, hopefully making people healthier and happier in the process.

Nowhere was that more evident than during the pandemic. I had a record number of people listening to my virtual shows, and I received thousands of e-mails and notes that those shows and that magical music helped sustain them. Steve ran the largest health system in Philadelphia, during one of the most difficult times in our history to be in healthcare, with a pandemic, a financial tsunami, and racial unrest as a backdrop, and his "radical communication" ended each week with a musical playlist that, as many of his 30,000 employees told me, helped sustain them through this difficult period. Those playlists ranged from songs like Curtis Mayfield's "Choice of Colors," about the difficult racial tensions we were dealing with, to Roberta Flack's "The First Time Ever I Saw Your Face," for people who were seeing colleagues for the first time without a mask!

For all these reasons, I love Steve Klasko and what he's done for the city we both care about. He's the man who brought the bop back to Philadelphia. He's Philly born and raised, and he learned to be a physician right here. Then he made a name for himself in other places and, like a prodigal son, came back to put the bomp, the ram, the dip into the city.

What I saw: Steve let Philadelphia and the health system he ran feel good about themselves again—like sugar and spice. People in this city need transformative leaders with creativity and passion. We need them for our kids to learn how to be professionals. We need the care it provides to all of us. And we needed Steve Klasko to give Jefferson Health his dose of optimism during his time as president and CEO.

This book has that spirit. You can see Philly Soul on every page. Healthcare and higher education face big challenges, but he's not going to let the size of the challenge stop us from winning. This is a book about solutions. If there's a message in Steve's music, it's to face the tough things and stay optimistic.

If you want to search for a brighter future in healthcare, read this book and hang out with Steve, and "You'll Never Walk Alone"!

Jerry Blavat, "The Geator with the Heater"

Playlist Index

Title	Artist	Year
Introduction		
Too Old to Rock 'n' Roll: Too Young to Die	Jethro Tull	1976
On a Carousel	The Hollies	1967
Take Time to Know Her	Percy Sledge	1968
We Are Never Ever Getting Back Together	Taylor Swift	2012
I'll Take You There	The Staple Singers	1972
The First Time Ever I Saw Your Face	Roberta Flack	1972
Hit Me With Your Best Shot	Pat Benatar	1980
Problems	The Everly Brothers	1958
Simple Solution	Nazareth	1979
Don't Be Afraid to Be Different	Logic, feat. Will Smith	2019
Don't Hang Up	The Orlons	1962
Take It to the Limit	Eagles	1975
Under Pressure	Queen, feat. David Bowie	1981
Human Touch	Bruce Springsteen	1992

Title	Artist	Year
Who Says You Can't Go Home Again	Bon Jovi, feat. Jennifer Nettles	2005
The A Team	Ed Sheeran	2011
Future Nostalgia	Dua Lipa	2020
It's Impossible	Perry Como	1970
We Can Do It	Jamiroquai	2017
Chapter 1		
Courage to Change	Sia	2020
Changes	David Bowie	1971
Waiting on the World to Change	John Mayer	2006
Chapter 2		
Keep the Customer Satisfied	Simon & Garfunkel	1970
Bridge Over Troubled Water	Simon & Garfunkel	1970
Stuck in the Middle with You	Stealers Wheel	1972
Two Different Worlds	Don Rondo	1956
Best of Both Worlds	Van Halen	1986
Future Starts Now	Kim Petras	2021
It's Time	Imagine Dragons	2011
The First Step (Is Admitting You Have a Problem)	Brother Moses	2015
Jump into the Fire	Harry Nilsson	1971
Chapter 3		
The Name Game	Shirley Ellis	1964
Should I Stay or Should I Go	The Clash	1982
Blaze of Glory	Jon Bon Jovi	1990
Feeling Myself	Nicki Minaj	2014

Title	Artist	Year
I Am What I Am	Gloria Gaynor	1984
I've Changed	Jaheim, feat. Keyshia Cole	2007
You Wear It Well	Rod Stewart	1972
Sitting on the Throne	Olamide	2013
Words	Bee Gees	1967
Chapter 4		
Mr. Roboto	Styx	1982
You Get What You Give	New Radicals	1998
Living in the Past	Jethro Tull	1969
Land of Confusion	Genesis	1986
Better Together	Jack Johnson	2005
Ironic	Alanis Morissette	1995
Chapter 5		
I Am Changing	Jennifer Hudson	2006
We Never Change	Coldplay	2000
Money for Nothing	Dire Straits	1985
You Must Be Kidding	Arcade Fire	2015
Nobody Does It Better	Carly Simon	1977
Nothing Compares 2 U	Sinéad O'Connor	1989
13 Questions	Seatrain	1970
Chapter 6		
For the Love of Money	The O'Jays	1973
Message in Our Music	The O'Jays	1976
Money Changes Everything	Cyndi Lauper	1983
I Want to Take You Higher	Sly and the Family Stone	1969

Title	Artist	Year
Two Out of Three Ain't Bad	Meat Loaf	1977
Honesty	Billy Joel	1978
The Twelfth of Never	Johnny Mathis	1957
You Never Give Me Your Money	The Beatles	1969
Mo Money Mo Problems	The Notorious B.I.G.	1997
Chapter 7		
(Simply) The Best	Tina Turner	1989
We Are the Champions	Queen	1977
It's All Wrong But It's Alright	Percy Sledge	1968
Hard to Imagine	Pearl Jam	1998
Somebody's Watching Me	Rockwell	1983
Big Brother	Stevie Wonder	1972
Peaceful Easy Feeling	Eagles	1972
Best of You	Foo Fighters	2005
Everyday People	Sly and the Family Stone	1968
Chapter 8		
Born This Way	Lady Gaga	2011
Living for the City	Stevie Wonder	1973
Paying the Cost to Be the Boss	B.B. King	1968
Babel	Mumford & Sons	2012
Radio	Beyoncé	2008
Change	Tracy Chapman	2005
Choice of Colors	The Impressions	1969
We Are Not Helpless	Stephen Stills	1971

Title	Artist	Year
Chapter 9		
An Honest Mistake	The Bravery	2005
I Don't Want to Do Wrong	Gladys Knight and the Pips	1971
Complicated	Avril Lavigne	2002
Don't Blame Me	UB40	1986
Make It Easy on Yourself	Jerry Butler	1962
Learn to Listen	Ramones	1989
There's No 'I' in Team	Taking Back Sunday	2002
Make Me Feel Better	Alex Adair	2014
The Safety Dance	Men Without Hats	1982
Chapter 10		
You Don't Learn That in School	The King Cole Trio	1946
Not Fair	Lily Allen	2009
Let Her Go	Passenger	2012
Another Brick in the Wall	Pink Floyd	1979
Epilogue		
Don't Stop Believin'	Journey	1981
The Myth of Trust	Billy Bragg	1984
Take the Long Way Home	Supertramp	1979
Invisible Connections	Vangelis	1985
Into the Groove	Madonna	1985
Breaking Free	Zac Efron, Drew Seeley, and Vanessa Hudgens	2006
Change the World	Eric Clapton	1996
So Close	Hall and Oates	1990

Introduction

"Too Old to Rock 'n' Roll: Too Young to Die" by Jethro Tull

I ALWAYS WANTED to be a DJ. In the 1960s, my brother and I created playlists and charts for WRSK (Ron and Steve Klasko). The radio station was in our living room and had two regular listeners (Ron and Steve Klasko) and occasionally a third: my father, who would yell at us to turn down the music. Even then, I realized that music could change the way you feel. For instance, the Hollies' "On a Carousel" always made me think of going to the shore in the summer. Phil Ochs made me understand that protesting was a way to initiate change, and Curtis Mayfield's "Choice of Colors" helped me understand that we had significant work to do to correct racial and gender inequities. In 1969, when I was 16 and my first girlfriend decided to leave me for an athlete, Percy Sledge's "Take Time to Know Her" was my virtual psychologist.

Fast-forward to 1974. I had just graduated from Lehigh University, and I got my first professional DJ job from midnight to 5 a.m. in Philadelphia, my hometown. The town of Dick Clark and *American Bandstand* and the legendary Jerry Blavat—the Geator with the Heater, the Boss with the Hot Sauce. I was "little Stevie Kent," partly because I was smaller than the national average at five feet seven and only 140 pounds, and my middle name is Kent. I was on my way!

My DJ dream was short-lived. I got fired from that job for not following a rule I disagreed with. So I decided to have a sit-down with my adviser at Lehigh University. Nothing like an academic adviser to bring you back to reality. "What do I do next?" I asked.

"Well, you're obviously not going to be a DJ," she said, "but you have a pretty good science GPA and you got an A in organic chemistry." (I was good at memorizing the enzymes in the Krebs cycle.) "If you take the MCAT and get a good grade, you could apply to medical school."

"Why would I want to do that?"

"Because, as I said before, you're obviously not going to be a DJ." Very logical.

My first med school interview was at Temple University. Let me preface this by saying that I was young, brash, and arrogant at the time. To say that interview didn't go well is an understatement. The interviewer (a neurosurgeon) questioned my motivation to be a doctor and informed me that he had three applicants from Penn State with higher GPAs than I had. I explained that Lehigh's chemistry program was light years tougher than Penn State's. He vehemently disagreed. "Just to get an interview at University of Pennsylvania Medical School, you would need a higher GPA than you have." Thinking this was a debate, I responded with, "Well, comparing Penn Med and Temple Med is like comparing Lehigh and Penn State." That ended the interview. I was clueless enough to think I'd won the debate, so I was a bit surprised when I got a special delivery rejection from Temple. This was before UPS and FedEx, so they wanted to make clear that Temple really, really didn't want me—in Taylor Swift's words, "We Are Never Ever Getting Back Together"!

I went back to my Lehigh adviser (yes, the same one that I went to after I got fired as a DJ). Her advice this time was slightly less sympathetic. It turns out that Temple had also notified Lehigh of what sounded like a rejection with prejudice. "Whether you ever get into medical school is immaterial," she said. "We would like some students from Lehigh to get in someday. So you have three choices:

Don't apply to any more medical schools, don't tell them you're from Lehigh, or don't be you." Very reasonable advice.

My next interview was at Hahnemann Medical College (now Drexel University College of Medicine, where I would later become dean of the medical school). The interviewer happened to be an ob-gyn physician. He had my one-page summary on his desk and was going down the page, clearly unimpressed by my vitals, when he saw at the bottom "Little Stevie Kent—midnight to 5 DJ." He beamed. "You're Little Stevie? I listen to you when I come in for deliveries. You're really funny. It would be great to have you come to Hahnemann."

My response—and I am not proud of the lack of veracity—went like this: "Well, Temple really wants me, but I'd much rather go to your school via early decision." Three weeks later, I was an admitted medical student. I was on my way, just not to a career as a DJ.

Even though I had to give up that dream, my DJ career taught me some important lessons that later helped me lead one of the largest health systems in the country in one of the poorest cities in the country during a once-in-a-century pandemic. The first lesson was that the artists are the stars, not the DJ. The 35,000 people who worked for me, our 8,000 students dealing with the physical and emotional challenges of getting their degree during a pandemic, and our patients were what mattered. I was just making the moves (spinning the tunes) that might help protect all these people.

Second, being a DJ is all about understanding your audience. As a physician, I had been taught that strategy, focus, and discipline were what mattered; but during the financial, medical, and racial crises of 2020–2022 I discovered that creativity, passion, flexibility, and concern for patients were the qualities that were needed most. A radio station or live DJ can let a robot play the songs, but understanding the audience, whether in person or on the air, is what separates the technically good DJs from the great ones. Similarly, self-awareness, empathy, communication skills, and cultural competence are what separate the great physicians from those who are champions at memorizing the Krebs cycle in biochemistry class.

By the way, Jerry (the Geator) and I are still rocking together!

So my DJ career paid off, and I promised that I would never forget the music. And I didn't. During the pandemic, as the president and CEO of Thomas Jefferson University and Jefferson Health, my radical communication strategy included a playlist that became a good part of my connection with the 35,000 people who worked for that organization. During the George Floyd protests, the playlist included "I'll Take You There" by the Staple Singers. Roberta Flack's recording of "The First Time Ever I Saw Your Face" was in rotation when the surge was abating and folks that had only met virtually were seeing the whole person unmasked, whether during a business meeting or first date. And I played "Hit Me With Your Best Shot" by Pat Benatar to encourage everyone to sign up for vaccinations. It was like nothing had changed in 45 years: Music and medicine were still inextricably linked in my life and professional success.

Of course, some things did change—including how I look. This was me in 1978:

And this is me now!

Everything I have learned personally and professionally in leading three different medical colleges and health systems for the past 30 years, I owe to and can trace back to lessons I learned from being a DJ for 40 years. Think of this book as "Ten Tunes for Transformation" or a "Mix for the 'Morrow of Medicine!" Ten songs, 10 chapters that I believe represent my best thoughts around the creative construction of a "health assurance" system to correct and transform the broken, fragmented, expensive, and inequitable care delivery system we have today.

Just to get you started, here is a song list that has guided me through my personal and professional life:

1958: "Problems" by the Everly Brothers

In many ways, both the pandemic and our response as healthcare workers and leaders have made me more optimistic that we can identify the problems in healthcare and find creative solutions. The miracle of vaccine development in less than a year, the fact that health systems that had previously only competed with each other went into a radical collaboration mode, and the fact that health inequities are at least being universally discussed are all encouraging signs. As Nazareth sang in 1979, there is no "Simple Solution," but to paraphrase Will Smith and Logic in 2019, we should not be afraid to think different!

1962: "Don't Hang Up" by the Orlons

What just about every patient says after waiting 15 minutes on the phone for a payer or hospital rep to answer a question. As one of my colleagues said, "We have Star Wars technology for individual patients in a Fred Flintstone healthcare delivery system!" Amazingly, in a 2021 Harris poll 62 percent of respondents agreed that the healthcare system "feels like it's intentionally set up to be confusing."

1975: "Take It to the Limit" by the Eagles

So much of healthcare delivery has involved incremental change of a system that needs an extreme makeover. My unlikely move from DJ to private practice obstetrician to CEO of a $9 billion, 18-hospital, two-campus university involved taking a "no limits" approach.

1981: "Under Pressure" by Queen and David Bowie

When people ask me what the pandemic has changed as it relates to my feelings about healthcare, I usually say "Actually, not much." In some respects, the fact that providers suffered while payers thrived just increases the pressure to create payer-provider alignment. The fact that some people in underserved areas died because they didn't have broadband internet and couldn't connect to providers through telemedicine makes it even more crucial to give everyone access to that technology. The stark health inequities revealed by the pandemic, meanwhile, turned social determinants of health, population health, and predictive analytics from philosophical and academic exercises into mainstream issues for clinical care, payment, and medical education.

1992: "Human Touch" by Bruce Springsteen
I discovered in my multifaceted career as an obstetrician, a healthcare leader, a university president, and a DJ that the only thing that matters is whether the people you are relating to—patients, faculty, students, or radio listeners—believe that you are talking directly to them. My most successful strategy at Jefferson was the "hot dog stand" strategy: Once a week during lunch I stopped by the hot dog stand outside the university hospital. What I learned there from employees and patients often became the most important components of a decision I made, eclipsing all the memos and suggestions I received from consultants and conferees.

2005: "Who Says You Can't Go Home" by Bon Jovi and Jennifer Nettles
Just as entertainment, shopping, and banking have moved away from "come to my office, urgent care center, emergency room, hospital," the emergence of telehealth during the pandemic has led many physicians and hospital administrators to ask the question that Jon and Jennifer asked, namely whether the default should be to bring healthcare to the patient where they live whenever possible. Simply put, healthcare needs to move from sick care to health assurance, starting at home, as outlined in the book I wrote

with Hemant Taneja and Kevin Maney, *UnHealthcare: A Manifesto for Health Assurance*.

2011:   "The A Team" by Ed Sheeran
My professor at Wharton Business School taught me early on that you should always have five people reporting to you who think they can do a better job than you, and three who are right. I have taken that dictum to heart, and in every one of my leadership jobs I have tried to bring in leaders who fill in my gaps and then leave them alone to do their job. Part of that A-team approach is being surrounded by loyal, creative leaders who will keep it real. In my professional life, much of the credit for creating academic medical centers that act like start-up companies goes to those kinds of people who shared multiple jobs with me, many of whom are mentioned by name in the acknowledgments at the end of this book.

2020:   "Future Nostalgia" by Dua Lipa
Science fiction has been a mainstay in my life. Three of my previous five books have had a science fiction medical business theme—*The Phantom Stethoscope*, *We Can Fix Healthcare: The Future Is Now*, and *Bless This Mess: A Picture Story of Healthcare in America*. The "history of the future" model, where you look back at today from a future where healthcare and education are much more accessible and strategize what you can do today to get there, creates much more creativity than thinking about today's problems. It's why I start all my current national talks as a hologram coming back from 2032 as the chief digital officer for President Taylor Swift (yes, the Swifties became a party), whose healthcare strategy is "make health tailored to the individual and the community and make it swift!"

I hope you enjoy this book and view it as the beginning of a discussion about how we can move from apathy to transformation to disruption to the creative construction of a new system that preserves the individuality of American medicine but allows for greater access, quality, and user experience and a decreased total cost. Perry Como sang a song called "It's Impossible." I hear that a lot about healthcare. I have replaced that in the playlist of choice with Jamiroquai's "We Can Do It," because there "ain't no problem / that we can't solve" with radical collaboration, radical communication, radical creativity, and a radical concentration on solving healthcare disparities.

CHAPTER 1

"Courage to Change" by Sia

You're not alone in all this / You're not alone,
I promise / Standing together, we can do / anything.

AT JEFFERSON HEALTH, Sia's "Courage to Change" became
something of a theme song for our frontline workers and their heroic
response to the COVID-19 pandemic. Every Friday I would send
out a playlist to inspire and recharge our 35,000 employees, and this
tune, released in September 2020 on her album *Together*, was on
one of those playlists. Sia begins the song by telling her audience
that she can relate to everyone's pain, and goes on to say that we all
need to embrace change to become better.

That's the theme of this chapter: Whatever role you play in the
healthcare ecosystem—patient, provider, hospital, pharmaceutical
firm, payer, founder, or tech company—do you have the courage to
change yourself in order to save the broken US healthcare system?

Even before the COVID-19 pandemic struck the healthcare system was a mess, and if nothing is done it will inevitably get worse. I
discussed this in a 2018 book entitled *Bless This Mess*, where I observed
that other "planets" (i.e., other sectors of the economy) were amazed
that policymakers were still talking about how to give more people
access to a broken, fragmented, expensive, and inequitable healthcare
system, instead of how to fundamentally change it. Imagine a retail
world before Amazon and Walmart, a hospitality convenience world
before Airbnb and Uber, or a banking world where you need to

get to the bank before 4 p.m. to cash your check. That's how other sectors (and probably other planets) view the nearly $4 trillion US healthcare system.

This is not an opinion. Consider a few statistics: In 2019, our country spent $10,948 per capita on healthcare. By comparison, the next 15 highest-spending countries spent an average of $5,718 per capita, a bit more than half of the US level (OECD 2021). "Yes, I know we're expensive, but we're the best and you get what you pay for, right?" No, wrong.

In the latest international comparison of healthcare systems from the Commonwealth Fund, the United States came in dead last among developed nations on overall measures of access to care, efficiency, equity, and healthcare outcomes. We had the highest infant mortality rate and the lowest life expectancy at age 60, and our rate of preventable deaths was more than double that of the best-performing country in the survey (Schneider et al. 2021).

In short, we're delivering inferior healthcare by some key measures, and we spend far more on it than other advanced nations do. Imagine another sector of the economy where you could say with a straight face, "Our business model is going to be one that will cost consumers ever more, while our service and their outcomes will be poorer than they should expect, and all of the players in the system will continue to expand and make increasing profits."

Moreover, US health costs are continuing to rise faster than family incomes or inflation. From 2011 to 2021, the average family premium jumped 47 percent, while the earnings of the average worker increased 31 percent and general inflation rose 19 percent. During the same period, the employee contribution to premium costs leaped from about $4,000 to $6,000 per year (Kaiser Family Foundation 2021).

Despite the rising costs, few employers are dropping health benefits. In fact, the percentage of employees eligible for health coverage increased from 75 percent in 2014 to 80 percent in 2020. However, only about half of employers offered insurance in 2020, and there was a slight decrease in the share of small firms that did (Fronstin 2021).

Instead of ditching health coverage, employers have shifted more of the cost to their employees. I've already mentioned rising premium contributions, and that's not all. From 2013 to 2018, the average deductible for employee-only coverage grew 52 percent to $1,100, and the average deductible for family coverage increased 45 percent to $2,225 (EBRI 2020).

It has often been said that the growth in US health costs is unsustainable, yet it has continued rising without a systemic collapse. However, the statistics just cited suggest that we're approaching a critical point where something has to give.

In my books and speeches, I've talked about disruption of the current system. I now hate the word *disruption*. It sounds too much like my older brother tearing down my sand castle without a plan to build another one. What this book will lay out, using music as a metaphor and as the message, is not disruption of the current system, but creative construction of a transformed, consumer-driven, wellness-centered and primary-care-oriented model that brings healthcare into the twenty-first century market economy. That will require creative partnerships between the "move-fast-and-break-things world" of Silicon Valley and the traditional healthcare ecosystem based on the mantra of "use my hospital, subscribe to my insurance, swallow my pills."

Medicare for All is not the answer. Its proponents have correctly identified the problem of fragmented, corporate-driven, disconnected payer and provider healthcare, which is the opposite of a consumer-driven model. But asking the federal government to create a more efficient, consumer-driven healthcare system is a bridge way too far. You only need to look at the disparate and disorganized vaccine distribution efforts across states and counties in the first phase of COVID-19 vaccination to understand what Medicare for All would look like. Government-run single-payer healthcare would do nothing to solve the problems of healthcare delivery. All it would do is guarantee that everyone had access to the same crappy healthcare. Costs would keep rising after a one-time reduction of provider payments to Medicare levels.

What's required to rescue our ailing healthcare system is a consumer revolution that harnesses the power of consumer preferences to bring about the necessary changes. The building blocks of this revolution are already in place; with some help from the government, especially in altering or retiring regulations, they could become an unstoppable force. While I mentioned the poorly coordinated vaccine policies during the pandemic, the government can be more effective in working with the private sector. Just look at the miraculous public-private partnerships during Operation Warp Speed, which led to the rapid creation and manufacturing of the COVID-19 vaccines.

The other factors that will help unleash the power of consumer choice are technological and entrepreneurial. A rapidly growing arsenal of healthcare technologies, ranging from telemedicine, remote monitoring, and mobile apps to artificial intelligence, genomics, and drones, will completely change how and where healthcare is delivered. And a broad range of technology companies and start-ups, supported by a flood of venture capital, is ready to collaborate with healthcare providers to transform healthcare from the ground up.

These must be creative partnerships that engage both sides in the work and the rewards of change; health systems can no longer be viewed just as customers and entities to sell to. The billions of dollars being spent on digital transformation need to be shared so that health systems with progressively decreasing traditional revenues (inpatient, outpatient, research funding) can share in the financial fruits of the consumer revolution.

The current phase of my career is working at doing just that by creating a consortium of the willing that includes the traditional healthcare ecosystem—payers, providers, pharma—and the digital and virtual "Silicon Valley" ecosystem of digital start-ups, private equity, and venture capital, all aimed at a new sort of radical collaboration and strategic partnerships for responsible innovation.

At Jefferson Health, where I was the CEO until the end of 2021, we called these efforts the new math. We diversified our portfolio through creative financial and strategic partnerships with venture capital firms, founders, and payers. Here's the logic: Hospital at home (HaH) might decrease a health system's traditional inpatient revenue, but sharing in the multibillion-dollar valuation of an HaH services company makes up for a lot of hospital admissions. Simply put, healthcare providers have not yet recognized that digital, telehealth, and technology companies need them to succeed—not just as customers, but also as partners that can share in the financial windfalls from the transformation brought about by their products.

We must also ensure that every person in our country—regardless of race, economic status, or zip code—shares equally in the healthcare improvements that this transformation can achieve. Today, the glaring disparities in our healthcare system subject people of color to fundamentally worse outcomes than those white people experience—a difference that has grown even worse during the pandemic. According to the Centers for Disease Control and Prevention (2020), a third of all deaths from COVID-19 have occurred among African Americans, even though that group forms just 12 percent of the population.

We will return to this theme throughout the book. As Martin Luther King Jr. said, "Of all the forms of inequality, injustice in healthcare is the most shocking and inhumane." This is why I tied 25 percent of my personal incentive compensation as Jefferson's leader to reducing health inequity in Philadelphia. And it is why I believe that the transformation we will see in healthcare over the next 10 years can fundamentally help us close the gap between care for the rich and care for the poor. Only through radical creativity, radical collaboration, and a radical concentration on inequity will we make the changes that will make us proud.

FROM THE STORE TO THE SCREEN

In every sphere of consumer goods and services but one, Americans now have plenty of choices that they can make with the tap of a finger on a smartphone screen. The sole exception is healthcare, where the consumer experience is not much different than it was in the 1990s.

Consider the difference between buying something on Amazon and making a doctor's appointment. To purchase a cutting board on Amazon, you go to the website, search for cutting boards and then scroll through a wide selection of items, with pictures, prices, and reviews all queued up for your inspection. Then you add the item you choose to your shopping cart, select the delivery address (if not your own), pay for it with a credit card already in the Amazon system, and you're done. A moment later, you get an e-mailed receipt that includes the promised delivery date.

When you want to make an appointment with your physician, in contrast, you may have to call the doctor's office, go through the voice-mail system, be placed on hold for several minutes, and then ask the receptionist when the physician will be able to see you. If you're lucky, you'll get an appointment while you can still be helped, but the earliest available time may not be convenient for you. Increasingly, practices are allowing patients to book their own appointments online, but the software isn't easy to navigate, and the next available slot isn't sooner or more convenient.

Unless health systems and physician practices change their approach, they'll get their primary care lunches eaten by the walk-in urgent care and retail clinics that have mushroomed across America. Obviously, health systems offer many other services beyond primary care, but as more consumer-friendly methods of healthcare delivery proliferate, healthcare leaders will have to ask themselves, "Does my system want to be the Blockbuster of healthcare, doomed to irrelevance by Netflix?"

The basic concepts of consumerism have not yet penetrated very far into the healthcare mentality. For example, the people who may come in contact with the system are still called "patients," although they're consumers until they actually visit a doctor. There's only a casual awareness that most of the factors that determine a person's health exist outside of healthcare settings. And healthcare providers stubbornly cling to the idea that nonminor acute care should be provided in hospitals and that chronic conditions can be adequately addressed by seeing a doctor two to four times a year. The key to future success will be creating loyalty among the 97 percent of people in your community (some of whom may have cancer, congestive heart failure, diabetes, or other chronic conditions) who don't want to think of themselves every day as a *patient*, but rather as a *person* who wants to be able to thrive without healthcare getting in the way.

Although telemedicine is starting to make a difference, healthcare usually still requires consumers to see a provider in person, whether in a doctor's office, a hospital, an ER, a pharmacy, an imaging center, or a lab. The hours of these healthcare settings are limited, except in ERs. People may have to take time off work, travel to an office, and wait in a waiting room for up to half an hour to see a doctor. In contrast, most other services can be obtained or ordered when a person is at home or on the move.

To bring healthcare into line with other sectors, we must not only incorporate the right technology but also fundamentally rebuild the system so that the technology can achieve its potential. At Jefferson, while everyone else was talking about telehealth we were talking about "healthcare at any address." We knew that the technology would continue to change and improve and that consumers, once they'd tasted real convenience, would thirst for more. Netflix started by sending DVDs to your mailbox so you didn't have to drive through the snow to the video store and pay late fees. Then the technology changed to streaming videos, and Netflix pounced. I imagine that in the metaverse we may all have Netflix chips in our brains so we can watch lost seasons of *Breaking Bad* whenever we want.

Consumers are starting to rebel against traditional healthcare. They want a choice in when, where, and how they'll be seen for care, and they want the same level of service and convenience in healthcare that they have in other areas of their lives. According to a consumer poll by Change Healthcare (2020), 81 percent of respondents said shopping for healthcare services should be as easy as shopping for other types of services. Sixty-seven percent said it feels like every step of the healthcare process is a chore, and 62 percent said that they felt like the healthcare experience is intentionally set up to be confusing. Compare that to Amazon, Netflix, or other successful online services.

One of the key changes during my tenure at Jefferson is that we recognized we no longer wanted to be defined by where our hospitals were or by the facilities where our sickest people were treated. Those facilities were important to our success, but we wanted to be defined by the quality of care and caring we could give, no matter where the patient was located. The future definition of success at Jefferson was that if you came to Philadelphia, no one would be able to tell you where the health system was physically located, because we'd be wherever the patient wanted us to be.

The inconvenient current healthcare model is much like banking long ago. Bank customers had to go to the bank on weekdays between 10 a.m. and 4 p.m. to deposit a check or make a withdrawal. Then some small local banks began to offer extended hours; they had the same FDIC insurance as the large banks, so customers started moving over to local banks. When that happened, the big banks recognized the importance of consumer choice. The next thing you know there were ATMs, and then digital banking. This was not "telebanking," but convenient banking at any address.

The upshot was that banking went from being 90 percent at the bank to 90 percent at home. The same kind of thing will happen in healthcare. People will see that Mary got her IV antibiotics safely at home while her mom was making her a home-cooked meal and she was watching TV on a nice set. Susan, meanwhile, went to the hospital where there was lousy food and a 19-inch TV set and it cost $35 to park—not to mention the out-of-pocket cost of hospitalization. Which care setting do you think most people will prefer when they have the choice?

Although I have abandoned the D-word, *disruption*, without a major change in thinking it will be catastrophic (with a capital C) for traditional healthcare systems. Their leaders are not thinking yet about what they're going to do when the demand for their beds craters; in fact, some systems are building more hospitals. But someday soon they're going to face the same choice that brick-and-mortar retailers did when Amazon and other online stores came along: resist or jump on board. Target and Walmart got onboard; Sears and JCPenney are basically gone.

As consultant Peter Diamandis said, "True disruption means threatening your existing product line and your past investments. Breakthrough products disrupt current lines of business."

TELEHEALTH EXPLOSION: A SIGN OF THINGS TO COME

There are signs that consumers are finally starting to move to center stage in healthcare. Some of these changes, like the rapid expansion of telehealth and the advent of HaH programs, were clearly spurred by the COVID-19 pandemic. But the continuing growth in retail and urgent care clinics long predates the health crisis, and the increasing importance of internet provider reviews is clearly related to the online retailing trends in other industries.

The explosive growth in the use of telehealth has been one of the most dramatic by-products of the pandemic. Initially, there was a huge increase in telehealth—both video visits and phone visits—because patients were avoiding physician offices and many practices temporarily suspended office visits. As the initial waves subsided, patients started returning to offices for in-person visits. By the end of 2020, only 8.4 percent of adult primary care visits in the United States were being conducted virtually (Mehrotra et al. 2021).

However, that number conceals some important shifts. To begin with, privately insured people used telehealth more than other patients did, partly because insurers eliminated telehealth copayments during the early phase of the pandemic. According to Cigna, virtual visits made up nearly 25 percent of its members' office visits in May 2021, compared to 1 percent pre-pandemic, and over

60 percent of behavioral health encounters were being conducted through telehealth (Lagasse 2021).

There was also a large increase in the percentage of Medicare enrollees who used telehealth after the Centers for Medicare & Medicaid Services (2021) temporarily lifted many of the coverage restrictions on virtual visits. The number of Medicare visits conducted through telehealth increased 63-fold to 52.7 million in 2020 from 840,000 in 2019. Whether Congress will authorize making these regulatory changes permanent is one of the major questions about the future of telemedicine.

The nature of telehealth also changed during the pandemic. The biggest shift was the rapid increase in the percentage of physicians who had virtual encounters with their own patients. Before the pandemic, telehealth services dominated the market and marketed to consumers or their employers. In these services' virtual visits, people saw physicians they didn't know, usually on a one-off basis and mostly for minor acute conditions. Most medical groups that offered telehealth visits either hired one of these outside services or assigned a few of their physicians to conduct online encounters.

During the pandemic, that landscape changed radically. Most physicians began seeing their patients virtually: According to a 2021 EBRI survey of people covered by employer-sponsored insurance, 62 percent of respondents had had a telehealth visit with their own physician, and 23 percent had had a virtual encounter with a provider in the same practice or health system as their doctor. This trend was boosted by the new payment parity between in-person and virtual visits.

Not surprisingly, as physicians began doing telehealth visits with their own patients, they also started managing chronic conditions through video or phone visits. As a result, the scope of telehealth was greatly enlarged. Some primary care physicians say as much as 40–50 percent of health problems can be safely diagnosed and treated virtually. And it's not unusual nowadays for telehealth to constitute 15–20 percent of visits to a primary care practice (Terry 2021b).

One of the advantages of telehealth is that it makes care more convenient than the traditional in-office approach. Through telehealth and other forms of digital care, one observer notes, "healthcare organizations deliver an experience that matches what consumers see elsewhere in their lives" (Bazzoli 2021).

In addition, telehealth can make healthcare more accessible. "For working adults with limited access to paid sick leave or affordable transportation, the convenience of virtual visits has dramatically lowered barriers to care" (Werner and Glied 2021, 869).

On the other hand, one survey found that telehealth adoption is highest among younger patients with relatively high incomes and educational levels. People who earn less than $35,000 a year, live in rural areas, or are uninsured are much less likely to have used telehealth. Forty percent of people in rural areas don't use telehealth (Olsen 2021a). Many have poor cellular or broadband connectivity, pointing to the need for more investment in rural broadband. The Infrastructure Investment and Jobs Act passed in 2021 will help with that. Start-ups like Homeward are also providing technology-enabled care specifically designed for people in rural areas.

Overall, the rise of telehealth is a marker for the consumer revolution. Even though some states have restored restrictions on the use of telehealth, consumers are used to a new way of interacting with their providers. Surveys show that rural consumers and others with previously limited access now prize telehealth access in their health plans, and they will continue to demand it from their providers (EBRI 2021).

One of the questions I get asked most frequently is "What will the pandemic fundamentally change in the delivery of healthcare?" As when I'm asked about anything else in the KAC (Kinda After COVID) world, my answer is "I don't know" and "it depends." That's because, to paraphrase Upton Sinclair, it's hard to get someone to do something when their salary depends on them not doing it. Only if providers continue to be fairly compensated for virtual visits—that is, paid at the same rate as for in-person visits—will they continue doing them. If that happens, and if consumers and providers are empowered to decide the best place for their interaction, and if this country ever achieves universal broadband access, telehealth will indeed become the revolution that we early adopters always hoped it would be.

RETAIL CLINICS AND URGENT CARE CLINICS

Another sign that consumers are being heard is the rapid growth of retail and urgent care clinics over the past decade. This signifies that many people prefer the convenience of going to a walk-in clinic with extended hours and little or no waiting time to driving to a primary care practice and cooling their heels for 15–30 minutes until the doctor is ready to see them. Moreover, many traditional practices still have office hours only on weekdays, requiring many employees to take off time from work to see a physician.

While the number of retail clinics inside pharmacies has leveled off at around 2,000, the big players are now launching full-scale primary care clinics within or alongside their pharmacies or superstores. CVS Health has built about 1,000 HealthHUB facilities that offer a wide spectrum of nonemergency care. Walgreens has partnered with VillageMD to develop 600 VillageMD clinics adjacent to Walgreens pharmacies by 2025; as of 2021, at least 50 of these clinics were already open. Walmart, which opened the first of its expanded primary care clinics in 2019, now has similar offices in its stores in four Southern states (Terry 2021a).

Meanwhile, the number of urgent care centers has grown by leaps and bounds. In 2019, there were over 9,000 of these fast-turnaround clinics in the United States (Terry 2021a). Hospitals have become major players in the urgent care business, using them to pull patients into their parent health systems when they have more complex needs. Whereas retail clinics are usually staffed by nurse practitioners, urgent care centers generally have physicians on staff; but that distinction will fade as full-service retail clinics spread across the country.

Primary care physicians in traditional practice are feeling the heat. Many doctors complain that their retail competitors are stealing the easy-to-provide services and the younger, healthier patients, leaving them to treat older patients with complex cases, for which they're poorly compensated (Terry 2021a). Most of these physicians—especially the older ones—are accustomed to having a single way for patients to see them, regardless of how consumer-unfriendly that model may be.

There will be a reckoning for this refusal to acknowledge change. The telehealth companies and retail companies that take care of many of the well-insured younger patients will increasingly steal market share from traditional providers. Eventually, these modes of care will become commoditized, and a new care delivery model will arise. To keep up with these changes in the healthcare consumer game of musical chairs, hospital and health system administrators will need to seek advice from digital health experts and entrepreneurs.

If you are a healthcare CEO, look around the room at your cabinet meetings. Make sure your chief digital officer, chief consumer segmentation officer, and chief medical social media information officer come from outside the healthcare system and that they represent the diversity in age, gender, race, and sexual preference of your population. And if you don't see those kinds of people around you, quickly change that scenario!

NEW DIRECT CARE OPTIONS

Other kinds of nontraditional companies have also begun offering healthcare directly to consumers. For starters, major insurance companies have created virtual-first health plans in partnership with telehealth services. In these plans, telehealth physicians are encouraged to form continuing relationships with their patients and may refer them to specialists (Terry 2021b).

UnitedHealthcare, for example, has partnered with Amwell to deliver virtual-first primary care. Cigna owns MDLIVE, and

Humana has teamed with Doctor On Demand. Humana is selling employers its virtual-first plan at about half the cost of its most popular traditional plan.

Teladoc, a telemedicine service, recently launched a virtual-first insurance plan, built around its primary care service. The plan, which combines telehealth with in-person care, is being sold to employers. It has been estimated that such plans could reduce premium costs by 10 percent (Olsen 2021b).

Start-up Medicare Advantage plans such as Alignment Healthcare, Bright Health, and Clover Health have also branched into direct delivery of care by employing physicians. Clover is using advanced analytic tools to help inform medical decision-making and offers a home care product (Livingston 2021).

Amazon has also started making waves in this field. Amazon Care, which launched in September 2019 and began winding down in late 2022, was a virtual-first clinical care service to combine telehealth with in-home care. Patients were provided with a smartphone app that allowed text or video interaction with a nurse and, if desired, a doctor. The nurse could do a home-based diagnostic assessment, and Amazon could deliver a prescription to the patient's home within two hours, using its online pharmacy (Rourke 2021). In 2022, Amazon switched course and purchased One Medical for $3.9 billion, setting up the possibility of an Amazon Prime-like subscription that could deliver primary care through both virtual and in-person visits.

Other direct-to-consumer companies are providing a better care experience than consumers get in most primary care practices, where they typically see a physician or nurse practitioner for only 10–15 minutes even if they have chronic conditions. Venture capital-backed primary care firms such as ChenMed, Oak Street Health, Iora Health, are changing this paradigm. ChenMed, for example, offers Medicare enrollees longer appointments and more personal attention than they'd get in most physician offices. The company stresses care coordination, incorporates innovative technology, and addresses social determinants of health. It partners with Medicare

Advantage plans, taking on financial risk through capitation contracts (Better Medicare Alliance 2017).

Another competitor to traditional physician offices is the direct primary care (DPC) movement, which now includes about 800 US practices. These practices don't accept insurance or participate in Medicare or Medicaid. Instead, they derive their income from monthly membership fees that generally range from $50–$100 a month (Terry 2020c). In return for these payments, patients can communicate with their physician by text or e-mail and have virtual or in-person visits that are longer than typical primary care visits. DPC physicians can spend more time with patients because they can make a good living with a smaller patient panel than a traditional doctor needs. In contrast to the 1,800–2,400 patients that a primary care panel generally includes, a DPC doctor may be responsible for only 800 people.

THE IMPORTANCE OF PROVIDER REVIEWS

Consumers are used to reading reviews and seeing ratings of the products they buy online. So it's not surprising that online reviews are now the most important factor in choosing a doctor, according to a consumer survey. Respondents said this information is more valid than another doctor's referral. In fact, 83 percent of the consumers said they went online to read reviews of a physician after receiving a referral from another provider (Terry 2021c).

Thomas Jeffrey, a patient experience consultant and president of the SullivanLuallin Group, told Medscape Medical News that the embrace of online reviews reflects not only consumers' familiarity with internet shopping, but also the shifting of more health costs to employees. "Historically, we didn't look at healthcare as a consumer product," he said. "But with high deductibles and copays, doctor visits can represent a pretty significant out-of-pocket expense. As it begins to hit folks' pocketbooks, they become more savvy shoppers" (Terry 2021c).

Consumers use a variety of web resources when selecting a doctor. Sixty-five percent of the survey respondents use internet search engines when they select a doctor. Many respondents also look up information on hospital and clinic sites, WebMD, Healthgrades, and Facebook. Besides reviews and ratings, they also pay attention to how physicians present themselves online.

This focus on the experience that other patients have had with healthcare providers is fairly shallow. Consumers have not yet seen much comparative data on out-of-pocket costs, quality, or outcomes. When they do, the landscape of healthcare will fundamentally change.

HOSPITAL (AND NEARLY EVERYTHING ELSE) AT HOME

Just as the pandemic accelerated the use of telehealth, it has also jump-started the implementation of HaH services. In this model, patients receive hospital-level acute care at home, where most of them would prefer to be. While it has been around for 25 years, HaH never spread beyond a handful of research institutions until the pandemic struck. Suddenly, overburdened hospitals began to use HaH to transfer out some patients who could be cared for at home, freeing up hospital beds for very sick COVID-19 patients (Terry 2020b).

In the HaH model deployed by Medically Home, a Boston-based company in which the Mayo Clinic and Kaiser Permanente have invested, patients who have certain medical conditions and meet other criteria can be admitted to HaH from a hospital, an emergency department, or a primary care clinic. A portion of the patient's house is converted into a hospital room, complete with a hospital bed, an IV stand, telemonitoring equipment, and an audiovisual conferencing setup. Mobile X-rays and lab tests can also be performed at home.

A nurse typically visits the patient at home a few times a day. Otherwise, the patient is cared for remotely by clinicians stationed at a command center that can be located anywhere. These doctors and nurses view the patient's vital signs and are automatically alerted to any concerning changes, as they would be in a traditional hospital. Whenever necessary, the clinicians conduct telehealth visits with the patient, who can also contact them 24/7.

Several HaH studies have been conducted over the years, both before and after home telemonitoring became available. These studies show that HaH is generally accepted by patients, improves the experience of patients and their caregivers, offers quality of care comparable to that of usual hospital care, improves physical functioning, and has better or equivalent disease outcomes. Some studies showed significantly lower costs with HaH. There is also evidence of fewer health complications and readmissions among HaH patients than among those in traditional hospitals (Terry 2020a). Among the acute-care patients who can be treated safely at home are those with COVID-19, congestive heart failure, pneumonia, exacerbations of asthma and chronic obstructive pulmonary disease, cellulitis, and urinary tract infections (Terry 2020b).

I believe we've barely scratched the surface of this trend. Someday, for example, it may be possible to do deliveries at home with hospital-level care. WellStar Health System in Atlanta has even experimented with a neonatal intensive care unit at home. Even deep vein thrombosis, which requires treatment with anticoagulants, can be managed safely at home; in fact, fewer complications were seen in the home setting (Ungerleider 2021).

Post-acute care can also be delivered at home in many cases. This starts with the early discharge of patients who still need hospital care such as intravenous antibiotic administration. Such patients have been shown to do very well in an HaH setting, and it's much less expensive than sending them to a rehab unit in a nursing home, where they're at risk of contracting infections (Terry 2020a).

Long-term care has increasingly been moved from institutional care to home-based services over the past three decades. The advent of bundled payments by Medicare accelerated this trend. Before that, if a patient had a low-risk hip or knee replacement, they'd go to rehab afterward. Once a hospital was on the hook for the cost of a procedure plus 30 days of post-acute care, it made sense to discharge the patient home with some rehabilitative equipment and physical therapy visits, which cost hundreds of dollars instead of $5,000 per case in rehab.

If telehealth visits can reduce the need for in-person primary care and specialty care, and if much acute care and post-acute care can also be provided at home, then a large portion of the sick care in our system—perhaps 60 percent of it—does not need to be provided outside the home.

Emergency departments would be far less crowded if consumers without clear emergencies first used a virtual triage system to talk to a clinician and see if a visit was necessary. Jefferson Health uses such a system for employees on its self-insured health plan: If a person utilizes this telehealth option and is directed to the emergency department, their deductible is waived. This approach reduced Jefferson's spending on unscheduled visits by 25 percent, and emergency department physicians found that they can diagnose and triage many conditions (even appendicitis) by starting virtually at home.

Meanwhile, some other kinds of care are migrating away from the hospital. Many procedures are now being provided in ambulatory surgery centers or physician offices; nearly anything that doesn't require a surgical intervention or an intensive care stay can be done at home. Even sepsis can be treated with antibiotics at home after the patient is stabilized. Under this scenario, acute hospital care of the future will consist mainly of emergent conditions such as trauma, severe infections, and organ failure; tertiary care such as treatment of advanced cancer; and complicated procedures such as heart surgery.

We need to go beyond the either/or of hospitalization or home care. Getting people home or keeping them there should be our objective. We can bring the doctors, the nurses, and the equipment into the home, as needed. It'll be much better for the patient, with far fewer hospital-acquired infections, and it will be much cheaper than a brick-and-mortar hospital.

It will take "Courage to Change," as Sia so aptly put it. Health system boards have to start incentivizing and hiring CEOs who are prepared for this future. CEOs and general counsels must have the courage to change from their risk-averse status quo mentality to one that diversifies their institution's portfolio and increases their risk tolerance. Only then can they form the creative partnerships that will diversify their revenue portfolios and move their organizations from a sick care model to a health assurance model.

Changes, as David Bowie said in 1971, are inevitable. What matters is whether you are leading the future or "Waiting on the World to Change" as John Mayer sang in 2006. Some healthcare providers will react to all the innovators creating companies that disrupt their old math of inpatient and outpatient revenue; others, who lack the courage to change, will play it safe and "risk-free" on a path to a slow decline into obsolescence.

We have a long way to go before the health assurance vision becomes a reality. But efforts to use technology to transform healthcare through consumer empowerment have a mighty ally, in addition to the consumer: the venture capitalists who are now pouring enormous sums of money into digital health. The next chapter will explain what's happening in this field and how healthcare organizations can participate in it.

REFERENCES

Bazzoli, F. 2021. "Can Digital Health Tech Make Patient Engagement Seem Seamless?" Health Data Management. Published December 21. www.healthdatamanagement.com/articles/can -digital-health-tech-make-patient-engagement-seem-seamless.

Better Medicare Alliance. 2017. "ChenMed: Patient-Centered Care for Medicare Advantage Patients." Published December. https://bettermedicarealliance.org/wp-content/uploads/2020 /03/BMA_ChenMed_Spotlight_2018_01_08.pdf.

Centers for Disease Control and Prevention. 2020. "Disparities in Deaths from COVID-19." Updated December 30. www.cdc.gov/coronavirus/2019-ncov/community/health-equity/racial-ethnic-disparities/disparities-deaths.html.

Centers for Medicare & Medicaid Services. 2021. "New HHS Study Shows 63-Fold Increase in Medicare Telehealth Utilization During the Pandemic" (press release). Published December 3. www.cms.gov/newsroom/press-releases/new-hhs-study-shows-63-fold-increase-medicare-telehealth-utilization-during-pandemic.

Change Healthcare. 2020. "Change Healthcare-Harris Poll Research: Half of Consumers Avoid Seeking Care Because It's Too Hard" (press release). Published July 13. www.businesswire.com/news/home/20200713005099/en/Change-Healthcare---Harris-Poll-Research-Half-of-Consumers-Avoid-Seeking-Care-Because-It's-Too-Hard.

EBRI (Employee Benefit Research Institute). 2021. "2021 Consumer Engagement in Health Care Survey." Published September. www.ebri.org/docs/default-source/cehcs/2021-cehcs-report.pdf.

———. 2020. "Health Plan Deductibles Are Increasing Across the Board." EBRI Fast Facts. Published September 3. www.ebri.org/content/health-plan-deductibles-are-increasing-across-the-board.

Fronstin, P. 2021. "A Buffeted Employer Health Care System Continues to Hold Firm: What Could Change That?" Employee Benefit Research Institute. Issue Brief. Published September 23. www.ebri.org/content/a-buffeted-employer-health-care-system-continues-to-hold-firm-what-could-change-that

Kaiser Family Foundation. 2021. "Average Family Premiums Top $22,000 in 2021." Private Insurance (news item). Published November 10. www.kff.org/private-insurance/.

Lagasse, J. 2021. "Telehealth Reimbursement Parity Spurs Insurer Concerns of Overutilization." Healthcare Finance, May 13. www

.healthcarefinancenews.com/news/telehealth-reimbursement
-parity-spurs-insurer-concerns-overutilization-though-future
-bright.

Livingston, S. 2021. "A New Breed of Health Insurers Is Taking
a Page out of UnitedHealth's Book . . ." *Insider*, July 7. www
.businessinsider.com/insurer-upstarts-alignment-bright-and
-clover-are-employing-doctors-and-providing-care-2021-7.

Mehrotra, A., M. E. Chernew, D. Linetsky, H. Hatch, D. A. Cutler,
and E. C. Schneider. 2021. "The Impact of COVID-19 on Outpatient Visits in 2020: Visits Remained Stable, Despite a Late
Surge in Cases." The Commonwealth Fund. Published February 22. www.commonwealthfund.org/publications/2021/feb
/impact-covid-19-outpatient-visits-2020-visits-stable-despite
-late-surge.

OECD (Organisation for Economic Co-operation and Development). 2021. "Health Spending" (online database). https://
data.oecd.org/healthres/health-spending.htm.

Olsen, E. 2021a. "Survey: Telehealth Adoption Highest Among the
Young, Educated and Wealthy." *MobiHealthNews*, December 14.
www.mobihealthnews.com/news/survey-telehealth-adoption
-highest-among-young-educated-and-wealthy.

———. 2021b. "Teladoc Partners to Offer Virtual-First Health
Plan." *MobiHealthNews*, November 8. www.mobihealthnews
.com/news/teladoc-partners-offer-virtual-first-health-plan.

Rourke, E. 2021. "In Clinical Care, What Will Amazon Deliver?"
New England Journal of Medicine 385 (26): 2401–03. https://doi
.org/10.1056/NEJMp2113702.

Schneider, E. C., A. Shah, M. M. Doty, R. Tikkanen, K. Fields, and
R. D. Williams II. 2021. "Mirror, Mirror 2021: Reflecting Poorly"
(report). The Commonwealth Fund. Published August 4. www
.commonwealthfund.org/publications/fund-reports/2021/aug
/mirror-mirror-2021-reflecting-poorly.

Terry, K. 2021a. "CVS, Walmart Plan Bigger In-Store Clinics: Will Primary Care Practices Suffer?" *Medscape Medical News*, December 28. www.medscape.com/viewarticle/965659.

———. 2021b. "More Competition for Docs as Insurers Boost New Telehealth Plans?" *Medscape Medical News*, March 3. www.medscape.com/viewarticle/946759.

———. 2021c. "Online Reviews Most Important Factor in Choosing a Doctor: Survey." *Medscape Medical News*, December 7. www.medscape.com/viewarticle/964264.

———. 2020a. "Has the Time Come for Hospital at Home?" *Next Avenue*, October 23. www.nextavenue.org/hospital-at-home/.

———. 2020b. "'Hospital at Home' Increases COVID Capacity in Large Study." *Medscape Medical News*, November 17. www.medscape.com/viewarticle/941173.

———. 2020c. *Physician-Led Healthcare Reform: A New Approach to Medicare for All.* Washington, DC: American Association for Physician Leadership.

Ungerleider, D. L. 2021. "DVT Treatment: Home Versus Hospital." Medpage Today. Published November 23. www.medpagetoday.com/resource-centers/advances-cvd/dvt-treatment-home-versus-hospital/3586.

Werner, R. M., and S. A. Glied. 2021. "Covid-Induced Changes in Health Care Delivery—Can They Last?" *New England Journal of Medicine* 385 (10): 868–70. https://doi.org/10.1056/NEJMp2110679.

CHAPTER 2

"Keep the Customer Satisfied" by Simon & Garfunkel

I'm oh, so tired / But I'm trying to
keep my customers satisfied.

"KEEP THE CUSTOMER Satisfied" was the B-side of one of the largest selling and most recorded songs in history, "Bridge over Troubled Water" by Simon & Garfunkel. The latter could also be an appropriate song for this chapter, because what I'm proposing can serve as a bridge over the troubled water of our current system from sick care and fee-for-service revenue to health assurance and providers taking financial responsibility for care.

To your health! L'Chaim! ¡Salud! За здоровье! Many cultures have a traditional toast acknowledging that health is our most important asset. But despite this customary tribute before taking a sip of wine or vodka (which one could argue is not necessarily a harbinger of wellness), neither most individuals nor traditional healthcare systems have been willing to do the hard work that will keep people or populations healthy.

It's not complicated: To remain healthy, manage their chronic conditions, and stay out of the hospital, people need easy, seamless access to primary care and wellness and they need to take care of themselves. An organized system should plan and coordinate patient care across multiple settings, and continuous care should be provided between office visits. Patients' social determinants of health should be addressed as much as possible, and health equity should be the rule throughout the health system (Terry 2020).

These are the basic tenets of population health management, a systems approach that has enabled some healthcare organizations to deliver excellent outcomes at a relatively low cost (Chuang, Luft, and Dudley 2004). However, this approach still hasn't caught on widely in the United States, where fee-for-service incentives induce providers to deliver more services rather than better health. The health systems, physician groups, and accountable care organizations that have embraced population health management tend to focus on what providers can do, such as improving care coordination and having care managers call very sick patients. Patient engagement is usually a lower priority.

In the new age of consumer empowerment, this is going to change. Consumers will be placed in charge of their own healthcare. They'll use a variety of apps, many running in the background, to keep themselves healthy and manage their chronic diseases between visits to their primary care physician. Clinicians will still be essential, but will function primarily as health coaches and monitors, serving as a backup in case people get severely ill.

Health systems will need to recognize that not all consumers are alike. Their marketing and growth departments will have to concentrate on consumer segmentation. That means learning how to communicate with different populations based on their food preferences, cultural differences, language, and many other variables. Clinicians will also have to learn how to take these factors into account, along with the traditional differentiators of how each person responds to diseases and medications, so they can better personalize care.

Some technology-driven, consumer-focused companies are already providing these kinds of services. For example, Livongo (www.livongo.com), which was piloted at my previous health system, started out as a health coaching company for people with diabetes. Livongo provides these patients with unlimited test strips, a smart meter, and personalized tips and coaching, all paid for by self-insured employers and health plans. The meter uploads blood sugar readings to the patient's secure account in the cloud through the Livongo smartphone app. AI-powered analytics are applied to the data, learn the patient's metabolic patterns, and tailor health advice to that person. The app provides real-time, 24/7 tips and insights after every blood glucose check. A Livongo coach calls the patient if a reading is out of range, and users can contact a coach at any time. The meter also reminds the patient when they need to order supplies.

The key to Livongo's success is empowering consumers to manage their diabetes by giving them instant feedback and guidance every day of the year. That is something that no primary care physician can do, and it is made possible by technology. The system doesn't replace the person's doctor; it just reduces the frequency of physician visits, and drastically reduces the likelihood of emergencies.

TECHNOLOGY-ENABLED WELLNESS

What Livongo does is an example of *health assurance*, a concept I developed with Hemant Taneja, managing partner of General Catalyst, the venture capital firm that helped fund Livongo as a start-up. The basic idea of health assurance is that, instead of relying on the healthcare system, consumers tap into services and apps that help them proactively improve their health, deal with chronic conditions, and navigate the sick care system when they need to use it (Taneja, Klasko, and Maney 2020).

Most people today find themselves in a very different situation. For the most part, individuals try to take care of themselves without the crucial support and monitoring they need to optimize their health. They go to a physician's office, an urgent care clinic, or an ER when they get sick, and they struggle to cope with their diabetes or hypertension or arthritis between office visits. Physicians do the best they can to educate patients and explain their treatment plans and medications, but they have a lot of patients and not much time to spend with any one of them.

Even those who have access to an executive physical in one of the top health systems in the country are just receiving a friendlier, more elaborate version of this episodic experience. I have been through several of these assessments, and they provide a great set of physical tests and baselines followed by one-off coaching that usually tells me that I am a bit overweight, a bit stressed, and a bit sleep deprived, and maybe I should spend more time with my wife and family. I then receive a digital report with pictures, texts, and suggestions. And after that, nothing—until the next year's $10,000 concierge experience, in which I'm told the same things. Average consumers come away from their annual physicals even less enlightened.

This is the central issue we must address before we can get a handle on out-of-control health spending. Consumers need regular support to optimize their health, but clinicians don't have the time or bandwidth to provide it. Health assurance solutions can help fill the gap.

Livongo, for example, takes the burden of managing diabetes (and some other chronic conditions) off the shoulders of the individual living with that disease. When Glen Tullman started Livongo, he effectively told people living with diabetes, "I'm going to be your invisible friend and treat you like a person. I'll let you know when you have to go to one of those places that will treat you like a patient, and we'll even arrange the appointment. But you shouldn't have to think about your diabetes. We'll do the thinking for you." That's the philosophy behind health assurance: The consumer doesn't have to think about their condition every day, because tools are doing that for them in the background. With health assurance, we can make it easier for people to manage their conditions without thinking of themselves as patients.

Of course, a lot of people won't avail themselves of these services, even if their physician recommends it. They need some kind of incentive. One approach to get them on board, which is explored further in chapter 6, would be to reduce their out-of-pocket costs.

By using digital health tools to become healthier and by choosing high-value providers, consumers can save money for their employers and health plans. If payers reciprocate by lowering these individuals' health costs, it will be a win for everyone. And if traditional payers don't get it, new entrants such as Amazon Care or Transcarent will.

Led by Glen Tullman, who left Livongo after it was sold to Teladoc in 2020, Transcarent supports employees of self-insured companies with personalized health and care support for many common conditions (Landi 2020). Its digitally enabled concierge service provides round-the-clock telehealth visits, telebehavioral healthcare, urgent care, reduced-price medications, surgeries, cancer care, and specialty care at home. According to the company's website, Transcarent members receive no bills and are not responsible for copays or coinsurance.

Tullman was happy to describe Transcarent's service in detail when I called. Employees of a firm that contracts with Transcarent download a smartphone app that can help them book appointments, renew prescriptions, and more. The app tells them which local pharmacy has the lowest price for a medication; if the prescription is filled there, the copay is waived. Transcarent members can also compare quality and cost data on clinics, hospitals, and medical procedures. Every member has access to a concierge team that answers questions about their treatment options.

If an individual needs elective surgery, they can use the app to compare hospitals and clinics, some of which may be in their health plan. If the user selects a high-quality provider based on Transcarent's advice, they get the full concierge experience and have no out-of-pocket cost. If they select a different option, they're subject to whatever copays and deductibles apply under their employer's health plan, and they book their own appointment.

Transcarent has three levels of providers, including local hospitals, other kinds of providers such as ambulatory surgery centers and specialty clinics, and top-rated providers in other parts of the country. It may defy conventional wisdom for an employer to, say, fly a janitor to the Cleveland Clinic for a heart operation, but Tullman says that Walmart does it for some associates—and it saves money by doing so.

By steering consumers to high-value providers and reducing the cost of care wherever possible, Transcarent saves money for employers. It doesn't charge them anything up front, but splits the savings with its clients. According to Tullman, the usual negotiated rate is about 30 percent.

OTHER HEALTH ASSURANCE COMPANIES

Livongo and Transcarent are two examples of a flock of health assurance start-ups that are creating a stir with the aid of venture capital money. Others include Tendo, Mindstrong, Mindful, Glooko, B.well, Noom, and Commure.

Tendo, which I brought to Jefferson Health early in its development, has created a patient engagement platform and a suite of applications that connect patients, clinicians, and caregivers throughout the care cycle. Tendo supports healthcare organizations as care shifts from episodic interactions to continuous engagement, and shifts focus from treating illness to enabling wellness (Tendo Systems 2021).

Mindstrong uses artificial intelligence (AI) to analyze what you type on your phone's keypad to understand whether you're depressed or manic. Mindstrong also has an AI-driven chatbot that periodically asks questions that help reveal a person's mental state. It can be customized to feel like an ally, and it knows when to bring in a human to help (Taneja, Klasko, and Maney 2020).

Mindful developed LifeXT, which combines digital tools with one-on-one coaching for a custom employee engagement program that optimizes well-being and performance. Both Mindstrong and Mindful recognize that the yearly physical does not end at the neck and that combining the digital and human aspects of care can improve behavioral health and physical well-being.

Glooko offers a digital platform for managing diabetes and other chronic diseases. The platform acts as a hub for connected monitoring devices and other disease-relevant data streams. Unlike Livongo, Glooko doesn't provide feedback or coaching to its users, but it allows people to import the data and review it alongside meal logs and activity data collected from fitness apps such as Fitbit and Strava. It also gives clinics remote monitoring reports that can be integrated with electronic health records (Muoio 2021).

B.well's platform can be used to access medical records from any healthcare provider that has cared for the individual, to manage medications and pharmacies, to connect with third-party apps and wearable sensors, and to send patients alerts and reminders about recommended care. ThedaCare, a Wisconsin health system, has incorporated these functions into a patient portal that includes data from remote monitoring devices and mobile health apps. Patient adoption to date has been significant (Siwicki 2022).

Noom, best-known for its weight-loss platform, now calls it a "behavior change" platform and is expanding it to help people with chronic conditions such as stress and anxiety, hypertension, and diabetes. Noom's digital tools, as described on the company's website, are based on evidence-based approaches such as cognitive behavioral therapy and are paired with human coaches.

Commure is a platform for healthcare apps, similar to the platforms for Apple and Android smartphone apps. Right now, nothing else like this exists in healthcare. Data are locked up in health systems' highly customized electronic health records, so an app developed for one health system is often incompatible with the technology used by other organizations. Commure aims to change that (Taneja, Klasko, and Maney 2020).

ADMINISTRATIVE STREAMLINING

Taneja, the managing partner of General Catalyst, estimates that 20 percent of digital health companies, including those that provide services and not just apps, provide administrative solutions. These firms are streamlining administrative functions such as billing and preauthorization in ways that make things simpler for consumers.

The United States spends several times more on healthcare administration than any other developed country. Companies such as Cedar, Akasa, and Olive use robotic process automation (RPA) to reduce that administrative burden. It is absurd that providers hire lots of people to appeal denials of insurance claims that payers hire lots of people to deny. For any of us caught in this maelstrom, the Stealers Wheel classic "Stuck in the Middle with You" should be playing on the phone while you are waiting for the payer or provider to blame the other for not following the rules. In an age of driverless cars and pilotless drones, these RPA companies and other start-ups focused on healthcare administration are creating "headless" administrative functions that will significantly reduce health costs.

Olive's website (www.oliveai.com) describes how the company uses RPA to help providers increase revenue from third-party payers. Cedar focuses on improving the healthcare administrative experience of payers and providers. It has integrations with the revenue cycle systems of 20 payer organizations across the United States and 35 healthcare organizations, including Yale New Haven Health, Summit Health, Novant Health, and Christiana Care (OODA Health 2021).

BIG INVESTMENTS IN DIGITAL HEALTH

Instead of focusing on only the clinical or administrative aspects of health assurance, some companies are trying to connect the two worlds. Take Avia, for example, which is funded by 7wireVentures and Abundant Venture Partners. Avia's home page (aviahealth.com) describes its aims to "accelerate digital transformation" and "enable healthcare organizations to achieve digital success with greater speed, discipline, and impact." More than 50 health systems employ Avia as the "horse whisperer" between their hospital/provider world and the virtual/digital transformation world. A health system CEO and a digital founder may live in "Two Different Worlds," as Don Rondo sang, but Avia channels Van Halen by bringing together the "Best of Both Worlds."

According to Rock Health, which tracks the industry, digital health start-ups raised $29.1 billion in 729 deals in 2021. That was nearly double the amount such companies raised in 2020. More than half of the year's funding came from 88 megadeals of $100 million or more, totaling $16.8 billion. Among the biggest fundraisers were Noom, which raised $540 million, and start-ups Ro, Mindbody, and Commure, which each raised $500 million (Landi 2022).

Transcarent (2022) has raised nearly $300 million and in 2022, just two years after its founding, was valued at $1.62 billion. Other top money raisers in 2021 included telebehavioral healthcare firms such as Lyra Health and NOCD. Diabetes start-ups also scored big, as did musculoskeletal healthcare firms such as Hinge Health and Sword Health.

The global expansion of digital health activity was even more striking. According to research published in StartUp Health, digital health deals worldwide were worth about $44 billion in 2021, twice the level in 2020. In 2012, the total figure was just $2.3 billion. The researchers attributed the huge leap in digital health investments mainly to the COVID-19 pandemic, which showed how much care could be provided virtually. The result, they noted, has been a historic shift in investment priorities toward telemedicine, remote patient monitoring, and other "next-gen health solutions" (Plaster 2022).

Having ingested those hefty investments and valuations, digital health is growing through its adolescence into maturity. For example, Teladoc bought Livongo for $18.5 billion in October 2020, but as of 2022 it was valued at less than $11 billion (Yahoo Finance 2022). Both Teladoc (2022) and Amwell (2022), the other big public tele-health provider, reported net losses for 2021. The shiny new thing is giving way to sustainable healthcare improvement and value plays. Although 2020 and 2021 were bull times for any company that had AI in its name, the keys to success in the future will be value, consistency, and impact.

SHIFTING PRIORITIES AT JEFFERSON HEALTH

A few years ago, I persuaded Jefferson Health to try out Livongo when the company was still a scrappy start-up looking for venture capital. At the time, it seemed like a good idea that might cut our employee health costs by improving diabetes care. I was right, and people were happier with this experience than with the old-fashioned way of treating diabetes. During the pandemic, moreover, many folks with diabetes were able to put off doctor visits and manage the disease on their own with Livongo's help.

But what I didn't know at the start was how profitable and successful Livongo would become. When it was sold for $18.5 billion, a light bulb went on in my head. Why shouldn't we—and other health systems like ours—partner with these health assurance companies from the get-go and participate in their financial upside?

Since then, Jefferson has done that with a few digital health start-ups. For example, we partnered with a company called Collateral Opportunities that makes a location-enabled badge that can be used to summon security if a nurse is threatened with violence (General Catalyst 2021). We piloted this at Jefferson after getting 15 percent of the company, which had no investors at the time. The pilot was successful, and other hospitals around the company adopted it. In 2021 the company was sold to Commure, and Jefferson's portion of that sale was an important part of our portfolio diversification strategy.

I have referred to this transformation as the "new math" model. The old math of inpatient revenue, outpatient revenue, NIH funding, and in-person tuition will increasingly be challenged. The new math of recouping some of that revenue through healthcare at home and digital health apps will be a game changer. I believe that the new math of digital transformation, strategic partnerships, philanthropy, and AI-driven automation will not only transform healthcare cost, quality, access, and patient experience but will also allow those of us who lead healthcare systems to diversify our portfolio and "participate" in those start-up valuations.

The shift described here is similar to what happened when Apple, Microsoft, and others recognized that the future belonged to the cloud and digital transformations of industries. Hospital stays and traditional health insurance, like PCs and MacBooks, will be commoditized. My current organization, General Catalyst, is partnering with healthcare systems around the country (what we call the consortium of the willing) ranging from HCA to Intermountain Health to Rush University Medical Center, all declaring that, as Kim Petras sang in 2021, the "Future Starts Now."

Jefferson took an even more proactive approach with Tendo, which acted as the system's patient engagement platform. Not only had Jefferson invested in the company, but its CEO, Dan Goldsmith, became a Jefferson "cabinet member" who reported to me before I left. Jefferson helped shape Tendo's vision, helped get it funded, and served as its beta site. In June 2021, Tendo received $50 million in funding, and in 2022, its market value expanded tenfold.

I brought Dan aboard not just to guide Tendo's development but also to advise us on future digital health opportunities. He listens to other leaders who tell him about their problems with quality or access or user experience. Then he looks at all the start-up companies involved in that space, and he may say, "Here's the best solution for your problem, and they'd love to partner with your health system."

HOW HEALTH SYSTEMS ARE WORKING WITH START-UPS

The operative word in Dan's pitch is *partner*, because health systems such as Jefferson are piloting, codeveloping, and in some cases participating in the valuations and royalties of these start-ups. The days of going to digital health conferences and having 500 young software engineers tell me that their app will transform healthcare are over. Health systems must be ready to partner, take the risk, and reap the rewards. A smart health system does not have to pretend it is a venture capital firm; it can create—as Jefferson did—a small investment fund to provide seed money to promising start-ups.

The health system's value is not in venture capital, but in serving as a spin-up partner to an early-stage company, helping the start-up hone its product for wider distribution. Payers understood this years ago. For example, UnitedHealthcare created Optum, and Humana Studio H accelerates digital health and analytics. Independence Blue Cross has partnered with Comcast to create Quil, a patient navigation firm.

This partnership approach has helped Jefferson and other innovative health systems in three ways. First, when health systems work closely with developers, the resulting solutions are changed in ways that make them much more useful to providers. Second, the health systems have been able to obtain wonderful apps that they never could have created in-house with the handful of people they could spare to work on digital innovation. Most providers don't have the resources of a Cleveland Clinic or a Mayo Clinic. And third, many of these systems have been able to co-develop and share in some of the app developers' financial gains.

In the past, health systems created their own apps and tried to market them, which was generally unsuccessful. Similarly, its spin-outs did not work as well for digital innovations as for drug research. A better approach is what I call the *spin-ins*, in which a start-up firm develops an app and approaches the healthcare system. The developers offer to pay the system a fee and some equity in exchange for piloting the product. Even better, and what became Jefferson's differentiator, are *spin-ups*, in which we take a promising technology firm that already has investors; co-develop, expand, and pilot its product; and then take financial risk in the expansion of the product and technology.

The best solution is for the system's innovation team to work with these firms' engineers and make suggestions about how to tweak the software. That makes a whole lot more sense than the old approach, where the developer came up with the product and the provider tried to adapt it to the process it was trying to improve.

INNOVATION SUPERCENTERS

The development of groundbreaking digital solutions could benefit from what I call *innovation supercenters*. In my vision, these are confederations of health systems that are interested in digital health and want to help promising start-ups pilot their solutions. Think of this as the Avia concept on steroids. What would happen if 55 health systems partnered to create these spin-up opportunities?

When a digital health entrepreneur has a good idea, it may not be easy to raise money to turn that idea into a business. Even if they can get seed capital, they still need to find a place to test their product. If just one healthcare system tries it in a few hospitals, it may not mean that much to venture capitalists, but if the app or service is piloted in several fair-sized health systems, the developer stands a good chance of getting significant funding.

The consortia I have in mind are patterned after clinical research supercenters, which consist of academic institutions that have agreed to standardize their legal requirements, such as institutional review boards. Instead of competing with each other for drug trials, they can go together to a pharmaceutical company and say, "We have seven clinical research sites that want to participate in this study." The pharmaceutical firm's costs are lower, and they can give the participants a better deal.

The innovation supercenter would make the proposition even more attractive to all parties. If you're a digital start-up company and you've got seed money or series A funding, you need places to test your app or service. And if the innovation supercenter decided to take on such a developer, that would create a lot of excitement among investment firms. If the pilot showed promising results, the start-up would probably get a big infusion of capital, which would make the supercenter members' equity stakes much more valuable.

Naturally, the innovation supercenter would have to be led by a healthcare outsider who understood the technology field. That person might say, "Here's how I'd rate the AI revenue cycle companies out there. Those three I wouldn't consider, but these two companies already have significant backing. Let me see what kind of deal I can negotiate on behalf of our innovation supercenter with each of those firms. Then your IT people and your revenue cycle people will meet with each company and you'll make a decision."

That academic–entrepreneurial approach is even being adopted by more traditional healthcare institutions. The American Cancer Society, for example, has taken a similar innovative approach through a subsidiary called BrightEdge. The BrightEdge About page describes the organization's mission as developing "groundbreaking patient-centric solutions" and accelerating the American Cancer Society's mission "to advance science, reduce disparities and promote health-care sustainability." The marriage of traditional healthcare and the entrepreneurial world has taken a while, but as Imagine Dragons said, "It's Time!"

THE MESSAGE FOR SMALLER HEALTH SYSTEMS

Big health systems, as I've mentioned, tend to have their own innovation divisions. But they also have a lot of surplus cash, and they're investing some of that in the digital start-ups and other innovative companies that are starting to change the industry. For example, Northwell Health, Intermountain Healthcare, and Rush University Medical Center have all invested in Transcarent (Schroeder 2022). Mayo Clinic and Kaiser Permanente are strategic partners in Medically Home, a leading provider of hospital at home services (Graphite Health 2021).

Other large health systems have joined together to form new companies that can benefit all of them. For example, SSM Health, Presbyterian Healthcare Services, Intermountain, and Kaiser Permanente have created Graphite Health, which focuses on overcoming interoperability challenges (Devereaux 2022). And a dozen systems founded Truveta, a for-profit data company (Cohen 2021).

But most other healthcare organizations are not investing in start-ups. What these systems don't realize is that, for a relatively small or zero investment in the right developer, they can set themselves up for a potentially big payday in the not too distant future. Moreover, they can improve their own care delivery and operations while contributing to the transformation of healthcare.

Health systems need to start thinking along these lines. As Eric Larsen, president of the Advisory Board Company, told the Jefferson Health board in 2021, traditional fee-for-service healthcare systems will continue to see their revenues shrink because they have become commodities, and many of their services are leaving the hospitals. Over the next five years, he said that those who have risk, who have access to the premium dollars, will be strengthened and better able to serve the industry than those who are price takers and further down the food chain as predominantly fee-for-service players. That applies to both hospitals and physicians. At Jefferson, our goal was to be a "a 197-year-old academic medical center thinking like a start-up company."

RESISTANCE TO VALUE-BASED CARE

Most hospitals and clinics are still not oriented to financial risk and population health management, which would empty beds and decrease the use of specialists. The tipping point for a health system to really manage population health, Larsen said, occurs when 23–29 percent of the system's revenues come from full capitation. "What percentage of health systems in this country have 23 percent to 29 percent capitation?" he asked the board in 2021. "I can count them on two hands." In fact, full-risk contracts account for less than 2 percent of the average system's income, he reported.

The early phase of the COVID-19 pandemic revealed how exposed acute-care hospitals and physician groups were as their fee-for-service revenue plummeted, Larsen noted in an advisory board report in March 2021. But the pandemic also "propelled forward a few important trends, such as site-of-care shifts, from inpatient to outpatient, from outpatient to retail settings, and from urgent care to home and virtualization. This shifting of care has been slingshot forward."

These site-of-care shifts all have one thing in common: They depend on the technologies discussed in this chapter. These shifts represent a big opportunity for health systems to transform themselves and the industry while benefiting from the upside of the technology start-ups.

Why would a healthcare organization want to embark on this unfamiliar journey? If I were talking to a health system board, I'd say there's no reason to do it, as long as you're happy about losing money or having a 1 percent margin or less. S&P and Moody's have both downgraded the healthcare provider sector because more and more services are exiting the hospital and are being provided elsewhere without the high fixed costs of brick-and-mortar facilities.

If you think you can be financially successful by continuing to see sick patients in your high-fixed-cost hospitals and getting more money from the insurers, then you shouldn't do anything. Just buy the things you think you need from app developers. But remember, a wide range of players—including health assurance companies, accountable care organizations, and new kinds of Medicare Advantage plans—are being incentivized to reduce your hospital admissions. So you'd better make sure you're not just contributing to someone else making all the money from providing consumer-centered, technology-driven care in nontraditional settings.

The healthcare industry has no viable alternative to changing its business model, because the current model is unsustainable. We have high costs and poor outcomes. We've rewarded inefficiency, because the more inefficient you are, the more you can earn under fee-for-service. And the insurers can just pass the cost on to employers. Denying that you have a problem doesn't make it go away.

Moody's and S&P have told healthcare organizations, in effect, that their fee-for-service model and dedication to being a sick care place have created a terminal condition while making new billionaires in Silicon Valley. Those technology companies can't make their billions without the health systems, so it's time for healthcare organizations to insist on sharing in their profits.

CHANGING WITH THE TIMES

When I was a healthcare executive, I didn't want to be a venture capitalist, but I also didn't want to wither away in an unsustainable financial model. I wanted to be Target or Walmart, not Sears or JCPenney. Target and Walmart recognized that they had great assets in their brick-and-mortar stores, but they also had to compete with Amazon in the "retail at any address" game. Sears and JCPenney did what many hospitals and payers are doing—they stuck to the old model that depended solely on customers coming into their stores and hoped the new competition would go away. It didn't. As Brother Moses sang in 2015, "The First Step (Is Admitting You Have a Problem)."

It's time for health systems to recognize that none of them will escape the consumer revolution. Consumers are having their "I'm as mad as hell and I'm not going to take this anymore" moment: "I'm not waiting half an hour in a waiting room. I'll go to somebody else," they say. And many of them have done just that. For example, when firms such as ChenMed, Oak Street, and One Medical started, experts said people weren't going to leave their primary care provider and go to One Medical or urgent care. But that's what's happening. Do I want to go in next Wednesday for my sore threat or go in now for a 15-minute appointment?

The changes being driven by digital health and alternative care sites don't require healthcare providers to go all-digital. At Jefferson, I would tell my board, "We have great hospitals, and if someone has pancreatic cancer or needs a transplant, they don't care what our digital strategy is; they want to extend their life with surgery and great nursing and medical care. But for the other 97 percent of people in the Philadelphia area, Jefferson also needs to be their partner, so that if they have a chronic condition or a minor acute issue, we are the first place they think of going to for a telehealth or in-person visit or home care."

Those people are looking for the most convenient way to obtain high-quality basic care. Health systems should continue to concentrate on what they do on the specialty side, because nobody else can do that. And then they should use their reputation for specialty care to market themselves as the place that is creating innovative care delivery methods and getting care out to where people are.

CONCLUSION

Health assurance companies and other firms offering innovative, technology-based solutions have the wherewithal—both creative and financial—to transform healthcare. When they join forces with healthcare providers, the cross-fertilization of their different kinds of knowledge will create new products and services that satisfy consumers' demand for better healthcare solutions. In the process, both the technology companies and the health systems will benefit, and most importantly people will get better healthcare closer to home. Health systems can also use some of these apps and services to deliver better care for less money as they cut huge swaths out of healthcare waste. Meanwhile, consumers will be treated better at home or in other nonhospital settings and will be more satisfied with their care.

What all this boils down to is one thing: "Keep the Customer Satisfied." This will be the key to success in the next decade, and the customer is multifocal. It includes consumers, employers, employees, payers, unions, and governments, each requiring a different approach. None of them will use your services based on billboards or 30-second commercials. You will have to build their loyalty by demonstrating value, giving consumers a single point of contact, creating a seamless experience across the continuum, and guiding consumers and employers by giving them the information they need to make good decisions about their health.

I can tell you from experience that when you challenge the traditional model and move to that new math approach, you may, as the song says, be slandered or libeled with words you "never heard in the Bible." These hateful words will be slung at you by those who don't want to do the hard work of transformation. Nevertheless, you must persist and embrace the future. Sometimes it feels like Harry Nilsson's 1971 song "Jump into the Fire," but those that come out the other side will survive and prosper in the coming years.

The current pandemic-driven surge in digital health solutions represents a flowering of the creative work that has been done in mobile health and telemedicine over the past decade. This work offers a "bridge over troubled water" that will enable those of us who have lived in the sick care world to enter the world of consumer-driven health assurance. But much more remains to be done, and the most innovative solutions of the next decade will be tied to artificial intelligence. The next chapter explains how and why.

REFERENCES

Amwell. 2022. "Amwell Announces Result for Fourth Quarter 2021 and Full Year 2021" (press release). Published February 24. https://business.amwell.com/press-release/amwell-announces -results-for-fourth-quarter-2021-and-full-year-2021/.

Chuang, K. H., H. S. Luft, and R. A. Dudley. 2004. "The Clinical and Economic Performance of Prepaid Group Practice." In *Toward a 21st Century Health System: The Contributions and Promise of Prepaid Group Practice*, edited by A. Enthoven and L. Tollen. San Francisco: Jossey-Bass.

Cohen, J. K. 2021. "Hospitals, Health Tech to Partner—and Compete—in 2022." *Modern Healthcare*, December 22. www .modernhealthcare.com/technology/hospitals-health-tech -partner-and-compete-2022-0.

Devereaux, M. 2022. "Kaiser Permanente Joins Digital Health Company Graphite Health." *Modern Healthcare*, January 13. www.modernhealthcare.com/technology/kaiser-permanente -joins-digital-health-company-graphite-health.

General Catalyst. 2021. "General Catalyst and Jefferson Health Announce Innovation Partnership" (press release). Published October 18. www.globenewswire.com/news-release/2021/10 /18/2315983/0/en/General-Catalyst-and-Jefferson-Health -Announce-Innovation-Partnership.html.

Graphite Health. 2021. "Leading Health Systems Launch Graphite Health, a New Member-Led Non-Profit Company to Accelerate Digital Transformation of Health Care" (press release). Published October 5. www.graphitehealth.io/launch -press-release.

Landi, H. 2022. "Digital Health Startups Banked Record-Breaking $29.1B Last Year. Will the Momentum Continue in 2022?" *Fierce Healthcare*, January 10. www.fiercehealthcare.com/digital-health /digital-health-funding-topped-29b-2021-almost-doubling-2020 -s-record-breaking-year.

———. 2020. "Teladoc Finalizes Blockbuster Deal with Livongo in Less than 3 Months." *Fierce Healthcare*, October 30. www .fiercehealthcare.com/finance/teladoc-finalizes-blockbuster -deal-livongo-less-than-three-months.

Muoio, D. 2021. "Diabetes Management Startup Glooko Collects $30M to Push Remote Monitoring, New Therapy Areas." *MobiHealthNews*, March 16. www.mobihealthnews.com/news /diabetes-management-startup-glooko-collects-30m-push -remote-monitoring-new-therapy-areas.

OODA Health. 2021. "Cedar Announces Agreement to Acquire OODA Health to Revolutionize the Consumer Financial Experience in Healthcare" (press release). Published May 13. www .ooda-health.com/cedar-announces-agreement-to-acquire-ooda

-health-to-revolutionize-the-consumer-financial-experience-in -healthcare.

Plaster, L. 2022. "2021 Year-End Insights Report: $44B Raised Globally in Health Innovation, Doubling Year Over Year." StartUp Health. Published January 7. https://healthtransformer .co/2021-year-end-insights-report-44b-raised-globally-in-health -innovation-doubling-year-over-year-90b19ff4a8a6.

Schroeder, M. 2022. "Hospital-at-Home Company Gets a $110M Shot in the Arm." MedCity News. Published January 10. https:// medcitynews.com/2022/01/hospital-care-at-home-company -gets-a-110m-shot-in-the-arm/.

Siwicki, B. 2022. "ThedaCare Health System Sees Huge Patient Adoption of New Digital Front Door." *Healthcare IT News,* January 7. www.healthcareitnews.com/news/thedacare-health -system-sees-huge-patient-adoption-new-digital-front-door.

Taneja, H., S. Klasko, and K. Maney. 2020. *UnHealthcare: A Manifesto for Health Assurance.* Philadelphia, PA: Thomas Jefferson University Press.

Teladoc. 2022. "Teladoc Health Reports Fourth Quarter and Full Year 2021 Results" (press release). Published February 22. https://ir.teladochealth.com/news-and-events/investor-news /press-release-details/2022/Teladoc-Health-Reports-Fourth -Quarter-and-Full-Year-2021-Results/default.aspx.

Tendo Systems. 2021. "Tendo Systems Secures $50 Million to Accelerate Digital Engagement Between Patients, Clinicians, and Caregivers" (press release). Published June 30. www .businesswire.com/news/home/20210630005353/en/Tendo -Systems-Secures-50-Million-to-Accelerate-Digital-Engagement -Between-Patients-Clinicians-and-Caregivers.

Terry, K. 2020. *Physician-Led Healthcare Reform: A New Approach to Medicare for All.* Washington, DC: American Association for Physician Leadership.

Transcarent. 2022. "Transcarent Raises $200 Million in Series C Funding Highlighting Growing Demand for a Different Health and Care Experience Aligned with the Needs of Self-Insured Employers" (press release). Published January 11. https://transcarent.com/posts/transcarent-raises-200-million-series-c-funding.

Yahoo Finance. 2022. Teladoc Health, Inc. (TDOC). Accessed April 20. https://finance.yahoo.com/quote/TDOC/key-statistics/.

CHAPTER 3

"The Name Game" by Shirley Ellis

Come on everybody, I say now let's play a game /
I betcha I can make a rhyme out of anybody's name.

ONE OF THE culture shocks I experienced when moving from
a health system to the technology world was the name game of
initials describing the new world of digital healthcare. RPA, RPM,
AI, NLP—it's a word salad of health information technology. The
trends these initials represent have received unprecedented investment and show incredible potential, but have not yet resulted in
measurable improvements in population health or health disparities.
In areas such as remote patient monitoring, however, these words
connote real promise.

No area better defines the maxim that we tend to overestimate
technology in the short term and underestimate its potential in the
long term. None of today's devices are life-changing, just as the
initial iPhones were mostly cool phones. But moving from sick care
to health assurance for all will require humans and technology to
come together to create a future of "healthcare at any address." When
that happens, the resulting devices will change the lives of millions.

Because of the pandemic and new reimbursement rules, remote
patient monitoring (RPM) has surged along with telehealth over
the past few years. In many cases, RPM has been combined with
virtual visits and health coaching. Meanwhile, artificial intelligence (AI) now informs some advanced RPM applications. As these

technologies come together, they promise to reduce the amount of time that physicians need to care for each patient while improving the quality of care. To the extent that they prevent avoidable hospitalizations, decrease the need for office visits, and enable most healthcare to be provided at home, the combination of RPM, telehealth, and AI can also reduce costs.

RPM is divided into two overlapping categories: mobile health, a.k.a. mHealth, and home monitoring. For several years after the advent of the smartphone, mHealth was the more glamorous branch of RPM. Mobile health apps proliferated, and by 2015 there were 165,000 apps on the US market. However, two-thirds of these apps just provided information on medical conditions. The majority of the others focused on fitness and wellness and were sold to healthy people who wanted to track their exercise, diet, or sleep patterns. Fairly few apps were designed to help people with chronic conditions such as diabetes or hypertension (Terry 2018). Fewer still were meant to help the underserved population better care for themselves and their families.

There was little effort to evaluate mHealth apps for either physicians or consumers. Doctors who wanted to prescribe them had little to go on; the early adopters tended to suggest apps they'd used themselves, or they just advised patients to shop in the app stores. A few health systems such as Ochsner and the Cleveland Clinic had their own app stores.

Consumers who downloaded these apps usually didn't stick with them for long. One reason is that most apps had no way for consumers to send data to their physicians. They could look at the data themselves, and the app might tell them what it meant, but it didn't really connect with their healthcare. What consumer marketers call "stickiness"—something that gets someone to tap on the app every day—was missing.

Meanwhile, the VA health system was showing the value of RPM. Besides reducing readmissions, a primary reason for the VA to use RPM was to keep veterans who required long-term care at home. As early as 2013, the VA had used remote monitoring for 119,000 veterans, more than one-third of whom had avoided institutionalization (Terry 2013). A 2021 VA pilot program found that veterans who actively shared vital signs weekly through an RPM platform had "a 75% decrease in emergency room visits and hospitalizations post-intervention, compared to pre-intervention" (McMillian 2021).

Some private health systems began using RPM with recently discharged patients, mainly those who had congestive heart failure, to prevent readmissions. But despite the cost savings the VA had achieved, only a handful of large organizations such as Kaiser Permanente, Partners Health Care, and Geisinger Health fully embraced remote monitoring. The biggest reason: Outside of healthcare organizations that took financial risk, providers were not being reimbursed for using RPM data in patient care. The core principle that it's hard to get someone to do something when their salary depends on them not doing it restricted RPM to those few systems that functioned as both payer and provider, such as Kaiser and University of Pittsburgh Medical Center (UPMC).

CMS REIMBURSEMENTS FOR RPM

Math is a wonderful thing, especially when it comes to reimbursement in healthcare. So when the country's largest payer, the Centers for Medicare & Medicaid Services (CMS), first began reimbursing physicians for RPM services provided to seniors with chronic conditions, both the implementation of RPM solutions by healthcare systems and the venture capital necessary to fuel research and development expanded greatly.

The initial CMS authorization in 2018 included the collection and interpretation of physiological data for at least 20 minutes per month (eHI 2018). In 2019, CMS added three new billing codes for RPM in chronic care. Coverage expanded further in 2020, allowing remote monitoring of patients with acute conditions such as COVID-19. In 2021, CMS proposed adding new codes for remote therapeutic monitoring that includes nonphysiologic data on medication adherence and mental status (Mecklai et al. 2021).

Private insurers are increasingly following CMS's lead. United-Healthcare, for example, now covers remote physiological monitoring services in its Medicare Advantage plans and some commercial plans (UnitedHealthcare 2022). In 2021, Humana rolled out a new program combining home health, RPM, and telehealth services (Wicklund 2021a). And in 2022, telehealth firm MDLIVE, which is owned by Cigna, introduced an RPM program for patients with chronic conditions (Torrence 2022).

Worldwide, the RPM market has exploded. In 2016, about 7 million patients globally were being remotely monitored (Mack 2017); by 2020, that number had ballooned to 45.6 million, according to Berg Insight (2021). The company projects that this number will jump to 115.7 million by 2026.

There are signs that RPM is growing rapidly in the United States as well, says Joseph Kvedar, MD, vice president of connected health partners at Mass General Brigham and professor of dermatology at Harvard Medical School. In an interview, Kvedar told me that "before the pandemic, remote monitoring was mostly confined to the VA and home care. Now lots of large physician practices are getting into the space." The reasons include improved reimbursement and hospitals' desire to avoid readmissions because of CMS penalties.

But fee-for-service coverage of remote monitoring is a clunky compromise, Kvedar argues. RPM will not achieve its full potential, he predicts, until value-based reimbursement makes it economically desirable to monitor and care for people between encounters with physicians.

"We're generally not set up to keep people healthy in their home," he points out. "We're set up to take care of them when they get sick. So, all those wonderful things that come from remote monitoring don't happen unless there's an economic reason for it to happen."

THE DEBATE OVER RPM BENEFITS

Since the VA's initial successes, a number of studies have shown positive outcomes from remotely monitoring certain kinds of patients. The Geisinger Health System found that telemonitoring reduced the readmission rate of congestive heart failure patients within 30 days by 44 percent (*Becker's Hospital Review* 2014). During the pandemic, Geisinger employed telemonitoring by giving patients an oximeter and thermometer to use at home. RPM patients provided daily updates on their subjective symptoms and objective pO2 (partial pressure of oxygen) and basal temperature. The combination of home monitoring and daily check-ins was a major component in reducing patient anxiety (Minemyer 2020). In another program, UPMC showed that 13 percent of monitored congestive heart failure patients were readmitted within 30 days, compared to 20 percent of those not enrolled in the RPM program (*Becker's Health IT* 2015b).

Systems that began RPM early, such as the VA, Geisinger, and UPMC, have taken those initial results as cause for expansion. In 2022, UPMC announced an app-like model with Vivify. Andrew Watson, MD, FACS, medical director of telemedicine at UPMC, described the system to NGPX (2020): "Patients simply open a box, then turn on a tablet or respond to a text message to access remote patient monitoring. The process has been streamlined to make it simple for them. Care is provided through survey questions, educational videos, scales, BP cuffs and pulse oximeters, and live video visits."

As described to NGPX, Vivify "provides a call center portal, equipment monitoring, reporting features, and integration with electronic health records (EHRs). It also offers BYOD (bring your own device) capabilities that allow patients to access the platform using their own personal devices." UPMC reported that the program reduced readmissions among Medicare enrollees by 76 percent, and patient satisfaction and compliance both exceeded 90 percent.

Ochsner Health System remotely monitors people with common chronic diseases such as hypertension, diabetes, and COPD. In 2021,

Ochsner added health wellness coaching personalized to each patient and started selling its RPM service to payers across the country. By using RPM to cut health costs, Ochsner claims, health plans and businesses can see a return on investment of 3:1 for diabetes and 4:1 for hypertension (Wicklund 2021b).

On the other hand, Mayo Clinic Platform president John Halamka, MD, and Paul Cerrato (2021) have pointed out that only some remote monitoring devices are reliable, and few of these products are supported by randomized controlled trials. Some devices, such as those of Digital Diagnostics and AliveCor, have received FDA approval or clearance, but the vast majority have not. Studies have shown variable effects of RPM on outcomes (Mecklai et al. 2021).

Kvedar attributes these varying results to differences in how the studies were conducted. Among the factors that might have influenced the results, he says, are "when a nurse or a doctor gets involved, who sees the data, what kind of data are they using, what kind of rules set is firing alerts, and how often they're communicating with the patients." For example, when Partners HealthCare (now Mass General Brigham) did RPM studies several years ago, "we had a 50 percent drop in heart failure and all-cause readmissions in the study groups. But an earlier study from Yale said RPM was ineffective." In that Yale study, "the intervention was that the patient weighed himself and then phoned the data into a robocall line. That's not a very sticky intervention; no wonder it didn't work. That's why there's so much difference between studies. The magic isn't in the scale or the blood pressure cuff, it's in how you use it."

Scales and blood pressure cuffs are just the "primordial ooze" of the potential for RPM, in much the same way that the iPod was the beginning of the digital revolution. The RPM devices most often prescribed by physicians today include equipment that tracks heart rate, blood glucose, oxygen saturation, and temperature. Patients with asthma or COPD are using remote spirometry devices. Patients with diabetes use glucometers to track their HbA1c and a pill bottle device to measure their medication adherence (Rosenthal 2020).

A more detailed explanation of the benefits that RPM can confer on patients and providers is presented in a report by eHI (2018, 1), which notes that RPM programs

> passively and continuously collect and transmit patient-generated health data (PGHD) from in-home medical devices to providers and care teams. PGHD, when compared to health data collected exclusively during in-person doctor's visits, more accurately and holistically reflects lifestyle choices, health history, symptoms, medication, treatment information, and biometric data such as heart rate, blood glucose, blood pressure, temperature, oxygen levels, and weight.
>
> ... There are tools currently available that identify data trends, elevate critical data points, and help aggregate, summarize, and visualize PGHD in meaningful ways. Investing resources in these tools makes PGHD useful at the point of care, while encouraging health professionals to embrace the available data and utilize these tools to further benefit their patients.

Beyond these uses of monitoring data, RPM supports the expansion of telehealth into chronic care, which is one of the reasons telehealth service Teladoc acquired Livongo. It also explains MDLIVE's decision to launch an RPM program. By providing real-time data on a patient's vital signs and chronic conditions, curated monitoring data gives doctors much of the information they need to make patient care decisions without seeing the patient in person.

RPM INTERFACES AND WORKFLOW

To make monitoring data useful at the point of care, RPM services need to do two things: (1) connect monitoring devices seamlessly with a provider's EHRs and (2) provide a mechanism to screen the data for important information that triggers alerts or shows meaningful patterns.

Validic, a leading RPM service, says on its website (www.validic.com/how-it-works/) that it "integrates directly with your existing clinical workflows, augmenting the functionality of your embedded systems and services to make remote care more efficient and effective." Validic has also teamed up with Philips, the medical device maker, which has integrations with a number of EHRs and clinical systems (HIT Consultant 2016).

One solution gaining ground with health systems is the Stel Life Vitals Hub, which securely and directly connects Bluetooth vitals devices in the patient's home to the EHR system without complex setup, Wi-Fi, or mobile applications.

Qualcomm Life, another RPM service, has had a partnership with Cerner since 2015. Under this arrangement, it transmits data to the Cerner EHR system via Cerner's device connectivity platform CareAware (*Becker's Health IT* 2015a).

Vivify Health provides EHR integration along with a call center portal, equipment monitoring, and reporting features. Physicians log into the Vivify portal to monitor alerts, bio-parameters, and patient survey results and to conduct video visits with patients. At UPMC, provider documentation flows from the Vivify portal into UPMC's EHR system, which is Cerner in the system's hospitals and Epic on the ambulatory side (Siwicki 2018a).

Beth Israel Deaconess Medical Center uses Apple's HealthKit in its RPM program. After passing through the RPM software and the Apple Health app, the monitoring data goes into the hospital's core EHR system via a specially designed app (Comstock 2016).

So it appears that remote monitoring data from a variety of devices can be transmitted to major EHR systems. But once the data is there, how is it analyzed and organized to separate the signal from the noise? The RPM services say they have found ways to do this so that physicians aren't overwhelmed by the volume of data and turned off by the extra workload. The key to RPM is to be an early warning sign for people with chronic conditions, but that requires separating out actionable data so that the person at home can answer the Clash's question: "Should I Stay or Should I Go" to the doctor's office or hospital.

Kvedar isn't convinced that the current solutions are up to the job. "I know it's a very soluble problem, because it's being done in other industries. If a healthcare provider has a need for that kind of a product, someone will build it. But what we've seen to date hasn't been that effective. Probably the reason we don't see it is no one has been willing to pay for it. The data science exists to build those signal-to-noise dashboards. It's not new technology."

AI TO THE RESCUE

Could AI be the key to analyzing monitoring data and delivering insights to clinicians in real time? Some vendors claim that their AI-based products can discover correlations in remote monitoring data for patients with chronic conditions (Johnson 2018). Whether they can reliably predict or detect events of clinical significance is uncertain. But if the right kind of algorithm parsed the records of thousands of patients similar to the person a clinician was treating, it could theoretically assess what was going on with that patient at any point in time, based on the remote monitoring data.

AI tools are already being used to predict the likelihood of read-mission, remission, and survival for patients with conditions such as blood cancer and brain cancer (Slabodkin 2017, 2018). They have also been used to predict the risk of individual cardiovascular events (Muise 2018). Machine learning algorithms can also predict the onset of sepsis, screen for diabetic retinopathy, and detect breast cancer from digital mammograms with a high degree of accuracy (Slabodkin 2019a; Muise 2018).

Some health systems have begun using AI tools to improve the outcomes of individual patients. UPMC has used predictive analytics to reduce hospitalizations and give discharged patients the diagnostic tools to manage their own conditions at home, so they don't need to see their doctor (Muise 2018). Intermountain has been at the forefront of using AI to assess patient disease risk and optimize care for a variety of conditions (Woolman 2020). And Northwell has applied AI to augment its postdischarge workflows, reducing readmissions by 24 percent. Its clinical AI tool stratifies patients for their risk of readmissions, identifies the clinical and nonclinical factors driving patient risk, and recommends targeted outreach and interventions to reduce that risk (Siwicki 2021).

Flagler Hospital in Saint Augustine, Florida, has used AI tools to improve the treatment of pneumonia and sepsis. A machine-learning program automatically revealed new, improved care pathways for these conditions after analyzing thousands of patient records from the hospital and identifying the common traits of those individuals with the best outcomes. Flagler was able to implement the new pneumonia pathway by changing the order sets in its EHRs. As a result, it reduced the readmission rate for pneumonia from 2.9 percent to 0.4 percent and saved $1,356 per patient (Siwicki 2018b).

AI's Rapid Growth

Nowhere has the word salad in healthcare tech been more prevalent than in the use of AI. Even its name is debated: Is it really artificial intelligence? I see AI as just an adjunct to the human being; a better name might be *augmented intelligence*. If it's operating in the background, rather than as a robot standing next to the human, we might use the term *ambient intelligence*. (Think unnoticed white noise vs. Jon Bon Jovi's "Blaze of Glory"). Those tech entrepreneurs who believe that the AI funding bubble of 2019–2021 is sustainable have yet to encounter an AI winter. Since 1984, the field has experienced several hype cycles, followed by disappointment and criticism, followed by funding cuts, followed by renewed interest years or decades later.

Healthcare in 2022 is clearly in an AI spring, despite decreased valuations among companies that are neither differentiated nor revenue sustainable. How long that blossom will remain depends on the ability to show that these techniques make a quantifiable difference in the conundrum of optimizing cost, access, quality, equity, and user experience that American healthcare now faces. Simply put, AI and machine learning will be a game changer in creating a healthier future, but just as spring gardening involves some pruning, several companies have been pruned down in this AI spring because they could not prove sustainable value.

AI has been spreading through the healthcare industry for the past several years. So far, it has gained more traction in administrative than in clinical applications, but the latter are catching up. According to a 2021 Accenture white paper, the top 10 AI applications in the 2020s will include robot-assisted surgery, virtual nursing assistants, administrative workflow assistance, fraud detection, dosage error reduction, connected machines, clinical trial participant identifier, preliminary diagnosis, automated image diagnosis, and cybersecurity.

To that point, one of the most exciting and executable areas of AI is in clinical trial matching, especially getting more underserved populations involved in clinical trials. Deep Lens and Kyra both use AI to create patient identification solutions that accelerate oncology clinical trial enrollment by connecting trial sponsors to community oncology practices at scale. As importantly, AI matching allows for more democratized utilization of potential lifesaving clinical trials to underserved populations who have been left out of more traditional trial matching.

Another exciting AI application is what Accenture calls a virtual nursing assistant—a kind of clinical decision support tool based on remote monitoring data. "When AI solutions remotely assess a patient's symptoms and deliver alerts to clinicians only when patient care is needed, it reduces unnecessary hospital visits," the company notes, adding that AI tools can also help people avoid unwarranted office visits (Accenture 2021, 4). Over the next few years, Accenture predicts, this function will expand from virtual triage to AI-based care recommendations to patients.

Hemant Taneja of investment firm General Catalyst sounds a note of caution about this rush into AI. Most of the digital health start-ups pitching him and his colleagues right now, he told me, claim they use AI in some way, but not many do. This is true of companies that have developed apps and services for population health management and of those that have created tools for use in the care of individual patients.

Taneja is much more likely to fund the former. When algorithms are applied to population health management, he says, they're seeking statistical correlations in data that might be used to improve the care of populations. Inaccuracies in some of that data are less likely to affect the outcome. But when AI is applied to the care of individuals, he says, the data must be highly accurate or it can harm patients. Taneja notes that the EHR data that these algorithms analyze may not be entirely correct, because billing considerations affect physician documentation (see chapter 4).

To use AI properly in digital health tools, Taneja says, you need to accumulate a lot of data pertaining to the outcomes of interest. That's why he won't invest in Silicon Valley start-ups that put AI first in their healthcare apps and services. Livongo, he says, avoided AI when it started and incorporated algorithms into its diabetes service only after it had built a large database.

AI Categories of Interest

The main AI categories in healthcare, besides robotic surgery, are natural language processing (NLP), predictive modeling, and prescriptive analytics. NLP and data mining will be explored in chapter 4 in the context of clinical decision support. From the viewpoint of interpreting remote monitoring data for patients, predictive modeling and its prescriptive cousin are more relevant—although more advanced NLP may someday play a role.

Predictive analytics is used to predict events and identify patterns, both in populations and in individuals. But it's really just a starting point to enact meaningful change. To apply predictive modeling to patient care, it's necessary to use prescriptive analytics that make specific recommendations to operationalize the data.

For example, Ochsner has used machine learning to predict the deterioration of patients in the hospital. The algorithm leverages more than 1 billion clinical data points to create a network capable of predicting deterioration outside of the ICU with 90 percent accuracy. Based on that model, the health system designed an intervention consisting of a response team and a notification process. This intervention has reduced adverse events outside the ICU by 44 percent (Slabodkin 2019b).

Supervised Versus Unsupervised Algorithms

Predictive analytics are typically based on algorithms that are trained through a "supervised learning" approach, in which the outcome is known ahead of time. That approach works fine when only certain kinds of data are being used, but the varieties of health data are increasing rapidly. For example, some health databases now encompass genomic data and social determinants of health, which include a dizzying number of variables. Moreover, individual responses to certain diseases and specific medications are very complex, and more is being learned about this all the time. So "unsupervised" algorithms that learn from experience are needed to accurately predict individual outcomes and responses to medical interventions (Hodach et al. 2016, 223).

The AI solution Flagler Hospital used to improve its clinical pathways, for instance, used unsupervised machine learning to identify common elements in the treatments of the pneumonia patients who had the best outcomes. The software did this by grouping patients who had been treated similarly and comparing those groups' outcomes, computing the direct variable costs, lengths of stay, readmission rates, and mortality rates for each of the cohorts. Comorbidities were also factored into the algorithm's calculations.

The Flagler team selected the cohort that had the shortest length of stay, the least readmissions, the lowest mortality rate, and the lowest cost. Then it used the algorithm to redesign its care pathway to reflect how that group of patients had been treated from the time they'd arrived in the ER until they were discharged. In some cases, the algorithm revealed relationships that the team would not have known to look for. For example, they found that the faster they started a pneumonia patient who also had COPD on nebulizer treatments, the shorter the stay, the lower the cost, and the lower the likelihood of readmission.

Flipping the Paradigm

AI tools are also starting to be used in the care of patients at home. Ochsner, for example, has begun to apply machine learning to its remote monitoring of patients with chronic diseases. Instead of going to a doctor's office three or four times a year, these patients get regular virtual checkups using real-time analyses of monitoring data fed continuously to their care team. More than 6,500 patients were participating in this program in 2019, and some hypertensive individuals were seeing their blood pressure fall as a result (Slabodkin 2019b).

As the technology improves and consumers gain greater control of their own care, AI-based health advisers will provide recommendations directly to people, based on their monitoring data and other information about them. Livongo, Homeward, and other health assurance companies are already doing some of this, but more can be done.

For example, people at risk of developing type 2 diabetes can benefit from evidence-based interventions listed in the CDC's National Diabetes Prevention Program. The intervention can be delivered in person, via telehealth, or online. High-quality virtual diabetes prevention programs use technology that reaches people where they are so they can be educated about key risk factors. Virtual counseling, including sessions powered by conversational AI bots, have been shown to help people make meaningful behavior changes that drive better outcomes (Gabbay and Hu 2021).

Another type of preventive care involves warning people when they are showing signs of a worrisome health condition. Apple smartwatches, for example, are now able to detect atrial fibrillation when paired with a deep neural network. While the AI-enhanced smartwatch data is slightly less specific than that of an electrocardiogram device, its accuracy is considerably greater than that of self-reporting (Lovett 2018b).

People who use such apps still can't diagnose themselves without the help of a clinician. Accenture (2021) discusses AI tools making "preliminary diagnoses" that must be confirmed by a physician. But in at least one area, algorithms have pushed beyond that barrier. The FDA has recognized IDx-DR, created by Digital Diagnostics, as a "breakthrough device" able to accurately diagnose retinopathy without involving an ophthalmologist (Preston 2018). Google researchers have confirmed that a trained algorithm can detect retinopathy as well as a physician can (Lovett 2018a).

If the FDA approves this technology, patients could test themselves without having to visit an eye doctor. Considering how many people with diabetes are referred for retinopathy exams but don't get them, this could be a major advance.

A NEW RELATIONSHIP WITH PHYSICIANS

So where are we going in the world of virtual care? Will the healthcare version of Nicki Minaj's "Feeling Myself" be "Diagnosing Myself?" Will we return to the paradigm of mHealth apps, which people use to manage their health and wellness without connecting to their physicians?

I don't believe that's going to happen. Even with the advent of health assurance services that provide automated feedback on RPM data about how to optimize health and manage chronic conditions, people will still seek advice and help from their care teams. But the relationship between individuals and their physicians will change.

In *The Patient Will See You Now*, the prescient 2015 book by Eric Topol, MD, the founder and director of the Scripps Research Translational Institute envisions a future in which each person has all their own medical data and the computing power to process it, and most care is provided at home. Here's how he describes the result:

> The doctor will see you now via your smartphone screen without an hour of waiting, at any time, day or night. It might not be your primary care doctor, but it will likely be a reputable physician who is conducting part of his or her practice through secure video consults. And those consults will involve doing parts of the standard physical examination remotely. More importantly, they will incorporate sharing your data—the full gamut from sensors, images, labs, and genomic sequence, well beyond an electronic medical record. We're talking about lots of terabytes of data about you, . . . from the womb to the tomb, in your personal cloud, stored and ready for ferreting out the signals from the noise, even to prevent an illness before it happens. (Topol 2015, 8)

I view the future in a similar way. At least for people with chronic conditions, and perhaps also for relatively healthy people, remote monitoring will become more or less continuous. The data from this real-time, always-on digital physical will be available both to the person and their care team. This represents the dream and reality of healthcare at any address, or health assurance, as described in the book I wrote with Hemant Taneja in 2020. Most important, RPM changes the definition of a health system or a physician practice, because most care will be provided at home rather than in the office or the hospital. The concept of a once-a-year physical should go the way of bloodletting and leeches.

The New Annual Physical

The implications of healthcare at any address are enormous. Take the annual physical. Today, this appointment is primarily a data collection opportunity. Your physician takes your blood pressure, weighs you, takes your temperature, does an electrocardiogram, draws blood for lab tests, looks in some orifices and pokes a few others, and then has about five minutes to ask how you're doing.

The data comes with no context over time—no sense, for instance, of what your heart rate or breathing rate is every day and whether it's showing troubling patterns. The data is connected to no other data about your life—nothing about what you eat, where you've been, how much stress you've been under. So, basically, the physician knows the state of your health only during the short time you're in the examination room, and has little time to talk to you because of the need to stay on schedule—and of course, collect all that data in the office.

An entirely new kind of "physical"—rich in data and deeply rooted in human empathy—will become the starting place for your health assurance. Some of this data will come from a comprehensive health record that will reflect everything that has been done for you by every provider you've come in contact with. In addition, the curated recent results and insights from your remote monitoring will be available. And there will also be information on other key parameters, including your genomic makeup, your personal and family history, and your social determinants of health. Think of a mix of Gloria Gaynor's "I Am What I Am" and Jaheim and Keyshia Cole's "I've Changed."

With the cost of genomic sequencing continuing to fall, in a few years genetic testing will be as routine as a blood test used to check cholesterol. However, people will have their umbilical cord DNA analyzed only once, because it will never change. It won't be long before everyone has their DNA tested at birth, making it part of each person's health record for life.

Privacy concerns around genomic data have become one of my primary areas of interest. Your genome tells doctors whether you have a predisposition for certain cancers or other diseases. It also provides clues about how to care for you, including what drugs are most likely to be effective for you. Your genetic data can even help you understand how fast you metabolize caffeine, which is important to know if you have insomnia. There are so many opportunities for commercialization and abuse, and the time to recognize the good, bad, and ugly is now.

If we knew that the social media revolution was not just a convenient way to communicate with others or to see your grandkids, but could also potentially affect elections and be used to spew hate, we would have put in some guardrails *before* implementation. Similarly, the genomic revolution—combined with continuous remote monitoring and, eventually, continuous blood analysis empowered by nanotechnology—opens up a new frontier for a healthier, more equitable society. Making sure that the unintended consequences of privacy issues, cybersecurity, commercial abuse, and racial inequities don't tarnish this potential will require (1) putting ethics into the equation at the beginning and (2) using technologies such as blockchain, deidentification, and tokenization to ensure that patients remain in control of not only their data but also the core of their being—their genomic makeup.

Another key source of data will be social determinants of health. These include social and economic factors as well as physical environmental factors, and account for 20 percent to 50 percent of health outcomes, as discussed in chapter 8 (Hodach et al. 2016). Some healthcare organizations use a range of apps to connect with community organizations that address components of social determinants, such as food insecurity and inadequate housing. In addition, they are turning to AI to accurately identify high-risk people with addressable social determinants and efficiently target interventions (Siwicki 2022).

When care teams have all this data at their fingertips, they'll be able to suggest appropriate interventions that will help people reduce their risk of developing or exacerbating chronic conditions. At the same time, automated health advisers will coach individuals about their health risks and opportunities to improve their health on a day-to-day basis.

As a result of these interventions, people will be healthier and better informed; thus, they'll need to visit doctors less often than they do now. When they do have a clinical encounter, it will be very different from today's routine interactions between doctors and patients. Instead of having to spend most of the visit investigating the person's physical condition and documenting it in an EHR, the physician will ask questions about recent trends in the individual's physiological data, find out more about their personal situation, and jointly prepare or adjust a treatment plan with the person.

It is beyond time for us to take advantage of these advancing technologies, not to just make the wealthy healthier, but also to move population health monitoring, social determinants, and predictive analytics from philosophic and academic exercises to the mainstream of clinical care and payment models.

Monitoring in the Background

Continuous health monitoring will not win many converts unless it can be done unobtrusively in the background. After all, most people don't want to regard themselves as patients unless they're very sick. One of the ways this can be accomplished is to develop improved wearable sensors, which will translate physical signs into data that can be transmitted via smartphones.

Wearables have been around for a decade or more. Ten years ago, Fitbit already existed, and so did AliveCor. A start-up named OMsignal was developing a compression undershirt with sensors that could reportedly capture electrocardiogram patterns, activity, breathing patterns, and emotive states (Dolan 2013).

Since then, the concept of wearable sensors has been dramatically upgraded. At Jefferson Health, for instance, we worked with an Australian company to codevelop a carbonized hemp wearable called Hemp Black, with sensors that help people stay connected with their health, track their steps, record their heart rates, and more. Michael Savarie, a Jefferson graduate and the sustainability enterprise catalyst for Hemp Black, told me in an e-mail, "There's a space that needs to be filled, and currently that space is being filled with clunky wires going into fabric." But Hemp Black has technology that could eliminate clunky, uncomfortable wires.

Sensor-laden clothing hasn't caught on yet, but in 2019 Current Health received FDA clearance for an upper-arm wearable monitor for home use in post-acute care. Paired with a dedicated tablet, educational content, medication reminders, and support for virtual visits, the wearable can monitor skin temperature, pulse rate, oxygen saturation, and movement (Muoio 2019a). Current has also partnered with Dexcom, which allows continuous monitoring of blood glucose through a wearable sensor, and Vivalink, which offers a wearable electrocardiogram monitor. Also in 2019, the FDA cleared an upgraded version of AliveCor's wearable six-lead electrocardiogram device, which is part of a cardiology service (Muoio 2019b). In February 2020, AliveCor rolled out a credit card-size electrocardiogram with a single lead that can be carried in a wallet (Lovett 2022a).

Apple leads the health wearables market with its Apple Watch, Beats, and AirPod products. I've already mentioned Apple's pilot for using the smartwatch to detect atrial fibrillation. Apple also makes 100 types of data available through the iPhone, Apple Watch, and third-party apps. People whose doctors use one of six leading EHRs will soon be able to send them tracked data on heart rate, sleep hours, exercise minutes, steps, and falls through Apple Health (Kaiser Health News 2021; Moeller 2020).

Fitbit, acquired by Google in 2021, sells a widely used wristband that tracks exercise. It also has a smartwatch that can measure blood oxygen, skin temperature, heart rhythm, heart rate, sleep patterns, and stress, as well as activity. Amazon has also entered the wearables race with its Halo wristband for health and fitness tracking (Moeller 2020).

The next stage in background monitoring will likely involve the Internet of Things. Smart speakers like Alexa and home control systems like Nest may serve as access points for low-power wearables and ambient sensors. They could also enable intelligent personal assistant capabilities such as medication reminders and exercise monitoring (Moeller 2020).

Meanwhile, the caricature of someone walking around with several devices stuck to their body is being replaced with almost imperceptible continuous monitoring techniques that don't require you to add or wear anything. These approaches use micro sensors attached to things you use in your daily life, much the way your car sends continuous signals about its own status. Rod Stewart's "You Wear It Well" may soon describe your health status, rather than your attire.

A pair of start-ups have beat the tech giants to the punch in the Internet of Things. Eight Sleep, which started out as a mattress that can heat or cool to your body's wishes, can now measure an increasing amount of healthcare data automatically. Casana, a smart-toilet maker, describes itself on the company home page as "the future of in-home health monitoring, where you least expect it!" Its "heart seat" seeks to capture reliable data during the three hours and nine minutes a week the average adult sits on the toilet—twice as much time as they spend exercising (Lee 2017). Olamide's song "Sitting on the Throne" might have a very different connotation someday.

Wearables are moving from the ring and watch to your everyday life. The cofounder of Jawbone, Hosain Rahman, is working with All.health to develop a comprehensive preventive and proactive healthcare platform that combines clinical-grade sensors, machine learning, patient histories, insurance claims data, and other information to provide real-time at-risk screening for several disease conditions. And *Digital Medicine*, of which Kvedar is the editor, has published an article about a remote device called Wellvii that can monitor 11 health parameters using medical grade sensors and algorithms which allow you to capture blood pressure variability, heart rate, heart rate variability, respiration rate, and SpO2 in 90 seconds (Polanco et al. 2019). The device provides an intuitive dashboard around balance, stress, vitality, and trends so you can "boost your health IQ" (wellvii.com).

No area of RPM and AI health data analysis will have a more rapid trajectory than advances in this direct-to-consumer area. What exists today will soon look like a first-generation iPod next to the wearables of the near future.

REDUCED SPENDING WHILE ENDING DISPARITIES

In a world of health assurance, consumers will stay healthier, manage conditions better, see doctors less often, get fewer tests, buy fewer drugs, and spend less overall on their health than they do today. This change will be a decisive factor in enabling the United States to bend the cost curve and make healthcare affordable. The aim will not be to make the sick care system more efficient, but to keep people as healthy as possible so they don't need sick care.

However, health equity must be a cornerstone of this transition. Today, as mentioned previously, racial minorities receive substantially worse care in the United States than white people do. Similarly, poor folks are at a healthcare disadvantage when compared with affluent people, and rural residents are losing access to healthcare for a variety of reasons, including hospital consolidations. All these disparities will get even worse in a health assurance world unless everyone is guaranteed access to computers or smartphones and a broadband internet connection.

There are also inequities in how AI algorithms are developed. To address these, says Paul Cerrato of the Mayo Clinic, "developers and researchers need to start by improving the data sets upon which their algorithms are based" (Lovett 2022b). In other words, those data sets must be more representative of the population. In addition, the design of the algorithms must be examined to determine what they seek to optimize: quality of care, outcomes, cost, or all three (Kent 2019).

To Taneja, health equity is a precondition of health assurance, and successful digital health entrepreneurs must be cognizant of that. "We need to build these companies so that we can shrink the overall amount that healthcare costs, and reinvest some of those savings in ensuring health equity. Because this is really a societal benefit that we believe everyone should enjoy."

When everything described in this chapter is fully achieved, AI will become a valued servant of consumers and providers without replacing the judgment of either party. But for AI to achieve its potential, we need much better and more comprehensive health data, and it must be universally available. Only then will physicians be able to trust the algorithms enough to focus mostly on health coaching and care coordination for their patients.

Just as in the Bee Gees song "Words," patients will need more than words to judge the health technology you want them to use; they will evaluate it based on how effective it is at assuring their health at work, home, and play. The next chapter examines the progress being made in these areas and offers some hypotheses on where that may lead for patients, providers, and the robots that will work alongside them.

REFERENCES

Accenture. 2021. "Artificial Intelligence: Healthcare's New Nervous System" (white paper). www.accenture.com/t20171215T032059Z__w__/us-en/_acnmedia/PDF-49/Accenture-Health-Artificial-Intelligence.pdf.

Becker's Health IT. 2015a. "Cerner to Advance Remote Patient Monitoring Connectivity with Qualcomm." April 14. www.beckershospitalreview.com/healthcare-information-technology/cerner-to-advance-remote-patient-monitoring-connectivity-with-qualcomm.html.

———. 2015b. "UPMC Uses Remote Monitoring to Reduce Admissions." February 17. www.beckershospitalreview.com/healthcare-information-technology/upmc-uses-remote-monitoring-to-reduce-admissions.html.

Becker's Hospital Review. 2014. "Telemonitoring Reduces Readmissions by 44%, Increases ROI, Finds Geisinger Study." October 6. www.beckershospitalreview.com/healthcare-information-technology/telemonitoring-reduces-readmissions-by-44-increases-roi-finds-geisinger-study.html.

Berg Insight. 2021. "Berg Insight Says 45.6 Million Patients Worldwide Are Remotely Monitored" (press release). Published December 20. www.berginsight.com/berg-insight-says-456-million-patients-worldwide-are-remotely-monitored.

Comstock, J. 2016. "Beth Israel Gears Up to Launch HealthKit-Enabled Remote Patient Monitoring Program." MobiHealth-News. Published January 28. www.mobihealthnews.com/content/beth-israel-gears-launch-healthkit-enabled-remote-patient-monitoring-program.

Dolan, B. 2013. "Digital health sensing clothes are next in wearables." MobiHealthNews. Published June 20. www.mobihealthnews.com/23227/digital-health-sensing-clothes-are-next-in-wearables/.

eHI (eHealth Initiative Foundation). 2018. "The Return on Investment of Patient-Generated Health Data & Remote Patient Monitoring" (Issue Brief). Published July 2018. Executives for Health Innovation website. www.ehidc.org/sites/default/files/resources/files/ROIPGHD_7.26.18_final.pdf.

Gabbay, R., and J. Hu. 2021. "Preventing Type 2 Diabetes Is a Minute-to-Minute Challenge; AI Can Help Provide Minute-to-Minute Care." MedCity News. Published December 22. https://medcitynews.com/2021/12/preventing-type-2-diabetes-is-a-minute-to-minute-challenge-ai-can-help-provide-minute-to-minute-care/.

Halamka, J., and P. Cerrato. 2021. "Taking a Balanced Approach to Remote Patient Monitoring." Mayo Clinic Platform (blog). Published December 9. www.mayoclinicplatform.org/2021/12/09/taking-a-balanced-approach-to-remote-patient-monitoring/.

HIT Consultant. 2016. "Philips, Validic Partner to Integrate Consumer-Generated Health Data from 3rd Party Apps/Devices." Published February 3. https://hitconsultant.net/2016/02/03/31719/.

Hodach, R., P. Grundy, A. Jain, and M. Weiner. 2016. *Provider-Led Population Health Management*, 2nd ed. Indianapolis, IN: John Wiley & Sons.

Johnson, S. R. 2018. "The Future Is Now?" *Modern Healthcare*, March 3. www.modernhealthcare.com/indepth/how-ai-plays-role-in-population-health-management/.

Kaiser Health News. 2021. "Apple Aims to Push More Patient Data to Doctors. But Who Can Gauge Its Impact on Health?" *Modern Healthcare*, August 12. www.modernhealthcare.com/technology/apple-aims-push-more-patient-data-doctors-who-can-gauge-its-impact-health.

Kent, J. 2019. "Could Artificial Intelligence Do More Harm Than Good in Healthcare?" *HealthITAnalytics*, June 25. https://healthitanalytics.com/news/could-artificial-intelligence-do-more-harm-than-good-in-healthcare.

Lee, B. Y. 2017. "Survey: British Spend Much More Time on the Toilet than Exercising." *Forbes* Healthcare blog. Published September

26. www.forbes.com/sites/brucelee/2017/09/26/british-time
-on-the-toilet-double-that-of-their-exercise-time/.

Lovett, L. 2022a. "AliveCor Rolls Out Credit Card-Sized ECG."
MobiHealthNews. Published February 1. www.mobihealthnews
.com/news/alivecor-rolls-out-credit-card-sized-ecg.

———. 2022b. "How the Digital Health Industry Can Innovate and
Improve Health Outcomes for All." MobiHealthNews. Published January 28. www.mobihealthnews.com/news/how-digital
-health-industry-can-innovate-and-improve-health-outcomes
-all.

———. 2018a. "Google Researchers Find Trained AI Detects Diabetic Retinopathy on Par with Experts." MobiHealthNews. Published March 14. www.mobihealthnews.com/content/google
-researchers-find-trained-ai-detects-diabetic-retinopathy-par
-experts.

———. 2018b. "Study: Apple Watches Paired with Cardiogram
Can Detect A-Fib." MobiHealthNews. Published March 21. www
.mobihealthnews.com/content/study-apple-watches-paired
-cardiogram-can-detect-fib.

Mack, H. 2017. "Remote Patient Monitoring Market Grew by 44
Percent in 2016, Report Says." MobiHealthNews. Published
February 8. www.mobihealthnews.com/content/remote-patient
-monitoring-market-grew-44-percent-2016-report-says.

McMillian, G. 2021. "Telehealth Improves Heart Care for Veterans."
Inside Veterans Health (blog). US Department of Veterans
Affairs. Published November 2. https://blogs.va.gov/VAntage
/96471/telehealth-improves-heart-care-for-veterans/.

Mecklai, K., N. Smith, A. D. Stern, and D. B. Kramer. 2021. "Remote
Patient Monitoring—Overdue or Overused?" *New England
Journal of Medicine* 384 (15): 1384–86. https://doi.org/10.1056
/NEJMp2033275.

Minemyer, P. 2020. "A look inside Geisinger's new remote monitoring program for COVID-19 patients." *Fierce Healthcare*, June 11. www.fiercehealthcare.com/hospitals/a-look-inside-geisinger-s-new-remote-monitoring-program-for-covid-19-patients.

Moeller, J. 2020. "Remote Patient Monitoring Sets Up Big Tech to Revolutionize Telemedicine and Healthcare." Health Care Blog. Published October 23. https://thehealthcareblog.com/blog/2020/10/23/remote-patient-monitoring-sets-up-big-tech-to-revolutionize-telemedicine-and-healthcare/.

Muise, J. 2018. "Small Wins vs. Big Losses: AI in Healthcare." MedCity News. Published March 12. https://medcitynews.com/2018/03/small-wins-vs-big-losses-ai-healthcare/.

Muoio, D. 2019a. "Current Health Partners with Fellow Connected Device Makers to Flesh Out Its Remote Monitoring Platform." MobiHealthNews. Published October 1. www.mobihealthnews.com/news/north-america/current-health-partners-fellow-connected-device-makers-flesh-out-its-remote.

———. 2019b. "FDA Clears AliveCor's Six-Lead Smartphone ECG." MobiHealthNews. Published May 13. www.mobihealthnews.com/content/north-america/fda-clears-alivecors-six-lead-smartphone-ecg.

NGPX. 2020. "How UPMC Is Using Remote Patient Monitoring and Telehealth" (blog). Published April 28. https://patientexperience.wbresearch.com/blog/upmc-remote-patient-monitoring-and-telehealth-strategy.

Polanco, N., S. Odametey, S. N. Derakhshani, M. Khachaturian, C. Devoe, K. Jethwani, and S. Kakarmath. 2019. "Evaluating the Accuracy of the VitalWellness Device." *Digital Medicine* 5 (3): 109–18. https://doi.org/10.4103/digm.digm_22_19.

Preston, J. 2018. "This AI Screening Tool for Diabetic Retinopathy Makes a Decision, not a Recommendation." MedCity News.

Published February 11. https://medcitynews.com/2018/02
/ai-screening-tool-diabetic-retinopathy-makes-decision-not
-recommendation/.

Rosenthal, J. 2020. "Benefits to remote patient monitoring." *Medical Economics*, November 5. www.medicaleconomics.com/view
/benefits-to-remote-patient-monitoring.

Siwicki, B. 2022. "How AI and Machine Learning Can Help Predict SDOH Needs." *Healthcare IT News*, January 18. www
.healthcareitnews.com/news/how-ai-and-machine-learning
-can-help-predict-sdoh-needs.

———. 2021. "Northwell Health uses Machine Learning to Reduce Readmissions by Nearly 24%." *Healthcare IT News*, July 12. www
.healthcareitnews.com/news/northwell-health-uses-machine
-learning-reduce-readmissions-nearly-24.

———. 2018a. "At UPMC, Remote Patient Monitoring Helps Reduce ER Utilization and Hospital Readmissions." *Healthcare IT News*, May 24. www.healthcareitnews.com/news/upmc
-remote-patient-monitoring-helps-reduce-er-utilization-and
-hospital-readmissions.

———. 2018b. "Flagler Hospital Uses AI to Create Clinical Pathways That Enhance Care and Slash Costs." *Healthcare IT News*,
August 13. www.healthcareitnews.com/news/flagler-hospital
-uses-ai-create-clinical-pathways-enhance-care-and-slash-costs.

Slabodkin, G. 2019a. "Duke Leverages AI to Identify Patients with Early Stage Sepsis." Health Data Management. Published September 3. www.healthdatamanagement.com/articles/duke-
leverages-ai-to-identify-patients-with-early-stage-sepsis.

———. 2019b. "Ochsner Integrates Healthcare Innovation into Clinical Workflows." Health Data Management. Published July 19. www.healthdatamanagement.com/articles/ochsner
-integrates-healthcare-innovation-into-clinical-workflows.

————. 2018. "AI Software Predicts Outcomes for Patients with Brain Tumors." Health Data Management. Published March 15. www.healthdatamanagement.com/articles/ai -software-predicts-outcomes-for-patients-with-brain-tumors.

————. 2017. "Machine-Learning Model Predicts Remission, Relapse in Cancer Patients." Health Data Management. Published February 15. www.healthdatamanagement.com/articles/machine -learning-model-predicts-remission-relapse-in-cancer-patients.

Terry, K. 2018. "How to make health apps valuable for physicians and patients." *Medical Economics*, February 10. www .medicaleconomics.com/view/how-make-health-apps-valuable -physicians-and-patients.

————. 2013. "Why the Private Sector Lags VA in Telehealth." *InformationWeek*, August 5. www.informationweek.com/leadership /why-the-private-sector-lags-va-in-telehealth.

Topol, E. J. 2015. *The Patient Will See You Now: The Future of Medicine Is in Your Hands.* New York: Basic Books.

Torrence, R. 2022. "MDLive Rolls Out Virtual-First Health Monitoring Program for Chronic Conditions." *Fierce Healthcare*, January 27. www.fiercehealthcare.com/tech/mdlive-launches -virtual-first-health-monitoring-program-for-chronic-conditions.

UnitedHealthcare. 2022. "Remote Patient Monitoring." Updated January 19, 2022. www.uhcprovider.com/en/resource-library /news/Novel-Coronavirus-COVID-19/covid19-telehealth -services/covid19-telehealth-remote-patient-monitoring.html.

Wicklund, E. 2021a. "Humana Launches Remote Patient Monitoring Program for Chronic Care." *mHealthIntelligence*, February 5. https://mhealthintelligence.com/news/humana-launches -remote-patient-monitoring-program-for-chronic-care.

————. 2021b. "Ochsner Health Takes Remote Patient Monitoring to a National Level." *mHealthIntelligence*, July 5. https://

mhealthintelligence.com/news/ochsner-health-takes-remote
-patient-monitoring-to-a-national-level.

Woolman, L. 2020. "Telehealth Growth During COVID-19 Reaches
1.4 Million Virtual Connections." Intermountain Caregiver
News. Published October 6. https://intermountainhealthcare
.org/caregiver-news/topics/stories/2020/10/telehealth-growth
-during-covid-19-reaches-14-million-virtual-connections/.

CHAPTER 4

"Mr. Roboto" by Styx

I'm not a robot without emotions, I'm not what you see. / I've come to help you with your problems, so we can be free. / I'm not a hero. I'm not a savior.

IN THIS PART-SCIENCE-FICTION, part-satirical ditty about the technological future, Styx thanks robots "for doing the jobs nobody wants to" and "for helping me escape just when I needed to." This is what doctors need to alleviate the burden of electronic health record (EHR) documentation. The right technology could also provide the clinical decision support that would simplify the job of diagnosing and treating patients, using the latest knowledge resources and all the available information about the patient.

Initially billed as technological progress that would make physicians' and nurses' lives easier and improve the quality of care, EHRs are also the only major technological advance that has required us to hire more humans just to restore the patient-doctor interaction we had before. This includes hiring scribes so we're not talking to a patient while looking at a computer screen. Physicians are often wary (for good reason) of any shiny new technology that promises to "make life easier." So far, that has been an unkept promise.

For EHRs to fulfill their promise, we'll need big advances—not only in machine learning but also in the ability of EHRs and other clinical and administrative systems to exchange patient data. In addition, we have to make EHRs easier to use, and their data must be more accurate and comprehensive. We also need to convince doctors and nurses that AI algorithms can provide reliable advice at the point of care.

Among other things, this change will require a major transformation in medical education (see chapter 10). I've long been telling people we need a Center for Intersentient Education. It took us 20 years to get doctors and nurses to work together as equals in teams, and it will take another 10 years to train clinicians and robots to act as partners. At one World Economic Forum meeting, Alibaba cofounder Jack Ma noted that "when we created cars, we didn't try to get humans to run faster; when we created planes, we didn't try to fly." In essence, as online meets offline, we need to be cognizant of the immensely changed role of the human in the middle.

Over the past few years, I've seen an explosion in tech advances and opportunities, but I've also seen weariness among healthcare leaders who are subjected to hundreds of aspiring tech entrepreneurs selling their wares. I fully understand the skepticism. Too many of the apps we see at health IT conferences or that bright-eyed, bushy-tailed salespeople bring to our door are vaporware. But the Gartner Hype Cycle remains true: We overestimate technology in the short term and underestimate it in the long run. Nurses and physicians—indeed, the entire clinical team—must let robots memorize and document while humans focus on the crucial question from a patient: "What does this mean to me and my family?" Computers can provide information, but clinicians provide meaning, context, and empathy. That will be our crucial role in the future.

Meanwhile, we have to figure out how to provide computable, digestible, and secure access to the key data that ambient intelligence will require in order to be truly useful. That means finally solving the puzzle of interoperability between different EHRs, which has plagued the healthcare industry for decades. While there are more pressing reasons for interoperability, machine learning needs to know what makes a patient tick, health-wise, before it can become a true partner with clinicians.

Moreover, consumer digital health apps cannot achieve their true potential until clinical data is accessible across platforms and provides actionable insights for the clinician (Jason 2021).

WANTED: MORE AND BETTER DATA

The type of data most often used in healthcare analytics is still paid claims data, because it has the widest reach across healthcare settings. But this data is neither timely nor rich, because it lacks critical elements such as a patient's blood pressure and weight. In essence, paid claims data captures the 20 percent of an individual's data that the doctor uses to generate a charge.

EHR data is available right away, and it has the basic clinical components that a doctor needs to assess, diagnose, and treat a patient. But an EHR that consists only of data collected by a single provider or health system is inherently limited. For a fuller picture, you need data from other providers who have seen a patient, as well as important parameters of a person's health that are not measured in a doctor's office, such as nutrition, exercise, tobacco and alcohol use, and medication adherence. As mentioned in chapter 3, data on genomics, social determinants, and other factors that influence a person's health will eventually be included in the palette of a patient's virtual record. A continuous stream of remote monitoring data will flow into the EHR and will have to be integrated. And when the outcomes of care become the primary basis of payment, there will be other patient-generated data related to how a person is feeling at regular intervals after treatment or surgery (see chapter 7).

In order to be actionable, the data in EHRs must also be more accurate than it is today. But EHRs were not designed for accuracy. These systems were built to optimize billing rather than to support patient care, because that's what the market wanted. Consequently, EHRs are built around templates that contain steps doctors must follow in order to meet billing requirements and increase revenue. Since this isn't necessarily the way physicians work, some of the details of patient encounters get lost, and some of the clinical documentation is there purely for billing purposes. It's no one's fault, but in essence we have analog systems in a digital world. We need to move to patient-centered care in a health assurance environment with value-based payment, but our data systems are built around a provider-centric fee-for-service motherboard.

Another thing that must change is the inability of digital health apps and services to easily access EHR data and write their data back to EHRs. There has been a lot of progress in this area, but it needs to go much further. That's why a concept like Commure—a platform that allows developers to create apps that can plug into any EHR and permits providers and patients to shop for such apps—is so badly needed.

It will take time to achieve these goals. Meanwhile, technologists and clinicians need to work together to advance the ability of machine learning to support patient care and population health management. Much of the requisite technology is already available, and the rest will be within the next decade. The real challenge will be in changing the business incentives to get software developers, providers, and payers on board. "You Get What You Give" by the New Radicals defines the problem. No matter how sophisticated the analytics, having access to all of the relevant data is the foundation.

INTEROPERABILITY: ALWAYS OVER THE NEXT HILL

Health IT interoperability has been a key goal of the federal government since President George W. Bush created the Office of the National Coordinator for Health Information Technology (ONC) in the early 2000s. The Meaningful Use program of the 2010s, while primarily aimed at increasing EHR adoption, also included requirements for providers to exchange clinical summaries; the program was eventually renamed Promoting Interoperability.

A number of interoperability efforts have emerged over the years, ranging from Direct secure messaging (a kind of healthcare-only e-mail) to regional and national health information exchanges (HIEs) and proprietary exchanges sponsored by individual EHR vendors. But true interoperability requires a seamless exchange of information that has encountered resistance on several fronts. Hospitals and health systems may see the easy exchange of medical histories as potentially helping competitors gain market share. Vendors frequently charge high prices for data exchange because they can, and because limiting information exchange can make it more difficult for providers to switch EHR systems.

The 21st Century Cures Act passed in 2016 prohibited this intentional withholding of patient health information between providers or between providers and patients—termed "information blocking." In the short term, the law had minimal effect. A January 2021 survey of HIEs, which are connected to both EHR vendors and providers, showed that information blocking was still occurring even as ONC was about to unveil its enforcement regulations. The problem seemed to be more widespread among EHR vendors than among healthcare organizations, but 15 percent of healthcare organizations reportedly refused to exchange information with other health systems (Jason 2021). So despite everyone agreeing that information fragmentation makes it difficult to coordinate care, self-interest across the healthcare ecosystem has led to at best slow and incremental progress.

REDEFINING THE PROCESS

Larger health systems are beginning to use a new kind of application programming interface (API) to exchange patient records and populate digital health apps, based on an emerging standards framework known as Fast Healthcare Interoperability Resources (FHIR). In essence, FHIR creates plug-ins that allow data exchange between EHRs, or between EHRs and third-party apps, without the need for interfaces. It does that by using web-linked snippets of data known as *resources* to represent clinical entities within EHRs (Terry 2015a).

An EHR system using this technology can, in theory, expose its data to outside digital health apps and import data from other EHRs. This could allow information exchange at a granular level, as opposed to the document-based information exchange that currently prevails. Most major EHR systems now have FHIR-based APIs, and because of a Cures Act requirement that patients be able to download their records through a standard API, all EHR systems certified for use in Centers for Medicare & Medicaid Services (CMS) incentive programs must include an FHIR API by December 31, 2022.

The Trusted Exchange Framework and Common Agreement (TEFCA), established by the Cures Act, is a voluntary framework for overall interoperability that incorporates a roadmap to increase FHIR adoption. This framework includes a common set of nonbinding principles for policies and practices to facilitate data sharing among qualified health information networks, or QHINs, that enable data sharing among their members (Frieden 2022; Siwicki 2022).

Another national network of networks already exists. As of 2022, CareQuality handles about 4 billion exchange transactions per year, according to Mariann Yeager. Yeager is CEO of the Sequoia Project, which manages CareQuality and is supervising TEFCA implementation for ONC. In addition, CareQuality collaborates with the CommonWell Health Alliance, a national network, sponsored by EHR vendors, that has a widely used record locator service (CommonWell Health Alliance 2016).

So what makes the TEFCA network different from CareQuality? Yeager says TEFCA is the first interoperability framework that includes a legal agreement on rules of the road and implementation guidance. In addition, TEFCA's framework applies to information on payments, healthcare operations, and patient access as well as to clinical data. It also sets a higher bar on privacy, security, and governance than CareQuality does, she says. Because technology is useless without trust, these concerns—especially as they relate to person-defining data such as genomics—will become increasingly important.

Initially, TEFCA will focus on document-based exchange, since that's what healthcare organizations are using. As for TEFCA's ability to move the needle on FHIR, Yeager told me that a real-world pilot of a very narrow use case and workflow will be required to begin with. "We have to do something where we're making it work between health systems within a network, with actual governance and an obligation for compliance and skin in the game."

She cautions, however, that there will be resistance to using FHIR in health information exchange, even though it could help physicians who are looking for particular pieces of data on a patient. "The EHR and HIE vendors think they've solved the data access and data exchange issues for patient treatment, and they don't want to reengineer it," she says. "So if they implement FHIR, it's going to be for other purposes. From what we've heard, they don't intend to implement a new technology stack to replace something they've already invested in."

While larger health systems have activated the FHIR APIs in their EHRs, some of these organizations question the value of FHIR because the return on investment is unclear. One IT executive noted that FHIR doesn't yet provide all the functionality for complete workflows and that the data generated by FHIR-based apps can't be written back to his EHR's database (CHIME and KLAS Research 2021).

Where Interoperability Stands Now

Despite all these barriers, Yeager says, interoperability has improved significantly. Her view is supported by a report from the College of Health Information Management Executives (CHIME) and KLAS Research (2021).

Two-thirds of the healthcare executives surveyed by CHIME and KLAS in 2020 reported that they often or nearly always had access to needed patient records from other providers using different EHRs. Four years earlier, only 28 percent of the respondents in a similar survey said that. The majority of respondents in the 2020 poll also said their EHR functionality had improved for tasks such as locating and viewing patient records. But only 15 percent of the healthcare executives said that data exchange had impacted patient care (up from 6 percent in 2016). Still, the ongoing consolidation of health systems into larger organizations, the report said, "has resulted in more needed connections with critical exchange partners, not fewer" (CHIME and KLAS Research 2021, 2). The researchers attributed this to an increase in information exchange between organizations using the same EHR.

That finding lines up with the results of an August 2019 survey of health IT executives. The most popular approach to improving interoperability within a health system, embraced by nearly 60 percent of respondents, was switching to a single integrated EHR. A third of the technology experts said their data-sharing efforts were insufficient, even within their own organizations. Less than 40 percent of the respondents said their organizations were successfully sharing data with other health systems (Siwicki 2019).

But what if health systems prioritize the cumbersome and costly task of consolidating EHR systems because they have yet to see an alternative technology with the sole purpose—and ability—to connect multiple point solutions in a meaningful way, all on one platform? One of these new technology leaders, Commure, is doing just that.

Beyond Point Solutions

Sharing data between health organizations is not the biggest problem facing healthcare chief information officers. Even more challenging is the ability to connect all the disparate data within a health system, says Ashwini Zenooz, MD, CEO of Commure. The data systems in a large health organization typically encompass 16–18 EHRs and one or more pathology systems, radiology systems, outpatient systems, and billing systems, she notes. In addition, the volume of medical device data and patient-generated data from consumer apps is increasing. Add to that all the point solutions that health systems buy or build to solve specific problems, and you have dozens of data systems that must be pulled together to supply actionable data at the point of care.

Currently, many health systems use data warehouses or data lakes to compile and normalize data from all these sources. The problem with this approach is that, by the time the data is available to clinicians, it's often no longer actionable. It can be used for retrospective analysis, but is of limited value in treating patients.

FHIR is a major step forward, Zenooz acknowledges, but it doesn't solve every problem. First, it's not really a single standard, as many flavors of FHIR are in use. Second, even as EHRs add FHIR APIs, many legacy applications used by health systems are not FHIR-based, so translations must be done between FHIR and non-FHIR applications. And third, FHIR doesn't solve the problem of semantic interoperability—for example, normalizing the many different terms used for medical concepts such as blood pressure or cardiac arrhythmia.

Commure functions as a technology infrastructure for the entire healthcare ecosystem, melding data from EHRs, other legacy technologies, digital health solutions, payers, and health applications into a single source of truth. According to Zenooz, Commure can give clinicians valuable patient data from a plethora of sources in real time. Once data from every source has been mapped to a single standard language—either by a healthcare organization or by an outside firm—it can flow from its source through Commure and then to the point of care without the normalization having to be performed again.

"With mergers and acquisitions playing such a large role in most health systems' growth strategy, it's unrealistic to think that these systems can consolidate their various EHRs every time they merge," she told me. "It's simply not a scalable model to achieve scalable growth. Instead of ripping and replacing technologies at every change in a health system's growth journey, health organizations need to connect their EHRs and other disparate systems to a single operating system—not only to unify their data sets, but also to make the most of their existing technology investments."

Faxing Still in the Mix

One of Jethro Tull's signature tunes was "Living in the Past." That phrase describes the many healthcare organizations that continue to use paper in health information exchange. An ONC survey conducted in 2018 found that 70 percent of hospitals still sent or received care summaries using mail or fax (Slabodkin 2018). There was also a big jump in Direct messaging in 2021, when CMS began to require hospitals to send admission-discharge-transfer alerts to other providers, including physician practices. While Direct messages are electronic, they're just one step up from faxes (Nelson 2021).

Yeager has a simple explanation for this: Many independent physicians who care for patients seen in health systems don't belong to a public health information exchange or don't use the same EHR as the hospital that is sending the alerts. So they must still be contacted by fax, mail, or Direct messaging.

Physician offices are definitely behind the curve on interoperability, unless they are affiliated with a health system. An ONC report released in 2019 found that only 10 percent of office-based practices and community health centers were engaged in interoperable exchange of health information with outside sources in 2017, about the same as in 2015. Significantly, practices with value-based-reimbursement contracts were more likely to use their EHRs to send, receive, find, and integrate patient data than were practices without such contracts (Burda 2019).

Meanwhile, accountable care organizations (ACOs), the centerpiece of the value-based care movement, predict that they'll have difficulty reporting quality measures to CMS under 2022 rules requiring electronic submissions, because their members' EHRs lack interoperability. Ninety percent of the surveyed ACOs have multiple EHRs, and 77 percent have six or more (Bazzoli 2022).

Sifting through these reports, I find reasons for hope as well as frustration. US healthcare is slowly moving toward interoperability, but it's not expected to reach the promised land anytime soon. FHIR APIs offer the best chance for universal interoperability at the level of discrete data, but adoption will continue to lag until the standards set matures and more developers and providers are willing to invest in this type of information exchange.

As Zenooz puts it, "Every clinician deserves to know their patient inside and out, regardless of which company they work for or which setting they work in. The technologies that will truly—finally—propel our industry forward will be the ones that prioritize collaboration above competition and build the roads between our historically siloed points of care."

Like remote patient monitoring, interoperability could benefit from a wholesale shift to value-based reimbursement. When healthcare organizations can achieve a return on investment by enabling clinicians and patients to obtain any piece of health information they need across the continuum of care, then interoperability will become real. The technology is here now; all that's lacking is the business case to perfect it and use it.

Further complicating the "actionable data" issue, patient data in the healthcare system is largely siloed for use by single health systems. Beyond interoperability for applications and technologies, clinicians and researchers want to collaborate across institutions for research and clinical purposes, but the process to share data can be lengthy and complex. Patients also want access to their data across time and across institutions, particularly those patients with medically complex histories.

Unfortunately, health systems don't have the technological, legal, or incentive structure to enable data sharing. To access health data for research purposes, research and pharmaceutical organizations often must partner with companies that make their money by charging large fees for transferring that data. Patients are largely unaware of how their data is being used, and while the current system is legal, it is often not strictly transparent or ethical. Furthermore, this system is inefficient and does not adequately serve patients, health systems, or researchers across the clinical and research landscape.

More efforts are underway to design a not-for-profit repository in which health systems and patients may participate in a clinical data-sharing ecosystem that is equitable, secure, and transparent. Health systems would set the rules for data usage and transfer, and patients and health systems would both benefit monetarily from data exchange. Patients would also be made aware of any data movement, so they could benefit clinically by participating in clinical trials or sharing their own data with research groups they believe should have access to it. The proposed ecosystem would rely on the use of blockchain and other novel methods for data storage and encryption and is being built today.

BUILDING THE DOCTOR'S AI ASSISTANT

EHR data, as noted earlier, is not very accurate; therefore, it can't be relied on for use in clinical decision support. One should also not depend on its accuracy in training algorithms, observes Hemant Taneja, managing partner of General Catalyst. "A lot of times, the data in the EHR is documented to optimize for billing codes, and it doesn't always exactly represent the patient," he says. "So if you use AI with this polluted data, you'll reach the wrong conclusions."

From the viewpoint of building an AI assistant that can some-day take the rote work of patient care away from physicians, this is a critical point. Until EHR documentation improves, we will be stuck in the classic conundrum of "garbage in, garbage out." Until we have seamless data transparency, we will be stuck in what the band Genesis called a "Land of Confusion," and the promise of the fourth Industrial Revolution will be unrealized.

I've already explained that physicians must follow EHR templates in order to justify billing codes. The resulting documentation doesn't necessarily reflect the work they did or the conclusions they reached. Moreover, the data fields in EHRs are often missing data or contain redundant data. In a 2020 study at Partners HealthCare, for example, diagnostic problem completeness varied from 72.9 percent for hypertension to 93.5 percent for asthma. Problem list duplications ranged up to 28.2 percent for diabetes (Wang and Wright 2020).

Computer-generated notes also create major issues. The over-reliance on boilerplate language creates "note bloat," making chart notes hard to read. Charting "by exception"—for example, setting up the EHR for a review of systems to default to normal findings and then changing the findings that are not normal—exacerbates the note bloat. Also, many physicians copy the unchanged parts of previous notes into the new visit document; this saves time, but also increases the risk of errors (Terry 2015b).

Physicians spend an average of just over 16 minutes on EHR-related tasks for every patient encounter, according to a Cerner study (Miliard 2020). The average primary care physician devotes more than half of their workday to EHR work, including chart review, documentation, and ordering. Eleven percent of the average doctor's EHR time occurs after hours, in the evening, or on weekends. EHR-linked patient portals such as Epic's MyChart give patients more control of and access to their records, but they also exacerbate physician burnout (Finnegan 2020). Providers and staff can spend hours each day answering patient questions on these portals, often with no or minimal reimbursement. For those of you who have reviewed your attorney's bill, you will notice that anomaly does not cross over to the legal profession!

To reduce the documentation burden, many doctors use voice recognition software that converts their speech to free text. The transcription accuracy, once the software has been trained to recognize a doctor's voice, is about 93 percent on average (Zhou et al.

2018). But physicians still have to spend time correcting transcription errors, and the data trapped in free text can't easily be retrieved when it's needed.

The promise of charting technology making physicians' lives easier turned out to be untrue. Until we can recover from, as one of my colleagues quipped, the "epic-demic" of administrative burden, it will be difficult to engage physicians with the next technology!

AI Assistants Proliferate

For years, physicians have been reading about new voice-enabled AI assistants designed to reduce the burden of medical documentation. These apps have advanced far beyond the simple voice-to-text capability of speech recognition programs.

One of the first tools of this kind was Suki, made by the company of the same name. Suki, which has also been deployed in Ascension Health and some other health systems, uses AI to understand simple voice commands. Suki can access patient data through an EHR interface and add notes or other inputs at a doctor's direction. It can create blocks of text based on a doctor's past documentation patterns, and it can automatically navigate the EHR to deposit transcribed text in the right place.

In 2019, the American Academy of Family Physicians (AAFP) tested Suki in a small number of practices and found it was able to reduce EHR documentation time significantly (Terry 2019). In late 2021, the AAFP released the results of a larger study. The primary care practices using Suki in the pilot reported a 72 percent drop in median documentation time; the clinicians saved an average of 3.3 hours per week and had improved job satisfaction. The physicians also reported that using the AI assistant made their notes more meaningful and professional. Steven Waldren, MD, vice president and chief medical informatics officer of the AAFP, described Suki as an "essential innovation for all FPs who have documentation burden and experience burnout."

Some leading EHR vendors, including Epic, Cerner, Allscripts, and eClinicalWorks, have created voice-enabled AI assistants of their own. Epic, working closely with Nuance, the leading voice recognition software firm, launched a mobile version of its AI assistant in 2018 and added it to its desktop EHR in 2020. Using this tool, clinicians can use voice commands to navigate the Epic EHR, place orders, and search for patient records, lab results, and visit summaries (Zieger 2020). Cerner's similar AI assistant facilitates clinicians' interaction with its EHR. Physicians can use it to query and retrieve patient data from the EHR, enter orders, and set up reminders. In addition, the robot can capture data from a physician-patient conversation and can help embed that data into the progress note, according to Cerner (Miliard 2020).

How Suki Does It

I asked Waldren how Suki reduces EHR documentation time. Here's how he explained it:

> In an EHR, if you're in a review of systems, that may be in a different screen than the history of present illness, which is in a different screen than the exam. If you're using voice recognition, you've got to navigate the EHR manually. But with Suki and similar types of AI assistants, you can just tell it, "Hey Suki, history of present illness" and then start talking. Or say, "Hey Suki, modify the asthma exam" and then tell it how, instead of having to navigate there. You can just focus in on what you want to talk about, using voice commands.

The next step for Suki is to populate certain EHR fields with discrete data. To do this, its natural language processing must reliably understand certain medical concepts, and it must also be able to write back to EHR databases. According to Waldren, Suki has met the first criterion, but it hasn't made much headway on write-back, because most EHR vendors won't allow it. Their main objection, he says, is that they have to create a different security profile for each outside party that seeks to send data directly into an EHR database. "It's challenging to do that," he notes, and they also have to do "translational work" to ensure that the data is in the right format when it's entered.

"The other thing is that from a business perspective, by integrating all of these added applications, you're eating away at the value that the EHR company is providing with their product," Waldren notes. "So there's a concern that at what point do you say, if all these apps work with these three different EHRs, now maybe I should switch over to another EHR."

The Coming of the Virtual Scribe

Assuming that one could get past the write-back obstacle, there are additional challenges to transforming the AI assistant into a true virtual scribe that would take most documentation duties off a doctor's hands. These challenges to what is known as ambient computing fall into three categories: (1) The AI assistant must be able to recognize who is speaking in the exam room, whether it's the doctor, the patient, or someone else; (2) physicians must say the right things during the encounter for the computer to understand what needs to be documented; and (3) the robot has to perceive the semantic structure of the medical concepts in the EHR.

Waldren expects that all these barriers will eventually fall. Someday, AI assistants will even be able to extract the relevant data from a doctor's dictation and place it in the right fields in the EHR, he says. The biggest obstacle he sees is not the ability of AI to learn all the synonyms for a medical concept, but its ability to grasp the EHR's semantic relationships.

"We need a 'knowledge graph' that really understands the inter-relationships of all the concepts in healthcare, like the knowledge graph that Google uses to power their search engine. If we had something similar in healthcare, you could put things into that graph, and the algorithm would understand that elevated blood sugar means the patient has diabetes."

None of this would necessarily improve the accuracy of data in a billing-oriented EHR. As long as the predominant payment method is fee-for-service, billing guidelines will continue to drive EHR documentation. If the healthcare payment system were value-based, however, there would be a strong incentive to restructure EHRs so that they were more clinically focused.

In Waldren's view, EHRs will always have to support some determination of value on which payments are based. Even in "direct" primary care, where doctors receive monthly fees from patients, he notes, the physicians "document a lot, because this is what they need to know to take care of those patients and track their health." For insurer value-based payments, "you have these quality measures and they become the proxy for value, instead of the note being the proxy for value.

"You want to record the care delivery and tracking. Because doctors and organizations want to know how they can become efficient, effective and systematic in what they do. But you don't necessarily care if somebody captures enough bullet points in a review of systems, or whether you documented enough in your assessment and plan, but rather what was done and why."

CLINICAL DECISION SUPPORT: A WORK IN PROGRESS

It's a big leap from AI-assisted documentation to AI-augmented clinical decision support (CDS). While documentation errors can and do lead to poor medical decisions, an algorithm that is used in CDS must be right nearly all the time, because it affects the physician's thinking process about how to diagnose and treat patients. Unless the physician believes that the AI assistant knows what it's doing and enables better clinical decisions, the doctor will not use it.

Even when AI-assisted CDS is much further along, it will augment, not replace, physician judgment. After all, physicians have the ultimate responsibility for patient care. They can't legally or morally allow a robot to decide what care will be delivered, even if the robot knows more than the human clinician does about a patient's characteristics and the latest clinical studies related to their care.

In addition, clinicians understand things about a patient that an algorithm could never comprehend. As one observer notes, "The practice of medicine is an art which takes into account multiple layers of variables before making a medical decision." These factors may include whether a patient can afford a treatment plan, whether they can take the medication as prescribed, their preferences, and whether the benefits of treatment outweigh its detriments (Balasubramanian 2021).

Nevertheless, AI is being used in some areas related to medical decision-making, such as reading cancer scans, interpreting dermatology images, and screening for retinopathy. It will take a while before AI reaches the level where doctors can trust AI-assisted CDS; but certain parameters are starting to emerge, according to Waldren.

> When we talked to a group of 20 of our FPs about this, they said that the physician needs to be able to retain control, because they're the ones who are liable for the care. If the AI is going to make a decision, it has to be preapproved, meaning, "here are the metrics of how the algorithm decides and how it all flows." The doc can look at that and say, "I agree with that, so I'll let the algorithm make those decisions." Or it makes a suggestion to the doc, and the doc has to confirm that before it gets put into action.

The physicians also felt it was important to understand how the algorithm arrived at a decision about a patient. They don't have to know all the details, Waldren says, but they want to know the most important aspects of the patient that went into making the determination. Also, they stressed the need for racial equity and for diversity in the data "to make sure that the tool applies to your population."

AI Doc is a good example of the sweet spot that doctors are seeking in AI. When IBM Watson won the "Jeopardy" contest (more on that in the next section), there were absurd predictions that AI robots would replace radiologists. Not surprisingly, given all the broken promises about new technology, radiologists were wary that AI would make their lives harder, rather than easier. However, AI Doc, started at Israel's Sheba Medical Center, empowers radiologists to detect urgent cases faster and reduces overall reporting time in the workflow.

As Jack Johnson articulated in the song "Better Together," we need to move beyond the EHR conundrum toward a future where robots and humans work together to improve health for all, and robots allow doctors and nurses to spend more time doing what they went to medical school and nursing school for.

The Fall of the House of Watson

While AI-assisted CDS has progressed slowly, one company leaped ahead of the pack a decade ago. IBM Watson, which called its healthcare AI strategy a "moon shot," ultimately failed to reach the moon. The healthcare assets of IBM Watson were sold to a private equity firm in San Francisco in 2022 (Miliard 2022).

Watson's inability to make headway in the healthcare industry underlines the relative immaturity of medical AI. A decade ago, IBM poured billions of dollars into Watson, which had garnered national attention by beating a human champion at "Jeopardy." Predictably, healthcare proved to be much more complex than a TV game show.

I was on the initial advisory board for IBM Watson Health, and in my opinion (and this should be a warning for all who believe robots will take over the world), the team began to believe their own commercials. You may remember those ads: IBM Watson in a white coat, IBM Watson helping the winery, and so on. Moving ambient intelligence from a pilot to a scalable partner is hard and slow work. It's worth it, but there are no magic bullets yet in the online-meets-offline world.

The fundamental assumption of IBM's "cognitive computing" was that natural language processing and other forms of machine learning could produce insights that would revolutionize medicine. In IBM's view, its supercomputer would be able to mine the medical concepts from the unstructured data comprising 80 percent of an EHR's content. It would comb the vast medical literature in seconds to obtain insights that could be applied in patient care. It would help healthcare organizations understand their populations' risk factors. And it would be able to integrate patients' genomic profiles with their clinical characteristics (Hodach et al. 2016).

In 2012, still riding on the crest of its "Jeopardy" fame, Watson "attended" medical school at the Cleveland Clinic to learn what physicians know and how they think. There were expectations that Watson might someday help teach medical students and contribute to CDS. If that happened, one Cleveland Clinic leader said, "it could be a paradigm change in how we practice medicine" (Terry 2012).

While tackling cancer care with such prestigious institutions as Memorial Sloan Kettering and MD Anderson Cancer Center, IBM Watson also bought Truven, Explorys, Phytel, and Merge Healthcare—all companies that had large volumes of patient data—to train its algorithms.

In the end, however, it all fell apart. The first blow came when MD Anderson put its partnership with IBM Watson on hold and later dropped it, dooming the Oncology Expert Advisor product the two organizations had developed. Watson's inability to understand doctors' notes and the lack of connection with MD Anderson's Epic EHR were said to be at the root of the problems (Harper 2017).

IBM developed a similar CDS product with Memorial Sloan Kettering in hopes that it would make the expertise of the center's oncologists available to patients everywhere. Eventually, Sloan Kettering also parted ways with IBM (Lohr 2021).

Difficulties also arose when IBM Watson worked on a genomics project with the University of North Carolina. "The IBM technologists were frustrated by the complexity, messiness and gaps in the genetic data at the cancer center," noted the *New York Times*. Nevertheless, they were able to show the value of Watson in searching the innumerable studies in the genomics field (Lohr 2021).

Some predicted that human physicians and nurses in certain specialties could be replaced by machine learning. In fact, some of these early failures accentuated the human role in healthcare. "Ironic," as Alanis Morissette sang on her landmark album, *Jagged Little Pill*.

According to Waldren, IBM went to market with Watson before the AI was ready. "They took too big a bite and it was a bit too broad. From what we know of AI, it does best when it has a very specific, specialized decision point, where there's a lot of data to back it up." He cites the dermatology, pathology, and imaging use cases, which have "black-and-white results."

BACK TO THE FUTURE OF AI

Despite IBM Watson's downfall, I believe that AI will develop to the point where it will be able to help physicians make better clinical decisions than they do today, with much less work. No longer will they have to memorize vast amounts of information; the robot will provide what they need to know in a particular case. Equally important, when doctors are trained to use AI-assisted CDS and trust its conclusions, they will be like the airline pilot who keeps an eye on the instruments and lets the autopilot do its job until it's time to land the plane.

When that happens, the nature of the physician's job will change. The machine-learning algorithm will combine the data gathered by remote monitoring devices and the information gleaned from the doctor-patient interaction with data on patient genomes and social determinants of health, the latest studies, and its knowledge of how thousands of similar patients have fared, and will use all that data to recommend a course of action that the doctor can either accept or override. With all that computing firepower at their command, clinicians can spend most of their time with patients asking how they feel, explaining the AI assistant's findings, and discussing how individual patients can improve their health.

This fits perfectly with our model of the changing "physical," in which data will be continuous and continuously analyzed. In that model, when a patient sees a doctor or a nurse, the clinician will do what humans do best—listen between the lines, advise in a customized fashion, given our experience with the patient, and empathize (which Mr. Roboto will never learn!).

In Styx's tune, the group sings, "I've got a secret I've been hiding under my skin / My heart is human, my blood is boiling, my brain IBM." No cyborg will ever be able to provide high-quality healthcare. While all this technology will help us provide better care for our patients and potentially free us from the tyranny of the legacy EHRs, AI and machine learning—even when mature—will be adjuncts to our ability to understand and treat our fellow humans.

Now that we've considered how medicine might be practiced in the future, using digital health apps, remote patient monitoring, and AI-assisted CDS, it's time to tackle the nuts and bolts of how healthcare systems can use these new technologies to "unscale" themselves and deliver the care that patients need where they live. That's what the next chapter is all about.

REFERENCES

AAFP (American Academy of Family Physicians). 2021. "Suki Assistant Significantly Reduces Primary Care Physician Documentation Burden" (press release). Published December 15. www.aafp.org/news/media-center/releases/suki-assistant.html.

Balasubramanian, S. 2021. "Can Doctors Truly Be Replaced by Technology?" *Forbes* Healthcare (blog). Published September 22. www.forbes.com/sites/saibala/2021/09/22/can-doctors -truly-be-replaced-by-technology/.

Bazzoli, F. 2022. "ACOs with Multiple EHRs May Struggle to Meet eCQM Targets." Health Data Management. Published January 27. www.healthdatamanagement.com/articles/acos -with-multiple-ehrs-May-struggle-to-meet-ecqm-targets.

Burda, D. 2019. "Hitting a Wall on EHR Interoperability, Patient Access." 4Sight Health. Published May 29. www.4sighthealth .com/hitting-a-wall-on-ehr-interoperability-patient-access/.

CHIME (College of Health Information Management Executives), and KLAS Research. 2021. "Trends in EHR Interoperability." Published January. https://chimecentral.org/wp-content /uploads/2021/01/Trends-in-EMR-Interoperability_CHIME _KLAS.pdf.

CommonWell Health Alliance. 2016. "Carequality and Common-Well Health Alliance Agree on Connectivity and Collaboration to Advance Interoperability" (press release). Published December 13. www.commonwellalliance.org/news-center/commonwell -news/carequality-commonwell-health-alliance-collaboration/.

Finnegan, J. 2020. "For Each Patient Visit, Physicians Spend About 16 Minutes on EHRs, Study Finds." *Fierce Healthcare*, January 14. www.fiercehealthcare.com/practices/for-each-patient-visit -physicians-spend-about-16-minutes-ehrs-study-finds.

Frieden, J. 2022. "ONC Releases Framework for Improving Health Record Interoperability." Medpage Today. Published January 19. www.medpagetoday.com/practicemanagement /informationtechnology/96758.

Harper, M. 2017. "MD Anderson Benches IBM Watson in Setback for Artificial Intelligence in Medicine." *Forbes* Healthcare (blog).

Published February 19. www.forbes.com/sites/matthewherper /2017/02/19/md-anderson-benches-ibm-watson-in-setback-for -artificial-intelligence-in-medicine/.

Hodach, R., P. Grundy, A. Jain, and M. Weiner. 2016. *Provider-Led Population Health Management*, 2nd ed. Indianapolis, IN: John Wiley & Sons.

Jason, C. 2021. "Information Blocking by EHR Vendors, Health Systems Still Prevalent." *EHR Intelligence*, January 11. https:// ehrintelligence.com/news/information-blocking-by-ehr-vendors -health-systems-still-prevalent.

Lohr, S. 2021. "What Ever Happened to IBM's Watson?" *New York Times*, July 17. www.nytimes.com/2021/07/16/technology/what -happened-ibm-watson.html.

Miliard, M. 2022. "IBM to Sell Watson Health Assets to Francisco Partners." *Healthcare IT News*, January 21. www.healthcareitnews .com/news/ibm-sell-watson-health-assets-francisco-partners.

————. 2020. " 'Hey Cerner': Company Seeks Health Systems to Help Test New Voice Assist Tech." *Healthcare IT News*, October 20. www.healthcareitnews.com/news/hey-cerner-company -seeks-health-systems-help-test-new-voice-assist-tech.

Nelson, H. 2021. "CMS Interoperability Rule, ADT, Fuels Direct Secure Messaging Growth." *EHR Intelligence*, August 4. https:// ehrintelligence.com/news/cms-interoperability-rule-adt-fuels -direct-secure-messaging-growth.

Siwicki, B. 2022. "Everything You Wanted to Know About TEFCA (but Were Afraid to Ask)." *Healthcare IT News*, January 27. www.healthcareitnews.com/news/everything-you-wanted-know -about-tefca-were-afraid-ask.

————. 2019. "Interoperability: Health Data-Sharing Is Lacking Inside and Outside of Hospitals, Survey Says." *Healthcare IT News*, August 19. www.healthcareitnews.com/news /interoperability-health-data-sharing-lacking-inside-and-outside -hospitals-survey-says.

Slabodkin, G. 2018. "Hospitals Still Use Paper to Send, Receive Summary of Care Records." Health Data Management. Published December 20. www.healthdatamanagement.com/articles/hospitals-still-use-paper-to-send-receive-summary-of-care-records.

Terry, K. 2019. "Voice-Enabled AI App May Reduce EHR Documentation Time." *Medscape Medical News*, November 20. www.medscape.com/viewarticle/921215.

———. 2015a. "The FHIR Train Leaves the Station." iHealthBeat. Published May 26. www.theusabilitypeople.com/article/fhir-train-leaves-station.

———. 2015b. "Why Electronic Health Records Aren't More Usable." *CIO*, December 1. www.cio.com/article/242791/why-electronic-health-records-arent-more-usable.html.

———. 2012. "IBM's Watson Hits Medical School." *InformationWeek*, November 2. www.informationweek.com/clinical-information-systems/ibm-s-watson-hits-medical-school.

Wang, E. C.-H., and A. Wright. 2020. "Characterizing Outpatient Problem List Completeness and Duplications in the Electronic Health Record." *Journal of the American Medical Informatics Association* 27 (8): 1190–97. https://doi.org/10.1093/jamia/ocaa125.

Zhou, L., S. V. Blackley, L. Kowalski, R. Doan, W. W. Acker, A. B. Landman, E. Kontrient, D. Mack, M. Meteer, D. W. Bates, and F. R. Goss. 2018. "Analysis of Errors in Dictated Clinical Documents Assisted by Speech Recognition Software and Professional Transcriptionists." *JAMA Network Open* 1 (3): e180530. https://doi.org/10.1001/jamanetworkopen.2018.0530.

Zieger, A. 2020. "Epic's Decision to Put Its Voice Assistant Front and Center Could Have a Big Impact." Healthcare IT Today. Published August 28. www.healthcareittoday.com/2020/08/28/epics-decision-to-put-its-voice-assistant-front-and-center-could-have-a-big-impact/.

CHAPTER 5

"I Am Changing" by Jennifer Hudson

I am changing, seeing everything so clear / I am changing, I'm gonna start right now, right here.

THIS UNFORGETTABLE SONG from the movie *Dreamgirls*, which is about the rise and struggles of Motown artists, could be the theme song for the American healthcare delivery system in the 2020s. In *Dreamgirls*, Effie White is the headliner of a Motown act who takes her position for granted until she is pushed aside for a more "marketable" singer. Effie only rebuilds her career after she hits rock bottom and changes her ways.

In many ways, that is what most of us in the traditional healthcare ecosystem are going through now. Until recently, hospitals could continue to do more and get paid more by insurance companies, who were themselves paid more to process more claims and to be the go-between for the patient and the hospital. Pharma companies could charge more for their drugs and had no reason to promote lower-cost alternatives. Patients could keep demanding more and more services because they weren't directly paying the bill. However, the fantasy mentality of the twentieth century is crashing down around us in the post-COVID world.

The problem is that not everyone has heard the crash yet. Despite the financial reverses experienced during the pandemic, many health systems continue to grow through mergers and build new hospitals. In 2022, a dozen health systems announced new construction projects collectively worth nearly $20 billion (Ellison 2022; Plescia 2022). Hospitals and health systems are also continuing to acquire more physician practices: They now employ, directly or indirectly, almost 40 percent of the US physicians involved in patient care (American Medical Association 2021).

Why health systems merge and expand depends on who you ask. At Jefferson, our merger strategy was about survival in a market dominated by large health systems and insurance companies. In order to fulfill our mission—We improve lives—we felt we could not survive as a "cute and cuddly" small hospital system in a hyper-competitive market.

In the world of insurers and regulators, the conventional wisdom is that health systems merge and expand mainly to strengthen their negotiating position with payers. This growth rarely improves a health system's quality or efficiency, these observers note, but it does raise health spending. Abundant research shows that increasing market share can make a health system a must-have provider that insurers and self-insured employers cannot leave out of their networks. Consequently, larger health systems can charge more to private insurers (Terry 2020c). The rates hospitals negotiate with health plans are now about 2.5 times higher than Medicare rates, on average (Berenson and Murray 2022).

Large health systems, particularly those that include academic health centers, also acquire smaller systems and community hospitals to build their referral base. Similarly, hospitals acquire practices and employ young physicians partly to guarantee their referrals in what is commonly called a "hub and spoke" system. Many of these employed doctors referred most of their patients to the same hospitals when they were independent, but the health systems don't want their competitors to acquire their practices (Terry 2020c).

All this consolidation is driven by the fee-for-service payment system that still predominates in healthcare. In designing their business strategies, the CEOs and boards of health systems, whether for-profit or not-for-profit, are thinking mainly about their hospitals' daily census, occupancy rate, average length of stay, payer mix, and revenues. Secondarily, they may think about how much money they're losing on their primary care practices, which nevertheless contribute to the bottom line through hospital admissions and referrals to hospital-owned labs, imaging centers, and outpatient facilities (Terry 2020c). Primary care practices that are losing money often contend that their hospital employers do not account for this "downstream revenue."

While there has been a lot of talk about value-based care and population health management, most health systems have been slow to embrace either. The reason is transparently obvious: In a value-based payment system, the systems' hospitals and other facilities become cost centers rather than revenue centers. To thrive under value-based contracts that include financial risk, they'd have to turn their business model upside down.

Because of their resistance to value-based care, large healthcare organizations pose the biggest obstacle to real healthcare reform that would keep the population healthier at a lower cost. To quote health policy expert David W. Johnson (2022), "The institutional drive to optimize revenues fragments care delivery, causes both overtreatment and undertreatment, tolerates medical errors, unnecessarily hurts and even kills some patients, limits care access, fosters care inequities and pushes far too many Americans into personal bankruptcy."

Fortunately for consumers, this business model is in greater danger now than ever before, as I posited in chapter 1. Consumers want relief from higher healthcare and drug prices; polls consistently show that this is one of their top issues (Heath 2018). And large employers are revolting and looking for alternative solutions. They're ready to work with providers willing to move away from fee-for-service. They don't like health system consolidation, which drives up costs. They want to know which digital health solutions live up to their promises and are turning to outside evaluators to find out. They are demanding transparency from providers (Mitchell and Morrison 2022).

Meanwhile, more nimble competitors are stealing business from health systems by hiring primary care physicians and aiming to make people healthier so they can share in the savings from lower health costs. UnitedHealthcare subsidiary Optum, the largest employer of physicians in the United States with 60,000 doctors (Haefner 2021), is building a care model that doesn't involve hospital ownership. Primary care companies such as One Medical, Oak Street, and ChenMed are thriving by reducing the cost of care, particularly for Medicare patients. Medicare Advantage plans are working with physicians to decrease avoidable hospital admissions. And digital health firms such as Livongo and Transcarent are improving care for patients with chronic diseases and helping patients navigate healthcare to get better value.

DINOSAURS DON'T EXPECT THE CRASH

Most health systems continue to buck this consumerist trend. Their business model is hospital-centric rather than patient-centric and focuses on sick care rather than prevention. They still don't understand that their brick-and-mortar facilities are dinosaurs that will ultimately be replaced by quicker, more intelligent mammals. At Jefferson, our "healthcare at any address" model looked to move our brand from providing care in our hospitals to providing care anywhere, starting at home. People are waking to the realization that hospitals are not necessarily the best places to get care for many conditions, and Jefferson was among the first to recognize this shift. "We Never Change" was a great Coldplay song but a poor healthcare strategy.

Emerging digital health technology will allow many hospital services to be delivered at home or in other care settings, and digital health tools and population health management will help people manage their health and avoid hospitalization. Instead of being mass produced in hospitals, care will be mass customized at any address. It will also be digitally enabled, tailored to the needs of each individual, and delivered efficiently at scale.

But for all these wonderful things to happen, the industry needs to move the needle on value-based care so that the incentives of healthcare providers and payers are aligned. Only when providers take a significant amount of financial risk will they be motivated to change how they deliver care. And only then will they be able to achieve the full potential of the new technologies that we explored in chapters 3 and 4.

This change will also require a new generation of health system leaders. The average age, gender, and experience of health system executives make it almost impossible to effect wholesale change. If you'd come up in a Hilton or Marriott management program, would you be likely to feel you could develop or lead an Airbnb hospitality model? But in the long run, the generational and diversity changes in leadership, the necessity of fixing the broken and fragmented healthcare delivery system, and the continuing market entrance of renegade start-ups will force the shift to population health management and value-based payment.

Value-based payment will shift the paradigm from hospital-centered to patient-centered care, from sick care to health assurance, and from scaling up to unscaling health systems. Moreover, when providers are responsible for population health, they will have to focus on health equity and social determinants of health (see chapter 8), because they will have a strong financial incentive to maintain the health of their entire population.

MY ODYSSEY IN PHILADELPHIA

In light of these ruminations, it might seem strange that I presided over arguably the largest consolidation of an academic medical center with other providers during the past 20 years. I'm referring to the rapid growth of Jefferson Health from 2013, when I joined the organization as president and CEO, to the end of 2021, when I retired. But I led this scaling up of Jefferson's size and reach partly because I knew the organization would need to become much bigger in order to unscale its operations and lay the groundwork for our vision of health assurance.

I became the head of the Jefferson Health System and the president of Thomas Jefferson University after serving as dean of the University of South Florida's Morsani College of Medicine and the CEO of USF Health. Previously, I'd served as dean of the Drexel University College of Medicine and had been an obstetrician/gynecologist for many years.

Jefferson Medical College goes back to 1824, and the academic hospital was opened in 1877. The university divested its hospitals in 1995 to Jefferson Health System, which was majority-owned by Main Line Health, another Philadelphia system. Knowing that Main Line was too conservative for the changes I believed were necessary, my team (with Main Line Health's consent) engineered the dissolution of Jefferson Health System in 2014 and formed Jefferson Health, entirely owned by the university. Then I persuaded the university board to merge with the health system board so there would be one line of authority for all decisions.

Before taking the CEO job, I'd told the board that the health system would have to grow to survive. I knew that we would have to become big enough to be essential to the community and to break the tyranny of the local payers, particularly Independence Blue Cross (IBC), which controlled almost two-thirds of the commercial insurance market in the Philadelphia area. This would require not only merging with other hospitals, but also selecting hospitals that had substantial primary care networks. If we didn't do that, I told the board, we would see our rates cut up to 5 percent per year, and we would go bankrupt or be sold. What I'd learned at Wharton Business School—that negotiating without leverage is begging—was never more true than when dealing with the big four insurers in the Philadelphia area.

I was interested in the hospital-owned primary care groups because I knew that value-based care would take over in the long run, and we'd be assuming financial risk from payers. To execute this strategy, we'd need scale and a presence in several areas of the market. In addition, most of the physicians employed by Jefferson at the time were specialists, and I knew we'd need a strong primary care base to keep people healthy and out of the hospital.

Building the Health System

Our first move was to merge Jefferson with the Abington Health System, centered around a hospital in the northern suburbs of Philadelphia. The University of Pennsylvania Health System was about to devour Abington when I came to them and offered to merge. They figured that whether they went with us or with Penn, they'd be a spoke in a hub-and-spoke system, referring patients to a big university hospital. Knowing that we didn't have the money that Penn did to spend on an acquisition, I said, "What if you weren't a hub and spoke? What if you were a hub and hub? My board will cede to you half of our board seats, and we will think globally while acting locally by preserving your regional service lines." They bought into the idea, and we did the deal without any money changing hands.

I repeated this approach, which we called "governance as currency," when we merged with Aria Health, a three-hospital system serving the areas of Frankford, Torresdale, and Bucks County, all north of Philadelphia. Because we couldn't give them half of the board after doing that with Abington, we expanded the board to provide equal representation to all three systems. Then we expanded into nearby southern New Jersey by merging with the Kennedy Health System, using the same game plan. Kennedy brought us three more hospitals and 1,000 more physicians.

By this time we were becoming a player in the market, but we weren't finished. In 2021, we finalized our merger with the Einstein Healthcare Network, which included an academic medical center. In addition, Einstein owned 25 percent of Health Partners Plans (HPP), a Medicaid and Medicare Advantage plan (mostly Medicaid). Jefferson already owned 25 percent of HPP through its merger with Aria, and the other half of the plan was owned by Temple Health.

Temple was willing to sell its interest to Jefferson if we could close the deal with Einstein.

When IBC, Cigna, and other health plans got wind of Jefferson's intention to merge with Einstein, they were afraid we'd be in a position to build Jefferson-Einstein-HPP into a real competitor in the mold of the University of Pittsburgh Medical Center (UPMC), which owns a large health plan and a premier hospital system. That part of the state had been roiled in controversy and infighting between UPMC and the large Blue insurance plan, Highmark, which eventually acquired a competitor to UPMC, Allegheny. There was an almost irrational fear that southeastern Pennsylvania would replicate this approach, given Jefferson's "aggressive" moves.

The local insurers' concerns fell on receptive ears when they complained to the US Federal Trade Commission (FTC), which spent more than two years attempting to stop the merger until a federal judge blocked the agency in December 2020 (Reed 2020). The FTC withdrew its challenge in March 2021 (King 2021).

After all our mergers were completed, Jefferson had grown from a three-hospital system with $1.6 billion in annual revenue to an 18-hospital system with $7 billion in revenue. That didn't include HPP, which added $1.1 billion more and made us the first integrated delivery and financial system in our area of Pennsylvania (Brubaker 2021). Despite the irrational fears, Jefferson's scale and health plan ownership have allowed the system to continue and expand its mission of caring for the underserved during a period when three other safety-net hospitals either went bankrupt or were sold to systems outside the area.

Why Own a Health Plan?

Having a health plan was important in a couple of respects. First, there was a lot we could do with a large Medicaid managed care plan to improve the health of our poorer patients in northern Philadelphia, which was a core mission for Jefferson. Hahnemann Hospital, the largest private safety-net hospital in the area, which had been owned by Tenet and had then been sold to another firm, had gone bankrupt with almost no advance notice. At the time, the CEO of Einstein and I called that the canary in the coal mine for the underserved.

Second, ownership of an insurer would help Jefferson start to realign its financial incentives. Besides taking financial risk through HPP, we had a large value-based contract with IBC and co-owns with Main Line an accountable care organization (ACO) that negotiated value-based contracts with Medicare Advantage plans. Jefferson also has a self-insured plan for its 50,000 employees. That employee cohort, for which the health system acts as employer, provider, and payer, allowed Jefferson to conduct a kind of "dress rehearsal" for value-based care.

For example, when Jefferson invested heavily in telehealth for emergency and urgent care in 2014, the move was considered financial suicide in the traditional fee-for-service world, but it provided great returns when used to care for a population for which Jefferson was at financial risk. That gave us confidence that we could survive and prosper in the "payvider" world. Our aha moment came when we realized that we didn't want to pay for unnecessary services that increased our health spending, even if the spending occurred at our own facilities. So Jefferson has begun to move from volume-based to value-based payment, although it's still far short of the level required to change its culture.

Jefferson has also made progress on the care delivery side. Its large primary care network is focused on population health management and on treating people close to home in the most cost-effective setting. Part of the reason we launched our telehealth program in 2016 is that we recognized that telehealth would be important in a "healthcare at any address" model. At that time, most healthcare systems either ignored telehealth or hired outside services to provide after-hours virtual care. When the pandemic hit in 2020, we were able to get more than 1,000 of our doctors trained on telehealth and conducting virtual visits within weeks.

Going forward, Jefferson board members told the Governance Institute (2017), the university hospital may become smaller as more care is moved into the communities where the health system has sites. Jefferson's acute general hospital footprint in central Philadelphia will probably shrink as the system builds more outpatient centers and what Jefferson calls "space stations between home and hospital." Meanwhile, some of the system's older hospitals will likely be repurposed as outpatient or other kinds of regional sites.

Improving Health Equity

On my watch and through the vision of our executive vice president for institutional advancement, Jefferson also created the Philadelphia Collaborative for Health Equity. The idea was to help improve healthcare for underserved people, partly by partnering with social service agencies that could address their social determinants of health.

In my long history as a healthcare leader, I recognized that the mission statements of most academic medical centers and health systems were noble—community engagement, diversity, health and academic equity, and so on—but our "philanthropic" efforts were often focused on constructing nicer buildings, bringing in programs to move us up in *U.S. News & World Report* rankings, and installing new technologies that differentiated us from competitors. In other words, not exactly Dire Straits' "Money for Nothing," but there was clearly a mismatch between what we said we wanted to invest in and where our investments actually were.

At Jefferson, our top philanthropic and investment goals were designed to break the intolerable healthcare gaps that made Philadelphia one of the best cities for healthcare if you made it to one of our hospitals or academic medical centers, but one of the worst cities for health outcomes for the underserved and people of color. Despite having several large and prestigious academic medical centers, Philadelphia ranks well below its Amtrak neighbors—Boston,

New York, and Washington, DC—in the overall health of its citizens (Field 2019).

Jefferson's focus on health equity attracted media interest and led to substantial donations. Hansjörg Wyss, a billionaire with no ties to Philadelphia, wanted to invest in better healthcare for the Southeast Asian community. There's a huge health gap between Southeast Asian Americans in Philadelphia and white residents of the city. Wyss gave us $3 million to build a wellness center that delivers full-spectrum primary care, social services, wellness activities, and other community-focused programming.

Andréa and Ken Frazier—he was the chairman and CEO of Merck at the time—noticed the huge gap in access and health between the neighborhood where Ken had grown up and their affluent suburb—a tenfold increase in heart disease, for example. So they made a several-million-dollar gift with a catch: the healthcare had to be delivered close to where Ken had grown up, which is now one of the poorest areas in Philadelphia. That led to a partnership with Temple University (a rare event at the time in Philadelphia) that has now created a true "healthcare at any address" model for stroke care. That relationship with Ken Frazier has led to my involvement after leaving Jefferson in a "food as medicine" initiative in the most underserved communities in Philadelphia.

REORGANIZING HEALTHCARE DELIVERY

A proof of concept for my ideas about unscaling came with the establishment of The Villages Health, whose birth I had a hand in when I was in Tampa. The Villages is an active living community for people aged 55 or older in central Florida; it has more than 140,000 residents. When I was at USF Health, we initiated a community-academic partnership discussion with The Villages. The Villages would build a primary care group for its residents, and the university would build a specialty group dedicated to the community. Eventually, we thought, the combined network would be able to take financial risk from health plans.

Like any good obstetrician, I was wise enough to hand the "baby" back to a great "parent," Elliot Sussman, MD, the former president and CEO of the Lehigh Valley Health Network in Pennsylvania. He met with The Villages' developer to discuss how the community's healthcare might be improved. The developer was considering building a third hospital in the area to improve acute care access. Instead, Elliot suggested, they should build a patient-centric community health system, driven by primary care physicians. He later became the chairman of The Villages Health (TVH), which launched in 2012.

Jeffrey Lowenkron, MD, an alumnus of Kaiser Permanente who had been my chief executive officer at USF Health, moved over to The Villages as their chief medical officer for TVH and helped guide its development. The USF connection was broken after the new dean of the USF medical school opposed expanding the health system beyond Tampa, he recalls. Since there had been almost no traction for USF specialists to provide specialty services in The Villages, TVH built its own specialty network. Instead, TVH sends its patients needing hospitalization to The Villages Hospital and Leesburg Hospital, both of which are now owned by the University of Florida. TVH has no financial interest in a hospital.

Changing Provider Incentives

With Sussman leading the design of the new health organization, the team decided to tackle the payment system in which their doctors operated. Fee-for-service was acknowledged as creating perverse incentives that harmed patient care and discouraged physicians from providing the best care they could.

TVH has about 45 care teams, each led by a primary care physician. A team is composed of the lead physician, a physician assistant or a nurse practitioner, and three medical assistants. Each physician-led team manages a maximum of 1,250 patients.

A primary care doctor can charge Medicare at its highest evaluation and management rate if they see a patient for 15 minutes, according to the coding guidelines from the Centers for Medicare & Medicaid Services (CMS). "As people get older, however, they tend to have multiple problems," Lowenkron explained in an interview. "If someone came in to see me with three problems, they'd want me to take care of those problems. I knew I wouldn't get paid extra for that, but if I referred them out to three specialists, everyone would get paid. That's the current comp model in the Medicare fee-for-service world, and it explains why care is so fragmented." If you are singing Arcade Fire's "You Must Be Kidding" about now, that's understandable!

The only way to get paid for taking care of all the patient's needs efficiently was to assume financial risk for a patient population. "So the decision was made to go with Medicare Advantage plans and take full risk." TVH receives a set amount per member per month from selected payers with Medicare Advantage plans. This payment covers all care provided to the people covered by those insurers, including primary, specialty, urgent, emergency, and hospital care, lab and imaging studies, and post-acute care.

The first payer that TVH took risk from was UnitedHealthcare's Medicare Advantage plan. After six years, "we expanded to Florida Blue and more recently, Humana. We have over 24,000 full-risk patients and we have another 36,000 patients who are not in Medicare Advantage. Some are commercial risk patients," which means gainsharing only, "and some, who receive specialty care only, are Medicare fee-for-service patients."

Almost 10 years later, Lowenkron says, TVH is making money on its Medicare risk contracts, and its quality of care is second to none. The health system was in the 99th percentile for quality in its second year of contracting with United. It also has a stunning track record on hospital admissions among its full-risk Medicare Advantage patients: "Of every 1,000 patients in traditional Medicare, about 370 are admitted yearly, on average. For Medicare Advantage patients, it's 249 per 1,000. For Villages Health, we're at 146, which is like the commercial population." To quote Carly Simon, "Nobody Does It Better."

One reason for this success, in my view, is the group's independence from hospitals. A system that does not own a high-fixed-cost facility that always needs to be fed more patients can provide better care in a less invasive environment, leading to improved access, quality, and patient experience.

Secrets of Success

The key to The Villages' achievement is ensuring that all patients receive appropriate preventive and chronic disease care. According to Lowenkron, this starts with longer appointments that allow clinicians to spend sufficient time with patients.

All full-risk patients receive an hour-long appointment when they're new to a TVH practice. After that, the standard primary care appointment for both full-risk and other patients lasts half an hour. This allows physicians to take care of a patient's minor acute, preventive, and chronic care needs and discuss all the other aspects of their life that might affect their health.

In addition, TVH employs nurse navigators who work closely between visits with patients who have chronic diseases. The health system is also piloting a paramedic-in-home program to help patients with urgent needs when their visiting nurse is unavailable, and there are social workers in each of its seven primary care centers.

The organization has about 150 clinicians, including primary care doctors, specialists, and advanced practice providers. Besides its employed specialists, it also uses a network of high-quality outside specialists. In addition, TVH has its own hospitalists who round on The Villages' patients when they're admitted to the hospital.

TVH doesn't have its own imaging facilities, preferring to work with a local imaging group instead. Lowenkron explained the decision this way:

We don't have to send anything to them, but we communicate well. They help us on the risk side, and we send them patients. We knew if we duplicated their facilities, we'd both have to overutilize services to make it work. Having a scanner is fine, but it's not a revenue source in our value-based world. Everything is a cost center, not a revenue center. The same thing is true with the hospital: If you recognize the hospital as a cost center, and you build your beds and services to align with it being a cost center rather than a revenue center, you might get to a different place.

For example, he says, hospital administrators use their daily census and revenue as measures of how well they're doing. If an activity doesn't generate revenue, it's not encouraged. But when an organization takes on risk, social work, home health care, and other activities that don't generate revenue make sense because they reduce overall costs. "Would you rather spend an hour with a patient or have the patient go to the hospital if you're writing the checks?" he asks.

The same philosophy applies to how TVH pays its physicians. Like doctors in many other groups, they're salaried; but where most groups give out bonuses based on the volume of services that their doctors produce, TVH bases its bonuses strictly on quality metrics. In other words, the payer-provider-patient alignment in this community setting could be summed up by Sinéad O'Connor's "Nothing Compares 2 U."

Limited Use of Technology

TVH offers its patients the option of telehealth visits. During the early phase of the pandemic, telehealth soared to 70 percent of primary care visits. But since then, Lowenkron says it has fallen to about 9–10 percent for primary care and 3 percent for specialty visits. "Most patients would rather come in. And it's patient-driven, so we'll do what they want."

Remote patient monitoring (RPM) is not used often at TVH, mainly because "you need decision support built into those tools to make remote monitoring worthwhile." In other words, what's missing is the ability to separate the signal from the noise automatically.

Lowenkron is agnostic on whether patients fare better in skilled nursing facilities or at home with home health nurses following hospitalization. "For us, it's a simple question: Where is the right place for the patient to be? And that's where we want them. If the patient goes back to the hospital, we end up paying the bill."

On the other hand, he stresses, his healthcare organization wants people to be hospitalized when necessary. "If the patients need to be in the hospital, we want them there. We want them in the right place, because if we try to keep them out of the hospital and they should be in there, they're more likely to end up in the ICU."

Hospitals Cooperate

The hospitals that TVH uses are very cooperative, Lowenkron says, and they don't create any obstacles for his hospitalists. "Our hospitalists are much more efficient and effective at getting people through the hospital, and readmissions are lower for our patients. We keep our census low for hospitalists, at around 12 patients each. It lets them think about the patients. If they need help from specialists, they'll get it. And if they don't need that, they manage the patients, since they have the time to do so."

From the hospital point of view this works well, because the average length of stay is shorter and the bed utilization is more efficient. Moreover, fewer readmissions means a lower chance of the hospital incurring a CMS penalty.

Summing up the health system's approach, he told me, "This is what happens when patients are the center of what you're doing. Our system aligns patient outcomes with our outcomes. If you have hospitals or doctors that are rewarded on the volume of tests and procedures, and if you have a group of doctors rewarded on how well their patients do, you can guess which group does more tests and procedures, and which group has better patient outcomes. It's not rocket science, it's just model design."

As an obstetrician, I am incredibly proud of the baby that I helped create in central Florida. Sussman, Lowenkron, the Morse family (the majority owner of TVH), and the organization's physicians and staff did an amazing job in creating this patient-centered, primary-care-driven model.

Lowenkron's comments about value-based care also remind me of a phenomenon that occurred when I was a practicing ob-gyn. When ultrasounds first became routine in pregnancy, there were few standards for when to perform them and how many to perform. Generally, I averaged about 1.5 ultrasounds per pregnancy; at the then prevailing rates, I received about $250 for that service. But I knew physicians who did six or seven ultrasounds per pregnancy. The patients loved it (they got to see the baby more often), and it didn't hurt them medically—or financially, because of insurance—but those doctors were making six times more than I was. The insurance companies caught on and created global fees for pregnancy that didn't increase when more services were provided in a healthy pregnancy. All of a sudden, doctors who were doing six ultrasounds went back to one or two.

POPULATION HEALTH MANAGEMENT

TVH's ability to deliver high-quality care within a budget is based on an approach known as population health management (PHM). Embraced to varying degrees by all healthcare organizations that take on financial risk, PHM is planned care that may encompass multiple care settings and providers. It also places individual care within the context of the care needs of the entire patient population. Instead of doing as much as possible for a patient, whether or not it's necessary or appropriate, PHM seeks to deliver the care that a patient needs without wasting the resources available to the organization.

Under PHM, the care process is viewed as ongoing and longitudinal, not confined to single episodes. The care provided to patients is more or less continuous, rather than being confined to office visits, ER visits, or hospitalizations. Fairly healthy patients receive preventive care and education on how to remain healthy, and chronic disease care is coordinated across settings and over time. Organizations that use this model assume they will be caring for their whole population for a long time, and that keeping people healthy or preventing them from getting sicker will not only benefit the patients but will also reduce the organization's costs.

PHM prioritizes good, thorough primary care because it can avoid the need for specialty referrals or hospitalizations. Instead of referring patients out to specialists if they have any type of complex condition, as is commonly done in fee-for-service medicine, primary care physicians use their full training to address as many of a patient's problems as they think is appropriate. They have no incentive not to if they're getting a salary plus a quality bonus, and the organization encourages them to do as much as they can for every patient.

It is important to remember that true primary care-driven PHM is different than the failed experiment of many HMOs in the 1990s. In that "gatekeeper" approach, primary care providers were encouraged *not* to send patients to specialists, resulting in underutilization. On the other hand, fee-for-service payment leads to overutilization. Our goal should be to promote and reward *optimal* utilization, and to employ the best technology to help providers in that pursuit (Terry 2020c).

Organizations that practice PHM go upstream of primary care by dealing with individuals' social determinants of health, which contribute greatly to poor health in many cases. Health systems and ACOs may do this by opening lines of communication with community social service agencies that address food security and housing for people who lack either or both. In some cases, they'll get people on Medicaid if they qualify but haven't applied for it. And, as will be explained in chapter 8, some risk-bearing organizations hire social workers and even repair people to ameliorate living conditions that harm people's health.

Nurse care managers or "navigators" are found in every organization that manages population health. These nurses usually work with high-risk patients to prevent exacerbations of their conditions and costly episodes of care. But many organizations also pay close attention to managing the care of "rising-risk" folks who may become high risk in the near future. The most successful organizations coordinate the care of everyone in their population when they get sick and educate them on how to manage their conditions. They also try to prevent them from getting sick in the first place.

Technology Stack Is Crucial

Success with value-based contracts requires dedicated software that can provide timely and complex data analysis. Crucial information can be discovered through patient risk stratification, identification of care gaps, measurement of provider utilization and quality, utilization analysis, and reports on out-of-network care, which can be costly to risk-taking organizations (Terry 2020c). Since 2015, telehealth and RPM have also become realistic adjuncts to PHM. To judge by Lowenkron's comments on how TVH manages care, however, these technologies are not yet widely used.

David Nash, MD, who is Dr. Raymond C. & Doris N. Grandon Professor of Health Policy and founding dean emeritus of the Jefferson College of Population Health at Thomas Jefferson University, predicts these programs will be more common once several challenges are overcome. The first challenge, he told me, is that "we have very few outcome measures for a telehealth visit." The American Telemedicine Association and some government agencies are trying to fill this gap, he adds. Second, physicians vary in their skill at diagnosing and treating patients online. Training on how best to use telehealth might improve that situation. Third, we're still in the early phase of establishing how to manage people with chronic diseases using telehealth and remote monitoring.

"There are organizations and companies like Teladoc and Livongo that are starting to pull together the ability to monitor patients and see their data at any given point, and this is being seen as a way to enhance chronic care management," Nash notes. "What some experts are seeing is the possibility of much more continuous management of chronic disease patients."

When that happens, he says, it will be applied first to people who have serious chronic illnesses. "Eventually, maybe we'll embrace health assurance, and the unscaling of healthcare could be more widespread. We're still a bit of a way from that." Among other things, methods must be found to "filter the data" so it doesn't add work for busy clinicians.

That last point is not trivial. Physician burnout has become endemic, and, as previously noted, in many cases technology has only served to increase a provider's load. For example, the My Chart patient portal of the Epic electronic health record is an effective way for patients to communicate with their provider, but it often adds significant unreimbursed hours to an already heavy workload, resulting in doctors spending less time with their families.

Nash agrees with the experts who think we won't achieve the full potential of telehealth or RPM until we have true value-based payments. Today, he notes, some physicians are taking advantage of the parity between payments for in-person and virtual visits to increase the number of times they see patients. Health services research, he says, must answer questions such as "How often do I have to do a telehealth visit with an otherwise healthy individual? Is the annual physical exam necessary? What's the correct number of visits, how long they should be, and should it be broken down into behavioral health and physical health?" Not quite the "13 Questions" that Seatrain sang about in their sophomore album, but they are core to finding the right balance between virtual and traditional healthcare.

BRINGING IT ALL HOME

If I'm right that most healthcare will eventually move out of hospitals to be provided at home, we should think about the kinds of technology that can enable that. These technologies must help ensure that patients receive care that is higher quality and less expensive outside the hospital than in it, except for things that only hospitals can do. Enabling technologies should also make it easier to manage population health.

One trend that seems to be gaining traction is the expansion of virtual care across care settings. For example, Intermountain Healthcare has built a suite of telehealth services, Intermountain at Home, covering a wide range of care types (Pennic 2019). Intermountain uses telehealth to connect recently discharged patients to a primary care physician or advanced practice clinician for hospital-level services at home, including

> remote monitoring
> expanded telemedicine capabilities
> virtual urgent care visits . . .
> appointment-based video visits . . .
> dialysis and intravenous (IV) medication
> physical therapy.

Hospital at home (HaH) was developed as an alternative to traditional inpatient acute care. Done properly, the benefits are obvious: improving patient and family care experience, reducing the rate of common hospital-associated complications, and reducing the costs of institutionalized acute care. Established models for delivering hospital-level care in a home setting have existed internationally for decades, including in Israel, Australia, the United Kingdom, Canada, and France.

Some companies are providing infrastructure for HaH. For example, Medically Home offers a turnkey HaH service to health systems. DispatchHealth and Maribel Health supply similar all-inclusive services. Current Health, which started in post-acute care, is now offering a broad range of RPM services and has expanded into HaH as well (Muoio 2019).

General Catalyst, where I serve as an executive in residence, is providing funding and strategy to Maribel, which was cofounded by Adam Groff, MD, and Ronald Paulus, MD. Maribel's HaH software can be integrated with health systems' technical infrastructure to ensure that care is safely, effectively, and efficiently provided to HaH patients. What differentiates Maribel is that they take partial or full risk for managing the HaH population while guaranteeing the health systems a return on investment.

HaH will eventually become the normal mode of acute care for many conditions. Post-acute care will be moved out of institutions, except for people who need care that can't be provided outside of a skilled nursing facility. Eventually, health systems and providers will be defined not by how they care for the sickest patients in the highest fixed cost settings but by how they help the other 97 percent of the population stay healthy and out of the hospital.

Remote Monitoring Evidence

Research on home care is starting to pile up. In chapter 1, I alluded to the studies supporting the efficacy of HaH and showing that it reduces costs. Most of these studies were done before the advent of telehealth, and more studies need to be done, but pandemic-era experiences with HaH have been largely positive for health systems and patients (Terry 2020a, 2020b).

At the height of the COVID-19 pandemic, for instance, some hospitals urged patients to stay home and be treated there if they had mild symptoms. Hospital safety experts have noted that remote pulse oximetry makes this remote monitoring feasible (Pronovost, Cole, and Hughes 2022). The pulse oximeters used in the hospital can also be deployed at home, and patient data can be relayed to "smartphones, secure cloud servers, and web-based dashboards where physicians and hospitals can monitor the patient's status in near real time." The review conducted by Pronovost and colleagues (2021) included an analysis estimating that

> daily assessment and 3-week follow-up of at-home pulse oximetry monitoring was projected to be potentially associated with a mortality rate of 6 per 1,000 patients with COVID-19, compared with 26 per 1,000 without at-home monitoring. Based on a hypothetical cohort of 3,100 patients, the study projected that remote patient monitoring could potentially be associated with 87% fewer hospitalizations, 77% fewer deaths, reduced per-patient costs of $11,472 over standard care, and gains of 0.013 quality-adjusted life-years.

Besides pulse oximetry, a broad range of other vital signs can be remotely monitored from home, they observed.

I am convinced that 10 years from now, monitoring pulse oximetry and other vital signs will be viewed as the beginning of the HaH evolution. Three years before you could rent a fancy Fifth Avenue Manhattan apartment or luxury seaside mansion in Thailand on Airbnb, the travel social network Couchsurfing was the place to fill up your sofa or spare bed with broke college kids or adventure seekers. Think of the current RPM activities as a precursor to a robust "health assurance at home" ecosystem.

A Sea Change Due to RPM

Jeffrey Gruen, MD, is the founder and CEO of Raziel Health, which has developed an RPM platform. He told me that the technology has gone through three distinct phases. Before 2018, "people used RPM in very limited, very small populations where there was thought to be a high readmission risk or a high risk of hospitalization." Hospitals or health plans paid for the service, hoping they'd see a return on investment in these high-risk cases.

Around 2018, he says, there was a "sea change" in attitudes when data demonstrated that RPM could benefit a larger portion of the population, including people with one or more chronic diseases. This was the second phase, when health plans began to establish mechanisms to reimburse providers for RPM.

In the third phase of RPM, which has already begun, the patient is comanaged by their physician and a third-party firm that provides analysis of the monitoring data coupled with care management.

Gruen admits that the evidence to date on the clinical benefits of RPM is not conclusive. "A lot of the current studies are flawed, and there's wide variation in the power of the intervention. A lot of times, the intervention is just the technology and isn't well-integrated with the high-touch component of care delivery. Or it is integrated, but the care is provided by parties with various levels of quality sophistication and impact."

Raziel's own data, he says, shows that RPM does have clinical benefit and can deliver a significant return on investment in the right settings. In addition, the algorithms his firm uses can pick out important information from the monitoring data about 95 percent of the time.

Changes in Post-Acute Care

The other major trend that will make home the center of care is the growth of home health care—which isn't as tautological as it sounds. Partly because of CMS's bundled payment programs, many hospitals have decreased the number of postdischarge referrals to skilled nursing facilities and increased the number of patients they send home with home health care, which costs less than institutional care (Minemyer 2018).

But home health care can come with unexpected "boomerang" costs if not done efficiently and appropriately. Nurses and doctors who were available with a push of a button are no longer there when patients return home. Patients and their families can get easily overwhelmed with the double duty of recovering and providing nursing and medical care. This leads to about 20 percent of home-discharged patients being readmitted to the hospital and more than a third transitioning to higher-cost nursing facilities.

Nursing homes themselves have had many quality issues over the years. Writing for the Kaiser Family Foundation, Harrington and colleagues (2017, 2) noted that "many nursing homes continue to fail to meet all federal quality standards, with about 93% receiving at least one inspection deficiency citation in 2015, about the same as in 2005." Yet home health agencies' quality scores have generally improved over time, with Medicare patient satisfaction scores in the 80 percent range.

Laguna Health, a digital at-home recovery service, acts as a "space station" of sorts when transitioning from the hospital or post-acute care facility to recover at home. "Recovery is a deeply personal experience and should take into consideration behavioral, emotional, environmental and socioeconomic factors" according to Yoni Shtein, CEO and cofounder of Laguna. "We extend the life cycle of care for patients through personalized recovery plans, clinical and behavioral support, and tech-enabled solutions to track their recovery journey."

These technologies will create a seamless post-acute care health assurance experience that will be a far cry from the underwhelming instruction sheet patients are currently handed on their way out of the hospital door.

Aid to Care Management

Home health agencies can incorporate RPM data to manage their patients' care, achieve care plan goals, and help providers adjust care plans (Rodriguez 2021). Monitoring a patient between visits could alert the provider of a significant change in a patient's health. For example, a congestive heart failure patient might experience weight gain over the course of a few days if their medications have been adjusted. Seeing the change in real time would allow clinicians to intervene before the problem worsened.

Since 2018, CMS has classified RPM as an allowable administrative cost if a home health agency uses it to augment the care planning process (Rodriguez 2021). To solidify the benefit, a bill introduced in Congress in November 2021 would establish an option for Medicare beneficiaries to recover at home after discharge while retaining the existing option of nursing home or rehab care. The benefit would combine Medicare-covered skilled nursing with personal care, transportation, meal supports, RPM, and telehealth. The bill's cosponsors argue that recovery at home would increase patient satisfaction, reduce exposure to infectious disease, and save big bucks for Medicare (Cuellar and Comer 2021).

Clearly, we are at the dawn of innovations in medical technology aiding in post-acute care, keeping patients out of acute care facilities and realizing the dream of "healthcare at any address." Ambient intelligence, natural language processing, voice biomarkers, and predictive analytics are already being used for problems ranging from medication nonadherence to cost management. The big leap, according to Yoni Shtein of Laguna Health, will be leveraging these technologies in a coordinated fashion in the care management space. Using machine learning to identify gaps and risks specific to individuals, creating automated mental health screening tools, and personalizing education and instruction to a person's specific learning style will allow caregivers to make more personalized and informed decisions and determine an effective intervention before a person gets readmitted to the hospital.

CONCLUSION

So, as Jennifer Hudson so beautifully sang, "I am changing, I'll be better than I am." For many reasons—COVID-19, logic, generational change—healthcare in America is changing (more slowly than some of us would like) from a broken, fragmented, expensive, inequitable fee-for-service system to one that will be truly patient-centered, rewarding health rather than healthcare, health assurance rather than sick care, and population health as opposed to maximizing the hospital's population.

The current trend of hospital consolidation and construction is nearing its peak. It will continue until the real payers—government, individuals, and employers—have reached their limit on health costs and political momentum for change becomes unstoppable. Sometime after we reach that inflection point, value-based payment will become the norm, and health systems will begin to see the advantage in moving more of their services from high-fixed-cost facilities into patients' homes and other less expensive settings.

But if hospitals and health systems tried to do this under the current economic model they'd hemorrhage money, and many would go out of business. To make unscaling feasible, the health-care financing system must be transformed into a patient-centered, value-based model in which providers take financial responsibility for care. Sounds impossible? Chapter 6 proposes one way to get there.

REFERENCES

American Medical Association. 2021. "AMA Analysis Shows Most Physicians Work Outside of Private Practice" (press release). Published May 5. www.ama-assn.org/press-center/press -releases/ama-analysis-shows-most-physicians-work-outside -private-practice.

Berenson, R. A., and R. B. Murray. 2022. "How Price Regulation Is Needed to Advance Market Competition." *Health Affairs* 41 (1): 26–34. www.healthaffairs.org/doi/epdf/10.1377/hlthaff .2021.01235.

Brubaker, H. 2021. "After Eight Years of Growth, Jefferson President Stephen K. Klasko Announces Retirement." *Philadelphia*

Inquirer, October 14. www.inquirer.com/business/health
/jefferson-health-stephen-klasko-retiring-20211014.html.

Cuellar, H., and J. Comer. 2021. "It's Time to Give Medicare Beneficiaries the Opportunity and Choice of Recovery at Home."
The Hill, November 15. https://thehill.com/blogs/congress
-blog/healthcare/581517-its-time-to-give-medicare-beneficiaries
-the-opportunity-and.

Ellison, A. 2022. "HCA, Tenet Invest More Than $10.7B in
Expansion." *Becker's Hospital Review,* February 7. www
.beckershospitalreview.com/strategy/hca-tenet-invest-more
-than-10–7b-in-expansion.html.

Field, R. I. 2019. "Survey Finds Philadelphia Less Healthy Than
Other Northeast Cities." *Philadelphia Inquirer,* February 18. www
.inquirer.com/health/survey-finds-philadelphia-less-healthy
-than-other-northeast-cities-20190218.html.

Governance Institute. 2017. "One Jefferson: Accelerating Reinven-
tion of Academic Medicine Through Growth, Integration, and
Innovation" (case study). Published December.

Haefner, M. 2021. "Optum Expects to Add 10,000 Physicians This
Year." *Becker's Payer Issues,* January 21. www.beckerspayer.com
/payer/optum-expects-to-add-10-000-physicians-this-year.html.

Harrington, C., J. M. Weiner, L. Ross, and M. Musumeci. 2017. "Key
Issues in Long-Term Services and Supports Quality." Kaiser
Family Foundation Issue Brief. Published October. https://
files.kff.org/attachment/Issue-Brief-Key-Issues-in-Long-Term
-Services-and-Supports-Quality.

Heath, S. 2018. "85% of Patients Concerned About Healthcare
Costs, Quality." Patient Engagement HIT. Published May
1. https://patientengagementhit.com/news/85-of-patients
-concerned-about-healthcare-costs-quality.

Johnson, D. W. 2022. "Big Lies, Tyranny, Healthcare and
American Democracy." Market Corner Commentary.

4sightHealth. Published January 13. https://mcusercontent.com
/8a4bf5d1617f86a90e5a909f0/files/7afca23c-c9f2-78bc-dbc7
-fa24552a2dcd/4sightHealth.BigLiesandHealthcare.MCC.1_13
_22.pdf.

King, R. 2021. "FTC to No Longer Challenge Jefferson Health-
Einstein Network Deal." *Fierce Healthcare*, March 1. www
.fiercehealthcare.com/hospitals/ftc-to-no-longer-challenge
-jefferson-health-einstein-network-deal.

Minemyer, P. 2018. "Study: Bundled Payments Drive Hospitals
to Reduce Referrals to SNFs, Improve Coordination." *Fierce
Healthcare*, August 6. www.fiercehealthcare.com/hospitals
-health-systems/study-bundled-payments-drive-hospitals-to
-cut-down-referrals-to-snfs.

Mitchell, E., and I. Morrison. 2022. "Large Employers Are Suiting
Up to Fix Healthcare." Medpage Today. Published February
19. www.medpagetoday.com/opinion/second-opinions/97277.

Muoio, D. 2019. "Current Health Partners with Fellow Connected
Device Makers to Flesh Out Its Remote Monitoring Platform."
MobiHealthNews, October 1. www.mobihealthnews.com/news
/north-america/current-health-partners-fellow-connected
-device-makers-flesh-out-its-remote.

Pennic, J. 2019. "New 'Intermountain at Home' Service Launches
with Remote Monitoring, Telemedicine Capabilities." HIT Consultant. Published March 12. https://hitconsultant.net/2019/03
/12/new-intermountain-at-home-service-launches-with-remote
-monitoring-telemedicine-capabilities/.

Plescia, M. 2022. "5 hospital construction projects worth
$1B or more." *Becker's Hospital Review*, February 9. www
.beckershospitalreview.com/capital/5-hospital-construction
-projects-worth-1b-or-more.html.

Pronovost, P. J., M. D. Cole, and R. M. Hughes. 2022. "Remote
Patient Monitoring During COVID." *Journal of the American*

Medical Association. Published online February 25. https://doi
.org/10.1001/jama.2022.2040.

Reed, T. 2020. "Judge Blocks FTC's Attempt to Stop Jefferson-
Einstein Merger Deal." *Fierce Healthcare*, December 9. www
.fiercehealthcare.com/hospitals/ftc-s-attempt-to-block-jefferson
-einstein-deal-stymied.

Rodriguez, J. 2021. "Home May Be the New Hospital." *HomeCare*,
October 8. www.homecaremag.com/october-2021/how-remote
-patient-monitoring-bolster-aging-in-place.

Terry, K. 2020a. "'Hospital at Home' Increases COVID Capacity
in Large Study." *Medscape Medical News*, November 17. www
.medscape.com/viewarticle/941173#vp_3.

———. 2020b. "'Hospital at Home' May Boost COVID-19 Inpatient
Capacity." *Medscape Medical News*, April 26. www.medscape
.com/viewarticle/929399.

———. 2020c. *Physician-Led Healthcare Reform: A New Approach
to Medicare for All.* Washington, DC: American Association for
Physician Leadership.

CHAPTER 6

"For the Love of Money"
by The O'Jays

All for the love of money / Don't let, don't let,
don't let money rule you / For the love of money
/ Money can change people sometimes.

THE GREAT PHILLY soul group, the O'Jays (also responsible for the song "Message in Our Music") provide a hard-hitting R&B warning about the effect that an obsession with money can have on your well-being. In the context of this book, "Money Changes Everything" by Cyndi Lauper might even be a better choice. As noted in earlier chapters, our system of paying for healthcare in many ways promotes the gross inequities that are the bane of US healthcare. Cheaper health plans sacrifice access and quality, while expensive ones are beyond the means of most consumers and employers.

The pandemic transformed our healthcare financing method from a problem to a life-and-death situation. Our fragmented system of OPM (other people's money) rewarded payers, who had received their premiums from employers before the pandemic, while almost bankrupting many providers who could not perform elective surgeries and procedures, and led to record stock prices for investor-owned pharma companies whose COVID-19 vaccines were approved. In some cases, money was literally the difference between life and death during the first acute phase of the pandemic, when poverty made it difficult for families to access adequate food and housing, transportation, or stable internet to receive virtual care. These are among the factors known as social determinants of health, which we'll explore further in chapter 8.

The obvious solution to the healthcare financing mess is for providers and payers to work together to reduce costs, with an assist from technology companies. (Think of The Villages Health from chapter 5, on a grander scale.) But how we get there is not obvious.

The current situation is bizarre and counterproductive. By fighting each other over money, providers and payers have created a huge administrative burden on both sides. The provider has to deal with prior authorization and claims denials; the insurance company tries to restrain utilization and deny claims where it can. Many thousands of provider and payer employees are engaged in this pointless struggle. Patients are trapped in between but don't benefit, no matter who wins. And our nonproductive administrative costs eclipse those of every other nation on Earth.

The main battlefield of this war is contract negotiations. The biggest, baddest provider in town makes off with the lion's share of the spoils, and smaller players are penalized with lower rates to compensate for what insurers are paying the dominant system. Not surprisingly, this motivates the community hospitals and smaller systems to join together through merger or acquisition, increasing the consolidation of healthcare systems and driving prices higher.

The battle between payers and providers goes even further. Big payers, for example, don't want health systems to own health plans that might compete with them, and many providers object to insurers making piles of money while they're having trouble breaking even. This happened in spades during the early part of the pandemic, when hospitals were hurting because of a sharp drop in non-COVID patient volume while insurance companies were declaring record profits because claims were far lower than expected.

Meanwhile, everyone else keeps losing. People skip needed care because of high prices, which leads to higher spending in the long run (Kearney et al. 2021). Employers continue looking for a silver bullet, as they have for decades, but nothing seems to work; whatever they try, providers, insurers, and Big Pharma find ways to obstruct them. If nothing is done, fewer and fewer people will be able to afford healthcare.

Could the system eventually collapse under its own weight? The sky has appeared to be falling on healthcare before. That was why the public demanded change in the early 1990s, when the Clintons proposed their national health plan, and in 2008, when momentum started to build for the Affordable Care Act. The country continued spending more on healthcare, however, and the sky didn't fall.

Nevertheless, there are disquieting signs that we may be approaching the point of no return. From 2011 to 2020, national health expenditures (NHEs) grew from $2.7 trillion to $4.124 trillion (Hartman et al. 2013). That included a 9.7 percent jump in 2020 because of federal spending to fight COVID-19; meanwhile, the economy contracted by 2.2 percent, yielding a ratio of health costs to GDP of 19.7 percent. In 2021, NHE growth dropped to 4.2 percent as the COVID-19 battle continued. While there is significant uncertainty about the future, NHE is expected to increase by an average 4.9 percent per year from 2022 to 2024 if the pandemic keeps waning. After that, NHE is projected to rise at an average annual rate of 5.3 percent, hitting $6.751 trillion, or 19.6 percent of GDP, in 2030 (Poisal et al. 2022).

If this prediction is accurate, health spending will have risen 57 percent over the decade. While that's only slightly greater than the spending increase during the previous 10 years, health costs might grow much faster if COVID-19 returns in force. Even if it doesn't, healthcare will continue eating up more and more of our economy as the population ages. One could argue that the only other sector in our economy that has had a greater increase in prices without appreciably better outcomes is higher education. As someone who has predominantly led academic healthcare institutions, I certainly share some of the guilt over this!

What happens if health spending hits $8 trillion in 2032 and $10 trillion in 2035? Will employers and individuals, including taxpayers, keep putting up with the burden that the healthcare industry imposes on them? Sly and the Family Stone's "I Want to Take You Higher" has been the theme around healthcare expenditures, which has certainly benefited health-related CEOs and shareholders. But will consumers rebel when they have to choose between paying for their utilities and covering their medical bills?

If I'm right in supposing that the public will eventually revolt, as several of the candidates in the 2020 presidential race predicted, the answer will not be three simple words like "Medicare for All." It's easy to say and a great talking point but, like many of the climate change "solutions" that make us feel good but don't achieve the desired results, Medicare for All is incredibly simplistic, short-sighted, and naive. It would lower costs one time—at providers' expense—and do nothing to improve healthcare quality. In fact, some of the current Medicare regulations make it *harder* to deliver quality care.

But there is a way to prevent a collapse. It's a private sector solution, but it will need to be set in motion and regulated by the federal and state governments. This kind of public-private collaboration has had excellent results in the past in the United States and in other countries, and I believe that it can succeed again if the major players are kept mostly whole.

A LONG HISTORY OF FAILURE

Public and private entities have tried many different strategies to reduce health spending to a sustainable level. But in the long run, none of these efforts have succeeded in making a real dent in cost growth, and the United States still spends twice as much on healthcare as other wealthy countries do, on average (OECD 2022). A brief survey of past trends explains why.

Managed care had its heyday in the 1990s after the Clinton Health Plan imploded and employers sought another way to hold down costs. California HMOs seemed to be saving money, so insurers tried to spread this concept across the country. They passed risk on to small, financially unprepared primary care groups that didn't know how to manage utilization after decades of fee-for-service payments (Terry 2007). Some groups went out of business. Other practices were sold to high-flying physician practice management companies that themselves went belly-up due to their flawed business model (Keckley 2016).

In the 1990s and 2000s, many health plans adopted pay for performance (P4P) schemes designed to improve healthcare quality, believing they would reduce costs. The quality results of P4P were mixed, however, and costs didn't fall (James 2012).

In 2016, the Centers for Medicare & Medicaid Services (CMS) launched a P4P initiative called the Quality Payment Program. Nearly all eligible clinicians who reported quality data in 2019 received small pay raises based on their scores, but the growth in Medicare spending didn't slow as a result (American Hospital Association 2020). Physician practices reported that participation in the Merit-Based Incentive Payment System, one of the program's two tracks, generated significant administrative costs (Khullar et al. 2021).

In the late 1990s, Congress tried to restrain physician spending with the Sustainable Growth Rate program, which was supposed to lower Medicare payment rates when service volume increased. After postponing reductions in physician pay several times, Congress finally repealed the law in 2015 (Guterman 2015).

THE IRON TRIANGLE

The Affordable Care Act (ACA) was supposed to reduce costs, increase access, and improve quality: quite a trick, considering that it would violate the "iron triangle" of health policy, which says you can achieve one of these goals, or maybe two, but not all three— unless you are willing to disrupt the system (Carroll 2012). But disruption is painful. So, not surprisingly, spending continued to rise under the ACA as more people gained access to care and some quality indices improved. Meat Loaf told us "Two Out of Three Ain't Bad," but in this case, that isn't good enough.

Despite a tax on insurers and a requirement that at least 85 percent of premiums be spent on patient care, the insurance industry enjoyed a boom during the ACA's launch period, partly because more people could buy coverage. While the ACA was supposed to bring down healthcare costs and provide more access, traditional "sick-care" stocks such as UnitedHealthcare and HCA soared.

To be fair, the ACA did lower the number of uninsured people and helped many low-paid working people gain access to care (Blumenthal, Collins, and Fowler 2020; Tavernise and Gebeloff 2016). It also authorized new CMS programs that improved the safety and quality of hospital care, including penalties for excessive readmissions and hospital-acquired conditions. The ACA's value-based purchasing programs, including two bundled payment initiatives, were less effective, although early results from the Comprehensive Care for Joint Replacement Program were promising (Terry 2020).

MSSP: MUCH ADO ABOUT LITTLE

Accountable care organizations (ACOs), associations of physicians and hospitals that are accountable for the cost and quality of care for a defined population, were highly favored by health policy experts in the 2010s. CMS created a program for ACOs called the Medicare Shared Savings Program (MSSP). Designed to promote value-based care, the MSSP allowed ACOs to share in any savings they generated for Medicare. More advanced or better-funded ACOs took two-sided risk: that is, they received a higher share of the savings in return for agreeing to reimburse CMS for any costs that exceeded the ACO's budget.

From the MSSP's inception in 2012 through 2019, participating ACOs produced small, although growing, savings for Medicare. Total annual shared savings jumped from $315 million in 2013 to

$983 million in 2018 and $1.47 billion in 2019 (CMS 2021). But 2019 savings were less than 3 percent of the *growth* in the Medicare budget that year (CMS 2020).

One reason for the relatively modest results is that in the early years of the MSSP, relatively few ACOs took two-sided risk. They were investing in infrastructure, but they weren't paying back CMS when they spent too much on care. Because of MSSP rule changes, 41 percent of participating ACOs were taking two-sided risk by 2021, but that shift coincided with a drop in the number of ACOs that remained in the program (CMS 2021).

Jefferson was part of a multicenter ACO that had every intention of taking two-sided risk. The ACO's greatest success came early, when spending was compared to a benchmark based on its historically high costs. As the ACO got better at managing care, the improvement targets became harder to achieve, and the MSSP model offered more risk than financial benefit.

The only government cost-reduction effort that has had a real impact over time is the Maryland all-payer rate-setting program and its successor, under which Maryland hospitals negotiate global budgets with the state (Emanuel et al. 2022a). I'll have more to say about this initiative later in the chapter.

CONSUMER-DIRECTED CARE

In the private sector, the most important cost-control initiative since managed care has been the consumer-directed care movement. Supporters of this approach believe that properly incentivized consumers can hold down costs through their care-seeking behavior and choice of providers.

To achieve this goal, employers offer their employees a high-deductible health plan (HDHP) with a tax-favored health savings account (HSA) attached to it. A 2021 analysis by EBRI and Greenwald Research shows that in many cases employers skip the HSA and simply shift the risk to their workers through an HDHP.

In 2019, 28 percent of US employers offered HDHPs with a savings option, but 55 percent of employees with an HSA didn't contribute any money to it—not surprising, since many lower-income people couldn't afford to. A third of HDHP enrollees did not have an HSA (Maciejewski and Hung 2020).

EBRI and Greenwald (2021) found that the rise in enrollment in high-deductible and consumer-driven plans has paused after reaching a record high. About 18 percent of employees were enrolled in either of these kinds of plans in 2021, down from 19 percent in 2020. Many workers rejected such plans if they had a choice: 42 percent of traditional plan enrollees were offered an HDHP, with or without an HSA. The same study found that HDHP enrollees are more cost-conscious than members of traditional health plans: They are more likely to check whether insurance will cover their medication costs, more likely to check the quality rating of a doctor or hospital, and more likely to check the price of doctor visits, medications, and other services before receiving care.

While it's unknown whether HDHPs save money in the long term, some health policy experts are concerned that they discourage people from seeking care when they need it (Aiken 2021; Yelorda, Rose, and Bundorf 2022). Overall, consumer-driven plans don't seem to be the silver bullet employers have been looking for.

Price Transparency

When consumers pay the bill, they'd like to get an estimate of how much a healthcare service will cost before it's delivered. Yet it's difficult for most consumers to learn their out-of-pocket costs in advance.

To alleviate this problem and increase competition, CMS adopted a hospital price transparency rule that became effective on January 1, 2021. The regulation requires hospitals to post their negotiated prices for all services in a machine-readable file, and to display the same information for 70 CMS-specified and 230 hospital-selected services (Bai, Jiang, and Makary 2021).

Unfortunately, most hospitals have yet to provide all the information required (Lagasse 2022). Some observers say hospitals are reluctant to reveal this kind of information because they don't want other payers to know what a particular plan is paying them. CMS can fine hospitals that don't comply with its rule, but as of 2022 it was just starting to do so (Cass and Plescia 2022).

Meanwhile, in an absurd scenario that would make Monty Python proud, there are consulting companies whose sole purpose is to help health systems adhere to the "letter of the transparency regulation" to avoid a fine while making it almost impossible for the average consumer to interpret what the data means. Imagine if Kayak presented travel price options, but only in a language you couldn't understand. By and large, that is the current state of transparency in healthcare. "Honesty" is a lovely word, according to Billy Joel, but for patients negotiating an increasingly byzantine healthcare financial system, honesty and transparency are hard to find.

Working at Cross Purposes

Despite the difficulties inherent in consumer-driven care, a consumer-directed intervention at Jefferson Health did manage to lower costs. We told the employees in our self-insured plan that, before going to the emergency department, they should go online to our JeffConnect service and discuss their problem with a Jefferson physician. If it wasn't a true emergency, the service would refer them to our urgent care center up the street from the hospital or would book an appointment with their personal doctor for the next day. The carrot was that if they used our JeffConnect telehealth system and were told to visit the emergency department they'd have no deductible and no copay; but if they went straight there for, say, an earache, they'd have a $200 deductible.

Using this very targeted kind of intervention, we were able to move roughly half of the nontrauma, nonambulance patients to less expensive, more efficient care. But here's the kicker: If we had done the same thing with patients who were not in our employee health plan, we would have lost over $1,000 per emergency department visit for every nonemergency patient who was redirected. Treating, say, a sprained ankle in urgent care would have cost far less, but we would have been reimbursed far less too. Clearly, it wouldn't have taken long for Jefferson to have negative financial consequences if we'd chosen that route.

Still, we saw no reason to waste all that money when we had invested in telehealth and urgent care. Also, using JeffConnect for triage started to solve the cost, access, and quality conundrum for unscheduled care. So, we went to the health plans and suggested that we split the savings if their members used JeffConnect.

This was back in 2014, when telehealth was relatively new and we were ahead of the curve. Some declined our offer, saying, essentially, "We're fine with the system as it is." But the plans said they loved telehealth and would gladly pay us $50 per virtual visit. "By the way," they added, "if you're doing too much stuff on an emergency basis, maybe we should take a closer look at what we're paying you for." It's another classic example of what happens when insurers and providers work at cross purposes. (Since then, several payers have worked with us on a more aligned "value-based" approach.)

PUBLIC-PRIVATE ACTION

Clearly, healthcare players that benefit from the status quo are not going to rescue our screwed-up healthcare financing system. The government has to prod them into action.

But there are limits to what CMS can do under current law. Congress authorized CMS to create Medicare Advantage, which now covers nearly half of Medicare enrollees, and it authorized the MSSP. In addition, CMS's Center for Medicare and Medicaid

Innovation has launched a number of demonstration projects such as the Comprehensive Primary Care initiative to support better care coordination. CMS has also granted waivers to let some states try out innovations in their Medicaid programs.

To bring about a major reorganization of the healthcare financing system, however, Congress would have to pass legislation on the scale of the ACA. Recalling the titanic struggle that the passage of that law entailed, I can confidently predict that the usual suspects—insurers, providers, and drug companies—would fight any such move with all the means at their disposal. But on the other side are employers and consumers, who have the wherewithal to fight for legislation they believe would benefit them.

The Relative Power of Lobbies

Let's look at the lobbying forces available to the healthcare industry. Open Secrets, a nonprofit transparency group that tracks money in politics, reports on their website that healthcare providers and pharma together spent $677.1 million on government lobbying in 2021. That total included $353.9 million for makers of pharmaceuticals and other health products; $117.4 million for hospitals and nursing homes; $84.9 million for health professionals; and $6.9 million for miscellaneous lobbying. In addition, America's Health Insurance Plans, the trade association for health insurers, spent $11.3 million on lobbying.

The US Chamber of Commerce spent "only" $66.4 million on lobbying for all purposes in 2021. But in 2009, when the fight over Obamacare ramped up, the Chamber expended $210 million on lobbying. If we add to that the possible spending by large employers and support from consumer advocacy organizations, a fairly large pro-reform war chest could be built. This would require, however, finding a policy that hits the trifecta of reducing costs to employers and employees, making care more accessible, and being pro-business growth.

In addition, insurers may support certain kinds of reform if their customers do and if they're guaranteed an important role in the new order. Even some healthcare providers, such as Kaiser Permanente, the Optum physician groups, risk-taking ACOs, and the private-equity-funded primary care companies would endorse a "radical" switch to value-based payment.

Of course, we can't forget about the power of the drug companies, which account for more than half of the industry's lobbying funds. But the pharmaceutical lobby may not oppose reform if the legislation doesn't directly target the drug companies. We can create a much better healthcare financing system without fundamentally changing how medications are paid for (as opposed to how much they cost). Drug prices must eventually come down, but how to accomplish that is beyond the purview of this book.

The other Loch Ness monster cruising beneath the still waters is the stock market. Ultimately, the boards and CEOs of all publicly traded companies must answer to their investors. If a major disruption of the status quo might cause the stocks of for-profit hospitals and other healthcare providers, insurance companies, and pharma companies to tank, investors would strongly oppose that change. So, any model that we design to reduce the growth of health spending has to take those concerns into account.

Whatever solution is adopted, it must move the healthcare industry to value-based care—defined here as high-quality, efficient care. It must incentivize providers to take financial risk so that their incentives are aligned with those of payers. It must meet the needs of patients, providers, and insurers while limiting cost growth. Technology companies, providers, and payers must be incentivized to work together to build a truly patient-centered system. Consumer choice must be a central element in the model. And the new model must guarantee health equity for all individuals, regardless of race, ethnicity, gender, or geography.

When you read the last few sentences, your first reaction was probably to mutter "that will never happen" or to start humming "The Twelfth of Never" by Johnny Mathis. You have every reason to be skeptical. But as with any major transformation, disruption, or creative construction of a new system, we have to start somewhere. So here we go.

BUILDING THE NEW MODEL

The year is 2035: A decade ago, the government set in motion and the private sector implemented a new model of healthcare financing that has had amazingly beneficial consequences. Contrary to the dire warnings of some observers back in 2025, when the Comprehensive Health Ethics and Equity Reform Act (CHEER Act) passed, healthcare providers and insurers are thriving, and technology companies are helping to transform the nature of healthcare. Americans are healthier than ever, and no one declares bankruptcy anymore because of medical bills.

The CHEER Act established that everyone has the right to receive first-rate healthcare. To make that possible, the law went beyond the ACA and required that every US resident have access to affordable care. For basic healthcare, including primary care and most kinds of specialty care, people purchase subscriptions to one of the competing basic care groups in their area with the help of their employers and/or the government. The government will buy a subscription for people who cannot afford one. The federal and state governments also provide subscriptions to people on Medicare and Medicaid.

In addition, everyone now has insurance for hospital and post-acute and specialist care, as well as expensive care provided in facilities such as ambulatory surgery centers and cancer treatment centers. Unlike the basic care subscriptions, this high-end insurance is provided by private insurance companies, which now enroll employed people, other nonelderly individuals, and Medicare and Medicaid beneficiaries. Like basic care, this "catastrophic insurance" is purchased with subsidies from the government and employers. The insurers pass most of the financial risk for this care to health systems that are willing to assume it. These organizations and their states negotiate all-payer global budgets covering hospital and post-acute care.

Redefining Insurance

How did we get there? First, we redefined health insurance. Traditional insurance policies covered services ranging from primary care to high-end care such as organ transplants and neurosurgery. Coverage was either first-dollar or was triggered by meeting a deductible. In the new model, insurance covers only expensive services, such as hospitalization, that most people can't afford on their own. The new type of insurance still covers most health spending, so insurance companies are still thriving. In addition, the government has incentivized most traditional Medicare beneficiaries to join Medicare Advantage plans, so insurers have greatly enlarged their business in that area.

Second, the federal government and participating states banned the purchase of private insurance for basic care and stopped allowing employers to self-insure. Those financing mechanisms were replaced by a consumer-driven subscription model in which people choose a primary care doctor in one of the competing basic care groups in their area. People control funds large enough to buy an annual subscription to any of these groups, but can't use the money to buy basic coverage from an insurance company. Those funds are a combination of the individual's own money and contributions from employers and the government, scaled to the individual's income and employment status. Government subsidies are similar to those offered on the obsolete ACA insurance exchanges.

This approach puts consumers, rather than employers, in the driver's seat and eliminates the bizarre dynamic of the person consuming the care and the person (or employer) paying for that care being two different parties. Before CHEER, people had to choose from among employer-selected health plans or resign themselves to the single plan their company selected. The insurer, in turn, decided which providers and health systems to contract with. Meanwhile, consumers paid ever-increasing percentages of their paychecks for insurance that limited their choices.

Now, people pick a basic care group, based on its subscription fee and published data on its quality, outcomes, and patient experience. In addition, consumers can see quality data on whatever hospital a group is affiliated with, which is the facility they'll likely be admitted to if they need hospital care. And the medically necessary services provided by the basic care groups are standardized, so consumers can compare the groups' subscription fees on an apples-to-apples basis.

Competition Between Provider Groups

Allowing individuals to choose from a menu of basic care groups places the competition where it should be: between care providers rather than insurance companies. The subscription fees, which are set by the providers, roll up to an annual care budget, so the provider groups are financially accountable for all the professional services, tests, and drugs they deliver, order, or subcontract. This includes all physician and advanced practitioner services (other than those listed in this section); lab and imaging tests; hearing, vision, and dental care; behavioral health care; and prescription drugs that cost less than a certain amount.

The competing groups are ranked by their quality scores. Individuals who select a group in the highest quality tier receive a 15 percent discount off their share of the subscription fee; people whose fees are mostly subsidized get a small bonus to spend on healthcare-related items if they select a high-quality group.

Another consumer-driven feature of the new model is related to health behavior. People who are willing to make health lifestyle choices—getting regular exercise, eating a healthy diet, allowing their vital signs and activities to be remotely monitored, for example—get another 15 percent off their portion of the subscription fee, with a similar bonus provision for those who are heavily subsidized. This aspect of the new model has grown steadily more important as the healthcare system has become more oriented to home care and as providers rely more extensively on remote monitoring data.

The subscription discounts don't reduce the care groups' budgets. Instead, the government makes up the difference. Even if a subscriber gets the full 30 percent discount, it's less than what the government saves on health costs.

Classification of Basic Care Groups

The basic care groups that are taking financial risk fall into several categories. The largest category is the care groups owned by health systems, which benefit from their groups' reduction of avoidable hospital admissions. Other types of basic care groups include independent primary care and multispecialty groups; organizations owned by insurance companies, such as the many groups belonging to UnitedHealthcare's Optum division; private-equity-owned groups such as those of Oak Street, ChenMed, and One Medical; subdivisions of integrated delivery systems such as Kaiser Permanente and Intermountain; ACOs; clinically integrated networks; and independent practice associations.

Under CHEER regulations, these groups must be of a certain size, neither too small to take risk nor so large that they squelch the competition. They must also contain a minimum percentage of primary care providers (physicians and nonphysician providers), who are essential to providing high-quality, efficient care, and demonstrate a certain level of proficiency in managing care and financial risk.

The basic care groups do not include hospital-based physicians such as radiologists, anesthesiologists, pathologists, emergency department physicians, and hospitalists. They also don't include surgeons, although the groups contract with them for nonsurgical services, such as the gynecological care provided by ob-gyns.

Independent Physicians

Around 70 percent of doctors were already in hospital- or corporation-owned groups capable of taking professional risk when the new model was announced in 2025 (Gamble 2022). However, not all independent physicians wanted to join a basic care group. Some primary care doctors elected to remain independent. Because there were no longer any privately insured patients and they couldn't take Medicare or Medicaid, their practices had to be cash-only. Most of these physicians followed the example of earlier direct primary care practices and charged subscription fees to cover their own services. But this was a hard way to eke out a living, especially for younger doctors who didn't have established practices. So as older doctors retired, independent primary care offices mostly faded out.

Independent specialists were in a different situation. While they faced the same dilemma as their primary care colleagues when insurance was cut off for basic care, they couldn't charge subscriptions for their services, which were less frequently needed by a smaller portion of the population. Nevertheless, these specialists didn't necessarily have to join one of the basic care groups. If they belonged to an established single-specialty group, they could contract with multiple basic care groups for their services.

Since basic care groups don't have all kinds of specialists, and some don't include any specialists, they all contract out for the specialties they lack. They try to make deals with high-quality, efficient specialty practices, providing business to these groups in return for moderate fees. If a specialty is in short supply in a particular market, those doctors' rates are specified by law. No doctor in an underrepresented specialty in a given region is allowed to turn away patients, regardless of which group they're with.

The healthcare financing system in rural areas differs from that in urban and suburban areas. Because there aren't enough rural physicians to form competing groups, they all work for or contract with one of the hospitals that have all-payer global budgets. Instead of just taking risk for acute and post-acute care, as other facilities do, these hospitals assume full risk that covers all professional services.

The digital health revolution also finally addressed some of the concerns related to rural health. Companies such as Homeward, begun by the former president of Livongo, used a combination of technology and healthcare professionals in areas such as home labs and mail-order prescriptions, longitudinal check-ins via telemedicine and remote monitoring, and ongoing care management to close gaps in care and address social needs.

Claims Processing Simplified and Subcontracted

Because the basic care groups contract for services not available internally, they receive claims from outside parties such as medical specialists, dentists, and pharmacy benefit managers. In most cases, they contract with insurers or third-party administrators to process these claims. The same entities also provide enrollment services to the groups.

One of the major advantages of switching from the old model to the new one is that insurance companies no longer second-guess physicians and force them to get prior authorization for many tests and treatments (an archaic process that ratchets up nonproductive administrative costs on both ends). Instead, each basic care group manages its own utilization, and its medical director makes decisions about what care is appropriate when a question comes up. In addition, the medical director pays close attention to the data on the cost and quality of individual physicians and discusses this with them when necessary.

In an ideal world, the care groups all would have established a system that paid physicians a base salary plus bonuses based on quality, cost, outcomes, and patient experience. Some groups experienced with managed care did that from the outset, but in many groups the doctors were used to being paid on the basis of production, using relative value units as the measure. Of course, when financial risk became the norm, this was counterproductive. So, most groups chose to split the difference: They based half of their doctors' bonuses on relative value units and half on quality and the other indexes. Over time, these groups phased out the volume-based component; within five years, most groups were using only quality- and value-based incentives.

MARYLAND'S PIONEERING EXPERIMENT

To understand the evolution of our 2035 mechanism for financing acute and post-acute care, it's helpful to review the history of the Maryland all-payer rate-setting system and its successor, the Maryland All-Payer Model (MD-APM), which mandated global budgets for hospitals.

In partnership with CMS, Maryland embarked on its rate-setting experiment back in 1977. Under its CMS waiver, the state negotiated all-payer rates with each hospital. Commercial plans, Medicare, and Medicaid all paid the hospital the same rates for its services. Those rates raised government payments and lowered those of private payers, but no hospital could use its market position to play hardball with health plans, or vice versa.

In 2022, commercial insurers in Maryland paid hospital prices that were 11–15 percent lower than in the rest of the nation, on average; Medicare paid hospital rates that were 30–44 percent higher than fee-for-service payments under its inpatient prospective payment system and 58–66 percent higher than payments under its outpatient prospective payment system (Jain et al. 2022).

Nevertheless, Medicare saved nearly $1 billion in Maryland from 2014 to 2018, following the introduction of the state's global budgeting system, and the annual savings have probably risen since then (Emanuel et al. 2022a). If the earlier savings had been projected to the entire country, they would have dwarfed the cost reductions of any other CMS program at the time, including the MSSP and CMS's primary care and bundled payment models.

The Transition to Global Budgeting

Maryland took a while to reach this position. When the state implemented its all-payer rate-setting in the 1970s, the mean cost of a Maryland hospital admission was 26 percent above the national average. In 2007, it was 2 percent below the national average. But starting in 2000, after the state eliminated payment adjustments based on the volume of admissions, hospital volume increased rapidly (Murray 2009). By the end of the decade, the CMS waiver that allowed Maryland to operate its rate-setting mechanism was threatened by the rising cost of hospital care (Kilaru, Crider, and Chiang 2022).

Because the all-payer system had served hospitals and insurers well, they united behind the state's proposal to switch to global budgeting, which was approved by CMS. After trying this approach with rural hospitals and achieving some success, Maryland inaugurated the global budgeting system statewide in 2014.

Under the MD-APM model, the state's Health Services Cost Review Commission (HSCRC) and the hospitals built an annual budget for each hospital's inpatient and outpatient costs, excluding post-acute care, using the hospital's revenues during a base period. The budget was adjusted yearly based on several variables. The HSCRC set the rates that each hospital used to bill all payers so that their total payments (based on expected utilization) would match the global budget.

The global budget established a ceiling on each hospital's revenues. If the revenues varied from the global budget, the following year the hospital either raised rates to meet its budget or lowered rates so payers could recoup the overage. To make it easier to navigate this requirement, hospitals were allowed to adjust their rates plus or minus 5 percent in order to stay within budget (RTI International 2019).

Promising Early Results

The CMS-commissioned report by RTI International (2019) found that from 2014 to 2018, Medicare beneficiaries had 2.8 percent slower growth in total expenditures ($975 million in savings) under the MD-APM relative to a comparison group. These savings were largely driven by 4.1 percent slower growth in total hospital expenditures ($796 million in savings) compared to the control group. According to the report,

> The additional reduction in total Medicare spending was due to savings on professional services in hospital settings and post-acute care (PAC). Although these services were not subject to global budgets, lower spending for professional services in hospital settings is consistent with decreases both in inpatient admissions and use of some hospital outpatient department services. The reduction in expenditures for PAC was likely due to the decrease in inpatient admissions, because an inpatient stay is required to qualify for these services. It could also reflect the significant investments hospitals made in post-discharge planning and care that may have allowed patients to avoid PAC services. (RTI 2019, ES-2)

RTI also found that commercial plan members had 6.1 percent slower growth in total hospital expenditures than a comparison group. However, the growth in total spending didn't slow among commercial plan members. This reflected different utilization patterns for the commercial population—especially increased spending on professional services that offset savings on inpatient care.

The Medicare data showed that the program's savings on hospital services were not due to cost shifting to sectors outside of the global budgets, the report said. Hospitals were "more likely to transfer patients to PAC providers following implementation of the All-Payer Model. However, hospital length of stay prior to a PAC transfer decreased slightly less in Maryland than in the [out-of-state] comparison group, suggesting the Maryland hospitals did not try to transfer patients out of hospital settings sooner as a result of the All-Payer Model" (RTI 2019, ES-8).

Significantly, RTI (2019, ES-1) found that "Maryland hospitals were able to operate within their global budgets without adverse effects on their financial status." But teaching hospitals and public hospitals with a disproportionate share of low- or nonpaying patients had worse financial outcomes than other facilities.

Global Budgeting Pros and Cons

Interviews with hospital executives, payer executives, and state and federal regulators generated a cluster of observations about the first several years of Maryland's global budgeting system. The researchers found that global budgets were viewed as essential to flipping hospital incentives in the right direction, but additional measures were required to soften the impact and pace of change.

Some hospitals shifted certain hospital-based services to outpatient settings not included in the global budget. However, quality incentives prevented hospitals from eliminating services or withholding care to reduce costs. The importance of a robust data infrastructure was cited by many respondents. There was extensive data sharing, including Medicare claims data and patient-level electronic health records obtained through the statewide health information exchange.

Certain areas proved challenging under the MD-APM, including setting global budgets through negotiations with the state, unpredictable shifts in hospital volume, funding of capital construction, and early adoption of novel therapies in academic medical centers (Kilaru, Crider, and Chiang 2022).

Total Cost of Care Model

While hospital costs dropped, nonhospital spending in Maryland, mainly in ambulatory and post-acute care, increased by 4.1 percent in 2016, greatly exceeding the national increase of 1.9 percent that year (Galarraga and Pines 2017). This rapid cost growth led to the conclusion that something more was needed to control spending growth in areas outside of hospitals' global budgets.

In 2019, CMS and Maryland launched the Total Cost of Care (TCOC) Model, which set a per capita limit on Medicare's spending in Maryland. While retaining global budgeting, this program allowed hospitals to use some or all of the savings they created for Medicare to make incentive payments to nonhospital providers that collaborated with the hospital to improve the quality of care. In addition, the hospitals could incentivize primary care physicians to coordinate care better and reduce the hospitalization rate of their patients (CMS 2022).

An analysis of TCOC published in July 2021 found that it was making some progress (Brennan 2022). Although the pandemic of 2020–2023 impacted Maryland hospitals, they didn't underperform hospitals in other states during the crisis. In fact, they fared somewhat better because they weren't dependent on fee-for-service revenue.

Ezekiel Emanuel, MD, David W. Johnson, and several other health policy experts argued in a pair of *Health Affairs* articles that the Maryland global budgeting model could be successfully introduced in other states. This would not only save money, they maintained, but would also "accelerate the adoption of innovative health care services, including virtual care delivery, hospital at home, enhanced primary care services and risk-based contracting" (Emanuel et al. 2022b).

HOW DID WE PERFORM IN THE NEW MODEL?

Once the decision was made to finance ambulatory care through subscription fees, the health policy experts who helped build the framework for the CHEER Act in 2025 took a close look at the MD-APM for ideas on how to structure the acute and post-acute care pieces of our model.

We concluded that the global budgeting mechanism that Maryland had adopted would work well if we made some key changes. First, since most ambulatory care providers—including physicians employed by health systems—would receive subscription fees, the hospitals' budgets could not include outpatient professional services. Second, while the Maryland hospitals did not take risk for post-acute care, we decided that the hospitals in our model should, since post-acute care is inextricably connected to acute care. (However, long-term care is not part of the hospital budget.) If hospitals were financially responsible for the cost of post-acute care, they would not unnecessarily refer patients to PAC providers and would try to ensure that the patients they did refer weren't readmitted.

In the CHEER model, the dividing line between hospital and ambulatory care budgets is unscheduled acute care, most notably in the emergency department. Emergency and urgent care is considered basic care until a patient is admitted to the hospital or transferred to another facility. A person who seeks emergency care for a nonurgent problem is diagnosed, treated, and released, as they would be in an ambulatory care setting. Moreover, the basic care groups must have an incentive to keep people out of the emergency department if they don't need to be there. So emergency care is part of the basic care groups' budgets.

On the other hand, emergency department doctors can't work for multiple groups; the hospital is the environment in which they practice, and they need to communicate with inpatient clinicians. So, like other hospital-based physicians, they work for or are contracted to their hospital, and their salaries are excluded from the basic-care budget.

Pulling the Insurance Trigger

The trigger for a person's catastrophic insurance to start financing their care can be pulled in one of two ways: If the individual is admitted to the hospital, catastrophic insurance would take over; there are no more "observation" stays. Alternatively, if a person receives hospital-level care at home, in ambulatory surgery centers, or in other venues, a dollar amount limit for out-of-pocket costs is chosen as the cutoff point. When the CHEER Act went into effect, this amount was $10,000; in 2035, it's $15,000.

Like the health plans on the old ACA exchanges, every catastrophic plan must provide standard benefits specified by law. These health plans fall into bronze, silver, and gold tiers, which provide 66 percent, 80 percent, and 90 percent, respectively, of the cost of covered benefits. People can buy additional coverage for benefits such as cosmetic surgery or a joint replacement that improves physical function but isn't medically necessary.

The government helps people with lower incomes pay for their share of their medical bills through cost-reduction subsidies, similar to those in the ACA, and those living below the poverty line pay nothing. The subsidies are phased out for middle income brackets, so these people can still receive substantial bills. Many people use HSAs, often bolstered by employers, to put away money for this contingency. Others buy supplemental insurance that resembles the old Medigap policies. There is even flexibility (an unlikely word in relation to government and healthcare in the past) for people undergoing changes in their employment or financial circumstances. The ability to increase or eliminate caps on HSAs is another tool to encourage consumers to take greater control of the financing of their acute and post-acute care.

The health plans compete on price and on the enhanced benefits they offer. Because they have far lower administrative costs under the new global budgeting model, their government-allowed medical loss ratios are higher under the CHEER Act. In most cases, this has resulted in lower profit margins, but insurers' overall businesses are larger because they now include the Medicare beneficiaries who used to be in traditional Medicare.

An Offer Hospitals Can't Refuse

Before the CHEER Act, hospitals and health systems typically tried to negotiate the highest rates they could with each of their private payers—rates which were then transferred to the employer or consumer. Some health systems had very robust margins, especially if they had facilities in suburban areas where a high percentage of people were privately insured. Of course, that wasn't true for all hospitals; those in rural areas and poor urban areas had difficulty making ends meet, and many closed. To make the new model work, we had to figure out how to persuade the more prosperous hospitals and health systems to accept global budgets while ensuring the survival of facilities in underserved areas.

The solution to the first problem was to go through the same evolution that Maryland hospitals did, only much faster. This entailed getting a critical mass of states to adopt the same all-payer rate-setting mechanism that Maryland had used successfully for decades. With health costs shooting up rapidly, the states were feeling excruciating pain in their Medicaid budgets, and they were looking for a way to moderate spending growth. When CMS added incentives—for example, guaranteeing waivers and providing technical support— many states got on board. Later, when health costs dropped substantially in these states, most of the others followed suit.

Leveraging All-Payer Rates

Hospitals had previously insisted that they had to charge private payers an average of 250 percent of Medicare rates to compensate for

Medicare and Medicaid rates that were below the cost of providing care, but health policy experts calculated that about 140 percent of Medicare would be enough (Berenson and Murray 2022). Translated to all-payer rates, that equals roughly 120 percent of Medicare.

So, our team of policy wonks suggested that the states set all-payer compensation for hospitals in the 120 percent range. This would be a stretch for most hospitals to make even a 1 percent margin, and these health systems would be coming out of a fee-for-service system. We knew they'd have to scramble to learn how to manage care and hold down costs.

When the states announced this provision in 2024, health systems saw that the jig was up. If they stuck with fee-for-service, they'd barely break even or perhaps even go broke. Ramping up their volume was the go-to alternative, but that wouldn't help if they were losing money on every unit of service.

Most health systems realized that the only way to come out whole would be to embrace global budgeting. For starters, the law allowed them to negotiate a higher base rate, pegged to the nature of the institution and the type of patients it had. Additionally, if they did a good job of operating under budget, they reasoned, they'd be able to increase their margins. That task would be greatly facilitated by the fact that their physician groups were also taking risk. That risk didn't cover inpatient costs, but to stay within their budgets the groups did their best to keep people healthy, reducing their odds of being hospitalized.

While the analyses of Maryland hospitals' status under MD-APM didn't say how well individual hospitals had fared, the CMS report said that overall the Maryland hospitals had not suffered adverse financial consequences. That was in an environment in which ambulatory care providers outside of hospital groups had no incentive to reduce utilization or improve the quality of care until the TCOC. What if all basic care groups had such an incentive and therefore decreased avoidable hospital admissions? Wouldn't hospitals taking risk for acute and post-acute care fare better financially than those in Maryland had?

Challenges in Underserved Areas

We took the plunge, and our strategy has succeeded, even with rural hospitals and teaching hospitals—both of which had financial challenges before the new model.

Rural hospitals always had difficulty coping with a higher percentage of Medicaid, Medicare, and uninsured patients than suburban facilities had. They also had a hard time attracting and retaining physicians and nurses. More than 135 rural hospitals closed between 2010 and 2022, and 435 rural facilities were vulnerable to closure at that point (Ellison 2022).

The Maryland global budget model didn't hurt rural hospitals, but it didn't give them much of a boost, either. According to one study, the MD-APM led to a decrease in rural outpatient visits but didn't produce a significant decline in hospital admissions. The researchers said that better alignment between hospitals and community physicians was necessary to move the needle on admissions (Minemyer 2019).

Our new model for full-service rural hospitals, as mentioned earlier, provides a global budget that includes not only acute and post-acute care but also all ambulatory care in the region. That aligns the incentives of doctors and hospitals to reduce utilization. Because of decreased admissions and emergency department visits, which helps them stay within their budgets, the rural hospitals have done better financially than they did under the old system.

In the early implementation of our plan, we made some allowances for rural systems as it related to payment for virtual services, which closed gaps in the availability of specialty care and behavioral health care. Only a portion of the payments these hospitals made for telehealth was included in their global budgets. Nevertheless, rural hospitals still suffer from a shortage of resources, including healthcare professionals. Larger government subsidies and inducements to doctors to practice in these communities, including student loan forgiveness, would improve the situation.

Academic medical centers (AMCs) include some giant, well-funded institutions. But many other AMCs were having a hard time before CHEER because of training and research costs, high faculty salaries, and patient populations that often tilted toward Medicaid and the uninsured. Under the new model, AMCs are having better financial results because the basic care groups are reducing avoidable admissions and readmissions. Some of the faculty specialists are now being paid by these groups for their clinical services.

But the AMCs still need more graduate medical education funding to cover their training costs. Also, trainees that choose to embark on mission-driven, lower-paying primary care careers need extensive loan forgiveness and government subsidies. And in this new future, the amount that resident physicians are paid during training is inversely proportional to what they can expect to earn when they graduate. So, for example, family physicians are paid more than orthopedic surgeons during residencies. Leveling the field that way will allow more primary care physicians to pay off student loans and begin a practice with less debt.

Community Wellness Centers

If a hospital doesn't have a good reputation, and the local basic care groups refer most patients to other institutions, that facility will be in trouble. You might think it should do well within a budget because of its low admission rate, but hospital budgets are adjusted every year, partly for volume. So, a hospital with very low patient volume won't have a large enough budget to cover its operational costs.

Quality issues aren't the only reason some facilities go under. Hospitals are always going out of business because of staffing difficulties or population shifts, or because the continuing movement of acute care out of facilities into the home and other care settings has reduced the need for hospital beds. In some cases, these hospitals have repurposed themselves as a combination of a freestanding emergency department and a community wellness center.

In the lobby of one such former hospital, people receive screenings and do group visits with others who have the same chronic condition. Health fairs are held there. Support groups, such as for breast cancer patients, meet there. In the winter, a farmers' market is held in the hospital atrium. Some of these hospitals have rebranded as "community centers of well-being."

Meanwhile, we now have universal access to healthcare, and everyone receives healthcare of equal quality, regardless of income, ethnicity, or race. Our national health statistics are trending upward: We're living longer and infant mortality has dropped sharply. The ratio of US health spending to GDP has finally fallen to around 17 percent, and we're shooting for 15 percent. The criticism of America having "Star Wars technology for individual patients in a Fred Flintstone healthcare delivery system" is no longer valid. And that iron triangle of cost, access, and quality is starting to take a more logical shape for the first time.

One more thing: While we were cleaning up the medical, insurance, and provider economics, the CHEER Act finally addressed the fact that we were the only wealthy country with unbridled malpractice liability. As part of the agreement between hospitals, insurers, and the federal government, common sense tort reform was passed. Among the provisions: physicians being held harmless if they followed agreed-upon evidence-based guidelines, caps on noneconomic damages, periodic rather than lump-sum payments, a sliding scale for attorneys' fees, and increased scrutiny of and disciplinary actions against reckless or incompetent physicians.

BACK TO THE PRESENT

That was fun, but enough of the back-to-the-future daydream. We're still in 2023, and we have much to do before and after the changes I propose. The O'Jays and Cyndi Lauper were right: much of healthcare financing exists "For the Love of Money," and "Money Changes Everything." When I was a hospital leader, I even pleaded to payers and CMS by singing karaoke to the Beatles' "You Never Give Me Your Money."

While the major change in healthcare financing proposed in this chapter would transform the system if it were adopted, that alone wouldn't move us from a nation of sick care to one in which health assurance is the norm. If we don't also deal with some of the other problems in our system, we could end up with "Mo Money Mo Problems," making the Notorious B.I.G. look like a healthcare prophet.

The first thing we need to do is to study other parts of healthcare the way we've studied Maryland's all-payer system so we know what works and what doesn't. We need more research on ways to measure the quality and outcomes of care, which we will need to rate and compare the basic care providers and hospitals in my proposed model. We also need to discuss how health behavior and social determinants of health can be integrated into these rankings. Those are the topics of the next chapter.

REFERENCES

Aiken, B. 2021. "High Deductible Health Insurance Is Bankrupting Americans." KevinMD (blog). Published December 24. www .kevinmd.com/blog/2021/12/high-deductible-health-insurance -is-bankrupting-americans.html.

American Hospital Association. 2020. "CMS Releases Quality Payment Program Results for 2019." Published October 28. www.aha.org/news/headline/2020-10-28-cms-releases-quality -payment-program-results-2019.

Bai, G., J. (X.) Jiang, and M. Makary. 2021. "Is the Hospital Price Transparency Rule Actually Lowering Costs?" Medpage Today. Published August 12. www.medpagetoday.com/opinion/second -opinions/94009.

Berenson, R. A., and R. B. Murray. 2022. "How Price Regulation is Needed to Advance Market Competition." *Health Affairs* 41 (1): 26–34. https://doi.org/10.1377/hlthaff.2021.01235.

Blumenthal, D., S. R. Collins, and E. Fowler. 2020. "The Affordable Care Act at 10 Years—Its Coverage and Access Provisions." The Commonwealth Fund. Published February 26. Originally published in the *New England Journal of Medicine* 2020 (382): 963–69. www.commonwealthfund.org/publications/journal -article/2020/feb/aca-at-10-years-effect-health-care-coverage -access.

Brennan, T. A. 2022. "Maryland Hospital All-Payer Model: Can It Be Emulated?" Health Affairs Forefront. Published May 31. www.healthaffairs.org/do/10.1377/forefront.20220526.939479.

Carroll, A. 2012. "The 'Iron Triangle' of Health Care: Access, Cost, and Quality." *JAMA Forum Archive*. Published online October 3. https://jamanetwork.com/channels/health-forum/fullarticle /2760240.

Cass, A., and M. Plescia. 2022. "Atlanta System 1st in US to Face CMS Fines for Price Transparency Violations." *Becker's Hospital Review*, June 9. www.beckershospitalreview.com /finance/atlanta-system-1st-in-us-to-face-cms-fines-for-price -transparency-violations.html.

CMS (Centers for Medicare & Medicaid Services). 2022. Innovation Center. "Maryland Total Cost of Care Model." Updated June 13. https://innovation.cms.gov/innovation-models/md-tccm.

———. 2021. "Shared Savings Program Fast Facts—as of Jan. 1, 2021." www.cms.gov/files/document/2021-shared-savings -program-fast-facts.pdf.

———. 2020. "CMS Office of the Actuary Releases 2019 National Health Expenditures" (press release). Published December 16. www.cms.gov/newsroom/press-releases/cms-office-actuary- releases-2019-national-health-expenditures.

EBRI (Employee Benefit Research Institute), and Greenwald Research. 2021. Consumer Engagement in Health Care Survey Report. Published September. www.ebri.org/docs/default -source/cehcs/2021-cehcs-report.pdf.

Ellison, A. 2022. "Staffing Crisis, Payment Cuts Put 453 Hospitals at Risk of Closure." *Becker's Hospital Review,* February 18. www .beckershospitalreview.com/finance/staffing-crisis-payment -cuts-put-453-hospitals-at-risk-of-closure.html.

Emanuel, E. J., D. W. Johnson, M. Guido, and M. Goozner. 2022a. "Meaningful Value-Based Payment Reform, Part 1: Maryland Leads the Way." Health Affairs Forefront. Published February 9. https://doi.org/10.1377/forefront.20220205.211264.

―――. 2022b. "Meaningful Value-Based Payment Reform, Part 2: Expanding the Maryland Model to Other States." Health Affairs Forefront. Published February 10. https://doi.org/10 .1377/forefront.20220207.85767.

Galarraga, J., and J. M. Pines. 2017. "The Challenging Transformation of Health Care Under Maryland's Global Budgets." Health Affairs Forefront. Published December 19. www.healthaffairs .org/do/10.1377/forefront.20171214.96251.

Gamble, M. 2022. "Hospitals Face Fiercer Competition for the Worst-Paying Specialty." *Becker's Hospital Review*, February 11. www.beckershospitalreview.com/hospital-physician -relationships/hospitals-face-fiercer-competition-for-the-worst -paying-specialty.html.

Guterman, S. 2015. "With SGR Repeal, Now We Can Proceed with Medicare Payment Reform." Controlling Health Care Costs (blog). The Commonwealth Fund. Published April 15. www .commonwealthfund.org/blog/2015/sgr-repeal-now-we-can -proceed-medicare-payment-reform.

Hartman, M., A. B. Martin, J. Benson, and A. Catlin. 2013. "National Health Spending in 2011: Overall Growth Remains Low, But

Some Payers and Services Show Signs of Acceleration." *Health Affairs* 32 (1): 87–99. https://doi.org/10.1377/hlthaff.2012.1206.

Jain, A., J. Levy, D. Polsky, and K. E. Anderson. 2022. "Medicare Advantage and the Maryland All-Payer Model." Health Affairs Forefront. Published March 18. https://doi.org/10.1377/forefront.20220316.50044.

James, J. 2012. "Health Policy Brief: Pay for Performance." *Health Affairs*, October 11. www.healthaffairs.org/do/10.1377/hpb20121011.90233/.

Kearney, A., L. Hamel, M. Stokes, and M. Brodie. 2021. "America's Challenges with Health Care Costs." Kaiser Family Foundation. Published December 14. www.kff.org/health-costs/issue-brief/americans-challenges-with-health-care-costs/.

Keckley, P. 2016. "Is Phycor 2.0 Ahead?" The Keckley Report. Published July 11. www.paulkeckley.com/the-keckley-report/2016/7/11/is-phycor-20-ahead.

Khullar D., A. M. Bond, E. M. O'Donnell, Y. Qian, D. N. Gans, and L. P. Casalino. 2021. "Time and Financial Costs for Physician Practices to Participate in the Medicare Merit-based Incentive Payment System: A Qualitative Study." *JAMA Health Forum* 2 (5): e210527. https://doi.org/10.1001/jamahealthforum.2021.0527.

Kilaru, A. S., C. R. Crider, and J. Chiang. 2022. "Health Care Leaders' Perspectives on the Maryland All-Payer Model." *JAMA Health Forum* 3 (2): e214920. https://doi.org/10.1001/jamahealthforum.2021.4920.

Lagasse, J. 2022. "Survey Finds Just 14% of Hospitals Are Compliant with Price Transparency." *Healthcare Finance*, February 10. www.healthcarefinancenews.com/news/survey-finds-just-14-hospitals-are-compliant-price-transparency.

Maciejewski, M. L., and A. Hung. 2020. "High-Deductible Health Plans and Health Savings Accounts: A Match Made in Heaven but Not for This Irrational World." Invited Commentary. *JAMA Network Open* 3 (7): e2011000. https://doi.org/10.1001/jamanetworkopen.2020.11000.

Minemyer, P. 2019. "Study Shows Maryland's Global Budget Had Limited Impact on Rural Hospitals." *Fierce Healthcare,* May 13. www.fiercehealthcare.com/hospitals-health-systems/study-shows-maryland-s-global-budget-had-limited-impact-rural-hospitals.

Murray, R. 2009. "Setting Hospital Rates to Control Costs and Boost Quality: The Maryland Experience." *Health Affairs* 28 (5):1395–1405. www.healthaffairs.org/doi/10.1377/hlthaff.28.5.1395.

OECD (Organisation for Economic Co-operation and Development). 2022. Health spending (indicator). https://doi.org/10.1787/8643de7e-en.

Poisal, J. A., A. M. Sisko, G. A. Cuckler, S. D. Smith, S. P. Keehan, J. A. Fiore, A. J. Madison, and K. E. Rennie. 2022. "National Health Expenditure Projections, 2021-30: Growth to Moderate As COVID-19 Impacts Wane." *Health Affairs* 41 (4): 474–86. https://doi.org/10.1377/hlthaff.2022.00113.

RTI International. 2019. "Evaluation of the Maryland All-Payer Model, Volume 1: Final Report." Published November. https://downloads.cms.gov/files/md-allpayer-finalevalrpt.pdf.

Tavernise, S., and R. Gebeloff. 2016. "Immigrants, the Poor and Minorities Gain Sharply Under Affordable Care Act." *New York Times*, April 17. www.nytimes.com/2016/04/18/health/immigrants-the-poor-and-minorities-gain-sharply-under-health-act.html.

Terry, K. 2020. *Physician-Led Healthcare Reform: A New Approach to Medicare for All.* Washington, DC: American Association for Physician Leadership.

———. 2007. *Rx for Health Care Reform.* Nashville, TN: Vanderbilt University Press.

Yelorda, K., L. Rose, and M. K. Bundorf. 2022. "Association Between High-Deductible Health Plans and Hernia Acuity." *JAMA Surgery* 157 (4): 321–26. Published online February 13. https://doi.org/10.1001/jamasurg.2021.7567.

CHAPTER 7

"(Simply) the Best" by Tina Turner

You're simply the best / Better than all the rest.

LEGIONS OF MARKETERS for cola makers, cell service companies, and more recently health systems have tried to associate Tina Turner's 1990s anthem with their brand and claim that they're "the best!" Unfortunately, some hospitals or healthcare systems claim to be the best at something with little or no basis for that assertion.

Often, the proclamation is based on a grading system that has little to do with what quality means to patients or physicians. Sometimes a reputation is overemphasized or underemphasized, and most of the claims are based on debatable measures such as a *U.S. News & World Report* ranking or patient experience surveys. But that does not stop health systems from spending tens of thousands of dollars letting everyone in the community know that they are "simply the best!"

People talk about healthcare quality all the time, but we still don't have a good definition of it. Even if we could pin down exactly what we wanted to measure, it would be difficult to measure it in a way that is fair to providers and represents what patients are or should be interested in. So, we have to acknowledge that quality measurement will never be more than an approximation of our goal. Yet it's still vitally important to figure out what we should measure and how to use the results to drive quality improvement.

In the healthcare financing model proposed in chapter 6, quality scores would be an important factor in choosing a basic care group. But quality metrics have a long way to go before they can serve that purpose. The current quality information system is broken, writes David Lansky (2022), former CEO and current senior advisor of PBGH (Purchaser Business Group on Health). "It's time to replace our system for measuring health care quality and putting quality information to use," he writes. "The current retrospective, transactional system for measuring and rewarding improvement is ineffective, expensive, burdensome, no longer credible, and does not measure health or the outcomes of health care."

After three decades of measuring the performance of health plans and providers, Lansky says, quality measurement is still based mostly on claims data and hasn't been shown to improve health. The financial incentives for providers to improve quality are relatively small and hard to understand, and they don't drive quality improvement or care redesign.

Moreover, he notes, payers continue to rely mainly on process rather than outcomes measures. "This approach cannot capture changes in patient health status resulting from care, nor the opportunity to recognize the impact of social factors on care delivery and effectiveness," he says. The fundamental problem, he argues, is that the current system does not assess the outcomes *people* are interested in, such as improvements in function, reduced symptom burden, quality of life, and longevity.

Except for longevity, those outcomes can be measured by surveying patients about functional status, pain, mental health, and quality of life. Based on these instruments, a substantial number of patient-reported outcome measures (PROMs) have been developed. Some PROMs can provide vital insights into how people feel and function during or after treatment or after surgery, and they can be used to collect longitudinal data. But as we'll see, PROMs are little used in performance measurement today for several reasons, not least of which is clinician resistance.

Until long-term outcomes measures are more widely used, we'll have to depend on conventional methods of quality measurement. These include patient experience surveys, process measures, intermediate outcomes measures such as HbA1c level and blood pressure, and broad metrics such as a hospital's or surgeon's observed-to-expected mortality, complication, and readmission rates.

When any of these data points are published, it's almost comical to see how the providers that top the list trumpet the accuracy of the scores while those on the bottom cry foul, asserting that their patients are sicker, poorer, or did not follow instructions. In my 40 years of following quality reports, especially in my discipline of maternal health, I have never seen a provider who ranked at the bottom say, "Yes, this is right and we have to do better." They're either singing Queen's "We Are the Champions" or Percy Sledge's "It's All Wrong but It's Alright."

Many of these rankings and reports lean heavily on process measures, which are at best inadequate for measuring overall quality and embody only a fraction of what a patient needs to make an informed decision about what doctor or group to choose to deliver their baby or provide care for their heart disease. Process measures are designed to show whether individual practitioners or physician groups follow evidence-based practice guidelines. Most of these measures focus on preventive or chronic disease care. Although by definition they concern processes of care, some of them also affect outcomes, says Peter Basch, MD, medical director of ambulatory electronic health records (EHRs) and health information technology policy at MedStar Health.

However, a handful of process measures don't show how good a doctor is, and they invite "teaching to the test": Physicians who are being evaluated on certain process measures are likely to pay attention to those activities and neglect other, equally important services, Basch notes. Moreover, when performance is inferred from claims data, numerous errors in the calculation may arise from misattribution of patients, missing diagnoses, or missing data for services that were performed but not specifically billed.

Process measures generally focus on specific steps in the prevention and management of disease, but should also measure how well hospitals and clinics manage the entire care process, from diagnosis and treatment through follow-up. In addition, a health system that continuously cares for its population and seeks to assure its patients' health must try to change health behavior in ways that improve outcomes. I'll discuss this later in the chapter.

Outcomes measures must be risk adjusted, at a minimum, for the age and health status of each individual. The measurement of health status, including the number and the severity of a person's chronic conditions, depends on the documentation of all a patient's diagnoses and the practitioner's assessment of their condition. Physicians don't always document how sick their patients are, Basch observes.

Patient experience surveys will also continue to be important quality indicators. These surveys show how easily people can access the system, how they're treated at every stage of their care, whether they feel cared about, and how well their care team educates them about their condition and how to manage it on their own. These are critical components of care that contribute directly to outcomes and long-term health.

A study commissioned by Change Healthcare (2020) demonstrated how important these measures are to consumers: In the related Harris poll, 56 percent of respondents knew people who had avoided seeking care because their healthcare experience had been so poor! And if access to care is restricted, the population health suffers.

Finally, it's important to measure the quality of care provided to all patients, regardless of their insurance coverage or lack thereof. This will supply a fuller picture of population health and help increase health equity over time. A universal quality measurement will be easier when everyone is covered in the same way and when providers have an incentive to keep all their patients as healthy as possible. When everyone's care is financed uniformly, the quality of care provided to the entire population can be fairly evaluated.

PATIENT-REPORTED OUTCOMES

"Performance measurement has traditionally relied on routinely collected clinical information such as rates of hospital readmission, infections, procedural complications, survival, or laboratory values," a group of quality experts assembled by the American Medical Association (AMA) said in a 2015 report. "But the ultimate impact on outcomes experienced by patients, such as symptoms, functional status, and health-related quality of life, have rarely been assessed" (Basch et al. 2015, 493).

While patient-reported outcomes are often used in clinical practice and research, the experts added, there have been few cases of PROMs being used in performance evaluation. Similarly, the National Quality Forum (NQF 2021), in a paper describing the environment for outcomes-based performance measures, said that only a few large payers had implemented PROMs in their quality programs.

When we spoke, Lansky, the senior adviser at PBGH, pointed out that this description applies mainly to the United States. "In the UK, they've been using these patient-reported measures for several major procedures across the whole country for ten years. Germany and the Scandinavian countries have registries for orthopedic and back procedures. In Stockholm, they don't pay surgeons until they look at their one-year outcomes for spine surgery. In Australia, there's a national registry. In Germany, there's a registry of general surgery outcomes. There are maternity registries in Kenya. It's all over the world."

He described a registry as a platform designed for the collection, analysis, and reporting of patient-reported outcomes data, as well as relevant clinical data and some administrative data. This infrastructure is almost entirely missing in the United States, but it could be built if we wanted to use PROMs in performance evaluation and reporting, he says.

Few Endorsed Measures

As of 2021, NQF had endorsed only 29 PRO-PMs (Patient-Reported Outcome-Based Performance Measures). These measures span outcomes such as health-related quality of life, functional status, symptoms and symptom burden, health behaviors, and experience with care for several conditions and care settings. Among the condition-specific PRO-PMs approved by NQF are measures related to pain and depression; functional status changes of patients with impairments of the knee, hip, foot and ankle, lower back, shoulder, neck, elbow, and wrist and hand; and functional status changes following lumbar spine fusion surgery, total knee replacements, and total hip replacement (NQF 2022).

In a news release about the report, NQF said "PROMs can be used to collect data over time, thereby measuring changes that are occurring for patients and populations. These longitudinal uses of PROMs can form the basis for performance measures (PRO-PMs), where the information is used to hold providers and payers accountable for the outcomes they achieve for their populations" (NQF 2021). However, the paucity of these measures underlines the difficulty of getting them adopted, at least in the United States. Among the challenges noted by NQF are clinician resistance, the burden of workflows related to data collection, and unclear funding sources to support the use of PROMs.

The burden on patients of repeatedly filling out surveys to measure their symptoms and functional abilities is another barrier to greater use of PROMs and PRO-PMs. Survey "length, layout, and cognitive load have been noted as factors that can affect the strain on patients and caregivers," the NQF report said. "While this insight has led to effective changes, such as shortened versions of existing questionnaires, it remains an obstacle to capturing what is most important to the patient as it relates to their health outcomes" (NQF 2022, 24).

Role of Medical Societies

Why do clinicians object to PROMs? According to Lansky, it's mainly because of medical societies. "Organized medicine has for a long time argued that providers or physicians should only be accountable for activities within their control," he notes. This view holds that a surgeon, for example, should be responsible only for operative mortality, complications such as wound infections, and adherence to surgical protocols. What happens to the patient three or six months later is not viewed as the doctor's responsibility, because it can be affected by factors not under the physician's control.

The other not-so-secret aspect of medical specialty societies is that their boards tend to be dominated by senior physicians, mainly from academic medical centers. The experience of those doctors has been predominately paternalistic and hierarchical; in many cases, their main goal is to protect the status quo and their specialty, rather than to look for innovative ways to measure quality and create transparent comparators for patients.

Lansky concedes that the medical societies may have a point in our current healthcare system, in which providers are not being paid for health assurance.

> It depends on how you view your job. If the reason you're there is to collaborate with other parties to help the person achieve improved health, then you need to structure the system to support that goal. If you're there to execute a technically proficient surgery and ignore everything else in the entire chain of diagnosis, treatment, recovery, you take a different view. You can be a plumber—go into the OR and do the operation and you're done. Whether the person goes to rehab or changes their diet or stops smoking—that's not your job. But if everyone takes that view, we end up with a lousy health system and an unhealthy patient.

Basch, of MedStar Health, believes many doctors oppose using PROMs in performance evaluation for other reasons. For one thing, he says, physicians have had a bad experience with quality measurement as a whole. Also, if a doctor treats a patient and that person gets better from a clinical viewpoint, the doctor may not understand why the patient should be asked how they feel. Finally, he notes, not all PROMs are equally valid.

"Some of the PROMs that are most mature are the ones that are most narrowly defined: for example, recovery after hip or knee surgery," he says. "When I look at some of the others, I don't think they've gone through the same rigorous analysis. Developing a good measure takes time, and if people don't think the concept is important, and measures are sitting out there for a while, they don't pay as close attention to them as they could."

Even NQF experts have questioned the validity of some PROMs, says Lansky. However, he attributes that mainly to the lack of an infrastructure for collecting and reporting PROMs data. "If you don't have a reasonably inexpensive way of collecting information from people and of doing it pretty completely, your data set looks incomplete and so it's technically not sound. But it's a circular argument. If you could inexpensively and reliably collect data from people three months after their hip replacement, you wouldn't have any problem demonstrating the technical soundness of the measure."

Adjusting for Bias and Health Behavior

Even if a PROM is shown to be valid, there are other challenges to using it for performance measurement. For example, the response rates—the percentage of patients who complete outcomes surveys—must be adjusted to avoid response bias. "Patients with worse outcomes are less likely to return a questionnaire, so those providers who are most vigilant about obtaining follow-up questionnaires may recover a higher proportion of responses from sicker individuals with worse outcomes, making their results look worse if analyses are unadjusted" (Basch et al. 2015).

Health behavior and social determinants of health (SDOHs) should also be considered in measuring long-term outcomes. However, that's easier said than done. Basch doesn't think it's possible, but Lansky suggests that we look at this problem the same way we view the challenge of adjusting surgical outcomes for prior health conditions.

"Someone who came in with low risk scores is not expected to achieve the same results as someone who came in with higher scores," Lansky says. "Similarly, you can adjust for socioeconomic status or prior health conditions. You can either stratify a population based on prior social determinants or you can risk adjust for those social factors. It's much harder to achieve good outcomes for people who have a lot of other things going on in their lives." The same is true for health behavior, he adds.

Jonathan Gleason, MD, executive vice president and chief clinical officer at Prisma Health in Greenville, South Carolina, and former executive vice president and chief clinical officer at Jefferson Health, agrees that it's possible to incorporate behavioral health and SDOH into performance measurement. However, he told me, "health systems would have to do all of this data collection, and they're not paid for that."

One alternative, he says, would be to bring in existing data sets on patient behavior and social and environmental factors from outside sources. For example, a company called Jvion marries health system data with "psychographic metadata" and analyzes that data to predict health outcomes such as the risk of falls. Jvion's SDOH data includes publicly available data that identifies vulnerable communities and the SDOH factors driving high health costs and avoidable utilization. While that data isn't being gathered for the purpose of risk-adjusting performance measurement, Gleason thinks it might be applied in this way.

Another start-up, KAID Health, applies natural language processing to EHRs to automatically identify and manage cohorts of patients in need of intervention. The Villages Health has used KAID's population health and risk-adjustment platform to calibrate each physician's reimbursement to the quality of care they deliver.

PROCESS AND SURGICAL MEASURES

As I explained earlier, process measures alone don't show the quality of a doctor or a hospital. Although these metrics, plus intermediate outcomes, have been the basis of consumer report cards across the country, those scorecards haven't had much impact on consumers' choices of providers. To some extent, this reflects the vagaries of insurance coverage and people's tendency to follow their primary care doctor's recommendations. But people are also less interested in and understand less about these quality scores than they do about the outcomes that matter to them, such as recovery time and quality of life after a treatment or a procedure.

As more direct-to-employer models (Transcarent, Amazon Care) blossom, real outcomes become the key. For employers, how quickly employees get back to work and can function at their highest level of productivity is often the most important driver. No employer wants a still-recuperating worker who is present but not producing.

Sports team managers, coaches, and owners have a similar view of an athlete's injury recovery. Neither management nor the athlete cares about an orthopedic provider's patient experience scores or where the institution ranks in the most recent national ranking. Their only interests are the experience of other athletes with similar conditions who have been treated by that orthopedist and how quickly the athlete will get back on the field functioning at close to 100 percent.

Nevertheless, Basch says, it may be valid to use certain process measures that have a proven correlation with outcomes. For example, MedStar Health uses four process measures to gauge the quality of primary care: breast cancer screening, colorectal cancer screening, avoidance of poor control in diabetes, and control of hypertension.

All these activities have a downstream effect on outcomes: colorectal cancer screening, for example, has been shown to reduce the incidence of colorectal cancer.

Lansky, in contrast, says that performing certain care processes well doesn't necessarily lead to better outcomes. For example, he says, the correlation between mammograms and breast cancer outcomes is not that strong. "Detecting cancer is not just about mammograms: it also includes self-care and self-exams and getting in and making appointments. The mammogram can also get done and then be ignored. Whether the mammogram is interpreted and used in the care chain is a more important question than whether the picture gets snapped."

What Lansky is getting at is the need for a more comprehensive method of measuring and reporting on care processes than is typical in today's quality programs. To use the mammogram example, consider the people I saw in my ob-gyn office who were eligible for mammograms. For how many of those patients did I document that I said they should get a mammogram? How many got the mammogram? What were my processes to make sure they got the mammogram, and how did I make sure they got the appropriate results and follow-up? That's true quality, because it will save lives. Similarly, for somebody who has heart disease, did the cardiologist put them on the appropriate medication? Did the person get it and take it, and what were the office's processes to check on that? Did they follow the doctor's diet and exercise recommendations? If we are going to talk about "real quality," it cannot begin when people walk into a doctor's office and end when they go home.

Combination of Measures Required

To measure quality with some degree of accuracy, Gleason says, we have to use a combination of PROMs and other patient-centered outcomes and process measures. "We need to be measuring safety, for example, and not relying on the patient to report on whether they felt safe or not. The goal should be a mixture of patient-reported measures and patient-centered measures and outcomes that could never be patient reported," whether we're talking about the outcomes of surgery or long-term chronic care.

The measures for chronic care will vary from one condition to another, but much of it can't be patient reported, Gleason notes. For the long-term outcomes of diabetes care, "We care about retinopathy and limb sparing and amputation rates, long-term mortality, and related cardiovascular disease. With someone who has cardiovascular disease, you have outcomes like heart attacks, ejection fraction, hospitalization, and quality of life." According to Gleason and the other experts I spoke with, remote patient monitoring can play a role in outcomes measurement. "We did a lot of that in Philadelphia, and we're doing it here at Prisma. I believe it's important both for health maintenance and for outcomes measures."

Gleason also stresses the importance of getting patients and communities involved in selecting and creating outcomes measures. "At Jefferson, for example, we built a robust patient-family advisory group that was deeply embedded in everything we were doing in quality and safety and quality improvement," he recalls. "The highest-level meetings on these issues were attended by community advocates. The whole idea was that we weren't doing things to or for the community, but only with them. We have to engage the community in determining what matters most to us and to our patients."

This engagement should have happened a few decades ago when large-scale quality measurement first emerged, he says. Instead of asking patients what was most important to them, he recalls, health plans picked quality measures—mostly process-related—that were easy to quantify using available claims data. Healthcare quality, like much of healthcare delivery, was handed over to unimaginative administrators who were checking boxes based on the data that was easily obtainable instead of building creative quality measures that would require patient input and additional effort and dollars.

"We need to do a restart," Gleason says. "Instead of what *can* we measure, we should look at what we *should* be measuring."

Like Pearl Jam, Gleason does not believe it's truly "Hard to Imagine" a more creative and meaningful set of quality measures in this country.

MEASURING INDIVIDUAL PROVIDERS

With an exception for surgeons, public reporting on the clinical quality of individual practitioners does not make much sense. Aside from the inadequacy of claims data, the pay for performance programs of health plans is applied only to each plan's members. Consequently, individual doctors are scored based on a subset of those members who have a particular condition, such as diabetes or asthma. In many cases, the sample sizes are too small to achieve statistical validity. In addition, the multiplicity of performance measures makes it difficult for clinicians to keep them straight; and, as noted earlier, focusing on particular metrics may result in other important dimensions of care being neglected (Terry 2007). Also, because patients are cared for by multiple providers, the doctor whose quality is being measured may not be the one responsible for delivering the services on which the scores are based (*NEJM Catalyst* 2018).

This hasn't stopped the Centers for Medicare & Medicaid Services (CMS) from publishing the quality scores of individual providers under its Quality Payment Program. But—fortunately or unfortunately, depending on how you look at it—this information is nearly impossible to find on the Medicare.gov website.

It's somewhat easier to locate ratings of physician groups and accountable care organizations, which are available from CMS and in several states, including Minnesota (www.mnhealthscores.org), Wisconsin (www.wchq.org), and California (www.opa.ca.gov). These scorecards offer data that is statistically significant and is relevant to people with certain chronic conditions. For example, the California Office of Managed Care lists clinical quality scores and patient experience ratings on 197 medical groups and independent physician associations, broken down by county.

In any case, whether the scorecards are for individual physicians or groups, consumers don't pay much attention to them. People are much more interested in online reviews of doctors and hospitals than they are in clinical ratings (Terry 2021). Few patients would understand those ratings even if they saw them. According to another report, of the consumers who saw clinical quality information on doctors or hospitals, only 4 percent used it in choosing a hospital and 6 percent used it in selecting a doctor (Findlay 2016).

In my clinical practice, I have been amazed at how many intelligent patients who objectively comparison shop for every other product in their life, and who are skeptical about nonverifiable claims related to automobiles, TVs, or even entertainment options, are often content to believe the hospital billboard proclaiming "we are the best."

Pay for Performance Endures

Pay for performance (P4P) programs, which provide the data for most public reporting, were an early effort to align the incentives of health plans and providers, and later, of Medicare and providers. The persistence of these programs, often rebranded as value-based payment, is a testament to the enduring prevalence of fee-for-service.

P4P has had a mixed record in quality improvement. According to a systematic review of 69 studies, "P4P programs may be associated with improved processes of care in ambulatory settings, but consistently positive associations with improved health outcomes have not been demonstrated in any setting" (Mendelson et al. 2017). The researchers pointed out that selection bias was a major concern in some of these studies because physicians had a strong incentive to attract healthier patients.

Another analysis of P4P programs noted that they "harm and reduce access for socioeconomically disadvantaged populations because, despite risk adjustments, providers who treat a larger share of low-income patients will not perform as well on P4P measures and therefore are incentivized to avoid treating them" (*NEJM Catalyst* 2018).

P4P financial incentives can also have unanticipated consequences. For example, a common intermediate outcome measure in P4P programs is the level of LDL cholesterol. Physicians normally try to get patients with high cholesterol to change their diet and exercise before putting them on a statin drug. But to get a good score on this measure, physicians may be incentivized to prescribe Lipitor or Crestor right away. "If I'm being incentivized to get everybody to goal right now, I'm a pill machine. I dispense to everybody," one New Jersey doctor told my collaborator Ken Terry (Terry 2007, 55).

In Basch's experience, some P4P measures show little understanding of clinical care.

> There's a process measure called adult BMI [body mass index] and follow-up. At least once a year, each patient should get a height/weight measurement and their BMI should be calculated. If the BMI is less than 18.5 or over 25, follow-up has to occur. The primary purpose is to address the obesity epidemic, which makes sense. But the action required for the purpose of the measure is the same for a person who has a BMI of 25.1 as for a patient who has a BMI of 50.
>
> Of the 25 to 30 patients a clinician sees each day, 60 percent of them might have a BMI over 25. Of those, half have a BMI of 25 to 26. Three have a BMI over 30. So let's say you ask the doctor, "Who would you refer to a nutritionist or to bariatrics?" The doctor might answer, "We do bariatrics for someone with a BMI over 40 or over 35, if he or she is comorbid." That's an appropriate use of resources. But that doctor would score low on the measure because he didn't send people to bariatrics for a BMI of 25.01.

Surgical Report Cards: A Work in Progress

Despite the drawbacks of rating individual physicians, anyone facing surgery is interested in the quality of surgeons. A great deal of discussion and analysis has been devoted to this topic. Yet in the United States, only cardiac surgeons have been rated using rigorous criteria, and only in New York, New Jersey, Pennsylvania, and California. The impact of these scores on patient care is unclear: There is evidence that some low-rated surgeons have stopped performing these procedures. But no clear connection exists between the publication of physician scorecards and patient outcomes. Moreover, most cardiologists in the affected states neither consider these ratings nor share them with their patients when they refer them to a surgeon (Xi 2015).

In 1989, New York State began collecting data on the risk-adjusted outcomes of coronary artery bypass graft (CABG) surgery, comparing the results for hospitals and individual surgeons. After privately giving the hospitals the data and allowing them a grace period to improve, the New York State Department of Health began releasing the data publicly. The performance records of individual heart surgeons weren't made public initially, but after a freedom-of-information lawsuit by *Newsday*, the state published those as well (Xi 2015).

The initial results of this process were positive: Death rates from heart surgery dropped 14 percent in New York hospitals for the first half of 1990 compared with the prior year (Altman 1990). Another study found that from 1989 to 1992, the risk-adjusted mortality rates for three groups of surgeons who had low, medium, and high rates at baseline dropped 10 percent, 33 percent, and 45 percent, respectively. The 30 hospitals in the study had similar results (Hannan et al. 1994).

According to the researchers, the most likely explanation for the drop was that "the information supplied to hospitals prompted them to make process and personnel changes that led to a reduction in the number of preventable deaths." In addition, it was later reported, New York hospitals restricted privileges for low-volume surgeons, who collectively had much higher mortality rates than the average (Xi 2015).

According to the New York State Department of Health (2019), the state's average risk-adjusted mortality rate for CABGs was 1.67 percent in 2016—a sharp drop from 1990, when it was 3.03 percent (Altman 1990). But the report cards on hospitals and surgeons may not have been the main reason for that decline. Mortality related to CABG procedures had dropped across the country in the previous decade because of significant advances in surgical techniques and postoperative care (Movahed et al. 2012).

The study of the early years of the New York program showed there was no change in the volume of cardiac surgery. This finding undercut critics' predictions that surgeons would avoid high-risk patients to boost their scores. In addition, it doesn't appear that CABG cases were sent out of state to boost scores (Xi 2015). Clearly it is possible to risk adjust clinical data on cardiac surgery. It's also feasible to gather data on the number of cases that individual surgeons have performed, which has been associated with outcomes.

Beyond providing objective data to patients, the healthcare industry should also seek to guarantee the competence of surgeons. The aviation industry requires pilots to regularly prove their competence on flight simulators. But we have no similar process to show continuing surgical competence, the need for which is becoming ever more pronounced with the aging of our physician population. As a private pilot, I must get my technical competence objectively assessed every two years; but no surgeon in the United States—regardless of age—undergoes standardized or mandated simulated technical competence assessments.

Innovative procedures such as robotic surgery can be equally problematic. For many conventional procedures, researchers have assembled data showing that a surgeon should perform a minimum number of cases per year to remain competent. But that is not necessarily a criterion in the robotics field. Limiting the number of surgeons who can perform these procedures is not in the best interests of the manufacturers, so these companies don't try to restrict their robots' use to experienced surgeons. Moreover, community hospitals may try to compete with academic medical centers by purchasing fancy new machines, but they don't necessarily risk upsetting their surgeons by taking steps to assure their competence with robots.

When a patient sees a billboard saying "come to our hospital for robotic surgery," their questions should not be about the robot, but about the human standing beside it. How many robotic procedures has the surgeon done? Have they gone through extensive training or just a short course? What is the advantage of robotic surgery in this surgeon's hands compared to laparoscopic or traditional surgery?

Appropriateness of Surgery

All that said, physicians recognize that no two patients are alike and that each patient comes to us with a different risk profile. But Gleason sounds a note of caution regarding risk adjustment. Particularly if surgeons' compensation is put at risk for their mortality rates, he says, "what you're incentivizing is for surgeons to do procedures on people who are less sick and who may not need those procedures. In very high-risk surgical specialties, mortality has gone down, but the people who are getting heart surgery and so forth are less sick than they've ever been."

While the perverse incentive is concerning, it's not a reason to stop measuring the quality of cardiac surgeons. Instead, he argues, the death rates should be "paired with measures of appropriateness." In addition, the risk adjustment of complication rates needs to be highly nuanced. "The best surgeons I know have some of the highest complication rates," he says.

So here's where I stand: It's complicated. I think patients deserve to know these facts about the surgeons whose skill is so important to them. The quality measurements need to be well thought out and carefully done, and the methodology should be explained to patients. I see no reason surgeons' compensation should be tied to their outcomes, but they should be accountable to the public and transparent to those who want the best surgeon they can find.

When you fly, while you may not know your pilot's name or where they studied, you can be assured that they are competent based on the ongoing and objective assessments of their technical skill and teamwork. As patients, we should demand and expect the same of those amazing folks with sharp instruments to whom we entrust our lives!

CHANGING HEALTH BEHAVIOR

Health behavior is a major factor in patient outcomes. According to one analysis, health behaviors such as diet and exercise, tobacco use, alcohol and drug use, and sexual activity account for 30 percent of health outcomes, compared to 20 percent for clinical care. Social and economic factors explain 40 percent, and physical environment 10 percent (Johnson, Jones, and Winkie 2022).

It has also been estimated that 40 percent of US deaths are related to modifiable behavioral issues such as smoking and obesity. Partly because of high drug prices, rates of adherence to prescribed medications are also low. In one study of drugs prescribed to heart attack survivors, including statins, beta blockers, ACE inhibitors and other antihypertensive medications, adherence ranged from 36 percent to 49 percent (Hodach et al. 2016).

The key to improvement of health behavior is patient engagement, and the doctor-patient relationship can play a key role in motivating patients. For example, when a doctor advises a patient to quit smoking, they are 30 percent more likely to do so (Hodach et al. 2016). But unless a patient is very sick, they're unlikely to see their physician more than a couple of times a year. The rest of the time, they're mostly on their own.

This can be a tough challenge for patients with serious chronic conditions. "Patients with chronic diseases must follow complex treatment regimens, monitor their conditions, make lifestyle changes, and make decisions about when they need to seek care and when they handle a problem on their own. Effectively functioning in the role of self-manager, particularly when living with one or more chronic illnesses, requires a high level of knowledge, skill and confidence" (Hibbard 2004).

Different activation models have been used or proposed to increase patients' ability to care for themselves and make necessary lifestyle changes. Some use care managers or health coaches to increase the patient's awareness of the need for change and help them build confidence in their ability to change their health behavior. In another model, patients are told they must change to avoid negative outcomes; in a fourth model, they are given small rewards or penalties for good or bad health behavior (Hodach et al. 2016).

None of this works with some people. They can't or won't change their health behavior because of their social and economic environment, cultural factors, lack of health literacy, knowledge deficits, or poor access to healthcare. As a physician, I learned early on that it is self-defeating to make a patient feel worse about themselves because of their smoking, overuse of alcohol, or use of dangerous substances. Many of these self-destructive habits arise because the patient already feels bad about themselves. Finding more constructive ways to link the destructive habit with their behavioral health issues requires time and consistency, neither of which is built into our current behavioral health system.

One of the key issues highlighted in previous chapters is that without radical collaboration with the consumer world, physicians and hospitals have little data concerning what their patients do when they leave the healthcare setting. In my role at General Catalyst, we partner with pharmacies and other entities that can, with the patient's consent, collect data to understand what they are doing in their daily lives that affects their health. For traditional healthcare providers to be part of this "Internet of You" culture, they will also need to stay in touch with patients between visits.

One of the companies we have invested in, Eleanor Health, recognizes that substance use and abuse is not just a physical or mental affliction and has taken a whole-person approach to the problem. A plan to recover from addiction needs to be personalized and comprehensive across physical, mental, emotional, and social issues. This requires a seamless and coordinated approach, including the use of technology and coaching from physicians and nonphysician providers.

Beyond Remote Patient Monitoring

In chapter 3, I discussed how remote patient monitoring might be used to provide continuous healthcare through background collection of physical data. The idea is to provide both care teams and patients with relevant data that can identify warning signs of an emerging health condition as well as exacerbations of existing conditions. This data, curated by AI apps, can be used to send patients online health advice tailored to their health status, including recommendations on health behavior. In addition, clinicians can intervene when the monitoring data reveals that somebody is getting into serious trouble.

Let's take this concept one step further. If we want healthier populations, we need data on individual patients that goes beyond their vital signs and how much they walk or stand. We also need to know what they're eating, how they live their lives, and what's going on around them. We can use some of this information, as well as related alerts, to urge changes in health behavior when it would do the most good.

I have had personal experience with this approach in an unrelated field. My car has a very powerful engine, and as a result, my auto insurance company charged an unusually high fee to cover me. But they said that if I was willing to install a device that would let them know whenever I drove faster than 60 miles per hour, they'd cut my premium in half. I went along with that, because I wanted to pay less for insurance and I don't (normally) drive too fast. If I were speeding, this would become one more factor in my decision to slow down.

A similar kind of technology is used in healthcare to improve medication adherence. My wife, for example, is in a clinical trial that requires her to use an electronic pill box. If she hasn't opened it by noon, it starts to flash. Both Colleen and her oncologist are alerted when she is not adhering to the protocol. All this exciting technology requires trust, which is why physicians and health systems must lead the charge, given our relationship with our patients and the trust we have built up over the years.

Trading Privacy for Health

The question is, how much privacy would people be willing to give up to use technology that could help improve their health behavior and their health? If you gave me access to your credit card information, for example, I'd know you go to Dunkin' Donuts every morning and get a coffee and two donuts. Based on that information, my monthly health advice to you would be to go to Dunkin' Donuts and get the egg white omelet bites instead. That's how you change behavior.

As discussed earlier, behavior can't be changed by using data from hospitals or primary care offices. I was on a panel once with a CVS executive who told me, "You guys are worthless in changing behavior. You don't know anything about a patient. They might visit their doctor's office once a year. In our stores and in our database, we know whether or not they buy condoms, whether they have eyeglasses, whether they've actually picked up their prescriptions, if they have a pet, and what else they buy at CVS. Do they buy candy or protein bars, for example?" Rockwell was right when he sang "Somebody's Watching Me."

Of course, even CVS purchases reveal only so much about a person. But if we could obtain a patient's data from Instacart and DoorDash, along with credit card data and Peloton data, and if we added activity data from Garmin or Fitbit, we'd know a lot about that individual. If we looked at healthcare as a continuous thing and not just as an annual physical, the coach that's calling me every month could say, "Gosh, Steve, your last two Instacarts were all junk. What's going on?" That's one way to change health behavior.

We cannot make our population significantly healthier if we have only 10 percent of the available data on them. Jenny Craig or Weight Watchers may charge you $100 a month for food that can help you lose weight, but they don't know whether you're eating it or what else you're eating. So if you really want to lose weight, you have to give up some privacy and let a coach monitor what you're doing and interact with you daily or monthly.

To some people, this may sound like Stevie Wonder's 1972 song "Big Brother." I understand that reaction, but we're already being monitored online in many other areas of our lives. Not only do apps and services observe what you're buying, many of them ask whether they can enable location services so they can "provide you with a better consumer experience." If you start to investigate flights to Tokyo, you may get an email from Airbnb telling you about the best places to stay in Japan. If you go to a website that sells outdoor pools, you may see ads for pools on Yahoo or Facebook. My son, an actor, was in a diaper commercial early in his career. I watched the ad a few times on YouTube, and I am still being asked online if I've had another baby and what diapers I use! We're willing to give up some privacy to get information we want. Maybe the time has come to think about doing the same in healthcare in return for better health.

Of course, as I've stressed throughout this book, most of us don't want to think about healthcare all the time. That's why remote monitoring should be done as unobtrusively as possible. In addition, if we're willing to have our health continuously monitored, we should be given the opportunity to dial up or dial down the response to the data we generate. Do you want to be contacted regularly, only if your signs take a turn for the worse, or only if a major health event is predicted? Similarly, how often do you want to receive advice on your health behavior?

Banking has this down. Most credit cards will let you adjust alerts based on dollars spent, billing dates, or frequency of use so that you can monitor your financial health on a customized, level. We deserve the same type of customized service for our physical and mental health.

Brain Health at Center Stage

Another important factor in health behavior is behavioral health—or brain health, as I prefer to call it. Problems such as depression and anxiety can have a major effect on physical health, and can contribute to poor health behavior.

Although this dimension of health is often downplayed and is usually segregated from medical care, brain health disorders affect nearly 20 percent of Americans, and the prevalence of these health issues has worsened during the pandemic. Individuals with brain health and substance abuse conditions cost 2.5 to 3.5 times more to care for than those with none of these issues. Conversely, people with serious health problems often have comorbid brain health issues, and up to 70 percent of primary care visits are related to psychosocial issues (Hodach et al. 2016).

Primary care physicians generally are not trained to handle these issues, so they tend to prescribe medications to such patients or refer them to brain health professionals. Primary care doctors often don't put patients on the best drugs for their conditions, and many patients don't follow through on their referral to a psychologist or licensed clinical social worker. Of the patients who receive treatment for mental health issues, 56 percent are seen in general medical settings (Hodach et al. 2016).

The obvious solution is to integrate primary care and brain care professionals wherever possible. This kind of integration is rare in today's healthcare system, according to a Commonwealth Fund study, but where the integrative approach has been tried for depression, it has been shown to be twice as effective as traditional depression care (Hodach et al. 2016).

During my tenure at Jefferson Health, most of our primary care doctors had access to nurse psychologists. When a patient made an appointment to see their doctor, they'd be prescreened for brain health issues. If the questionnaire revealed a problem, the physician would say, "I'd like you to come in 15 minutes early and see our nurse psychologist, and we'll talk after that." As a result, patients at high risk were seen by our brain health provider as an adjunct to their "physical." It just makes sense that a yearly exam should not be limited to "below the neck" disorders!

In other integrated practices, brain health professionals are colocated in doctors' offices, and physicians can refer patients to them after appointments. The close relationship between the doctors and psychologists makes it more likely that patients will comply.

Recognizing this need, Mindful Communications has expanded its corporate mindfulness programs, which are customized specifically for healthcare workers facing an unprecedented level of burnout, anxiety, and depression. A balance between brain health and physical health cannot be achieved solely through medications and psychiatric interventions. Having gone through counseling myself after leading our organization through the pandemic, I can attest that achieving the Eagles' "Peaceful Easy Feeling" takes work!

STRIVING FOR EXCELLENCE IMPROVES CARE

To sum up, if you are a healthcare provider, you want to be the best, and if you are a patient, you want your care team to be the best. While Tina Turner's assessment may have been subjective, healthcare assessments must be objective. In a world of health assurance and transparency, hospitals, their physicians and staff, and their patients must know where the goalposts are so incentives are aligned and the entire system improves.

For the patient of the future, the "Best of You" that the Foo Fighters sang about in 2005 will take a true partnership: patients examining their own behaviors, collaborating with their provider team, and using technology to monitor the results. Patients may have to give up some privacy, and trust must be built into the technology, but you can only be at your healthiest if you're willing to share your lifestyle successes (and failures) with your providers.

Along with health behavior and brain health, social determinants are major components of health outcomes. The American healthcare system cannot be the best until we provide access and customized care to everyone. As Sly and the Family Stone sang in "Everyday People," "I am no better and neither are you / We're all the same, whatever we do." We all want a healthy future for ourselves and our families.

Socioeconomic and environmental factors impose a particularly heavy burden on racial and ethnic minorities, as well as on people living in rural areas. The need for health equity demands that we pay attention to SDOH and other reasons for disparities in how people are treated, and how those disparities affect their health. In the next chapter, we will examine both of these contributors to health outcomes and discuss some solutions.

REFERENCES

Altman, L. 1990. "Heart-Surgery Death Rates Decline in New York." *New York Times*, December 5. https://timesmachine.nytimes .com/timesmachine/1990/12/05/issue.html.

Basch, E., J. Spertus, R. Adams Dudley, A. Wu, C. Chuahan, P. Cohen, M. L. Smith, N. Black, A. Crawford, K. Christensen, K. Black, and C. Goertz. 2015. "Methods for Developing Patient-Reported Outcome-Based Performance Measures (PRO-PMs)." *Value in Health* 18: 493–504. www.valueinhealthjournal.com /action/showPdf?pii=S1098-3015%2815%2901912-9.

Change Healthcare. 2020. "Harris Poll Research: Half of Consumers Avoid Seeking Care Because It's Too Hard" (press release). Published July 13. https://ir.changehealthcare.com /news-releases/news-release-details/change-healthcare-harris -poll-research-half-consumers-avoid.

Findlay, S. D. 2016. "Consumers' Interest in Provider Ratings Grows, and Improved Report Cards and Other Steps Could Accelerate Their Use." *Health Affairs* 35 (4). Published online. https://doi.org/10.1377/hlthaff.2015.1654.

Hannan, E. L., D. Kumar, M. Racz, A. L. Siu, and M. R. Chassin. 1994. "New York State's Cardiac Surgery Reporting System: Four Years Later." *Annals of Thoracic Surgery* 58 (6): 1852–57.

Hibbard, J. H. 2004. "Moving Toward a More Patient-Centered Health Care Delivery System." *Health Affairs* 23 (Suppl 2). Published online December 5, 2018. https://www.healthaffairs.org/doi/10.1377/hlthaff.var.133.

Hodach, R., P. Grundy, A. Jain, and M. Weiner. 2016. *Provider-Led Population Health Management*, 2nd ed. Indianapolis, IN: John Wiley & Sons.

Johnson, D. W., J. Jones, and D. Winkie. 2022. "Healthcare's Final Frontier: Engaging Consumers." 4sight Health. Published March 22. www.4sighthealth.com/healthcares-final-frontier-engaging-consumers/.

Lansky, D. 2022. "Reimagining a Quality Information System for US Health Care." Health Affairs Forefront. Published January 25. www.healthaffairs.org/do/10.1377/forefront.20220120.301087.

Mendelson, A., K. Kondo, C. Damberg, A. Low, M. Motúapuaka, M. Freeman, M. O'Neil, R. Relevo, and D. Kansagara. 2017. "The Effects of Pay-for-Performance Programs on Health, Health Care Use, and Process of Care: A Systematic Review." *Annals of Internal Medicine* 2017 (166): 341–53. Published online January 10, 2017. https://doi.org/10.7326/M16-1881.

Movahed, M. R., R. Ramaraj, A. Khoynezhad, M. Hashemzadeh, and M. Hashemzadeh. 2012. "Declining In-Hospital Mortality in Patients Undergoing Coronary Bypass Surgery in the United States Irrespective of Presence of Type 2 Diabetes or

Congestive Heart Failure." *Clinical Cardiology* 35 (5): 297–300. https://doi.org/10.1002/clc.21970

NQF (National Quality Forum). 2022. *Building a Roadmap from Patient-Reported Outcome Measures to Patient-Reported Outcome Performance Measures: Environmental Scan; Final Report.* Updated June 2022. www.qualityforum.org/Publications/2022 /06/Building_a_Roadmap_From_Patient-Reported_Outcome _Measures_to_Patient-Reported_Outcome_Performance _Measures_Environmental_Scan.aspx.

————. 2021. "NQF Releases a Roadmap Providing Guidance on Developing Digital Patient-Reported Outcome Performance Measures" (press release). December 15. www.qualityforum.org /News_And_Resources/Press_Releases/2021/NQF_Releases _a_Roadmap_Providing_Guidance_on_Developing_Digital _Patient-Reported_Outcome_Performance_Measures.aspx.

NEJM Catalyst. 2018. "What Is Pay for Performance in Healthcare?" March 1. https://catalyst.nejm.org/doi/full/10.1056/CAT.18.0245.

New York State Department of Health. 2019. "Adult Cardiac Surgery in New York State 2014-2016." Published April 2019. https://health.ny.gov/statistics/diseases/cardiovascular/heart _disease/docs/2014-2016_adult_cardiac_surgery.pdf.

Terry, K. 2021. "Online Reviews Most Important Factor in Choosing a Doctor: Survey." *Medscape Medical News*, December 7. www.medscape.com/viewarticle/964264#vp_2.

————. 2007. *Rx for Health Care Reform.* Nashville, TN: Vanderbilt University Press.

Xi, A. S. 2015. "The New Generation of Physician Report Cards." *AMA Journal of Ethics* 17 (7): 647–50. https://doi.org/10.1001 /journalofethics.2015.17.7.stas2-1507.

CHAPTER 8

"Born This Way" by Lady Gaga

Don't hide yourself in regret, just love
yourself and you're set / I'm on the right
track, baby, I was born this way.

LADY GAGA'S SONG rose in the charts and roused America when
she asserted that we were all on the right track as long as we cared
about ourselves. Unfortunately, the same affirmation does not apply
to healthcare in America. In fact, nothing can be further from the
truth. The COVID-19 pandemic proved that your zip code and
living conditions are more important to your health status and life
expectancy than your genetic code and whether you were "born
this way."

When I was the CEO of Jefferson Health, we participated in
a documentary project featuring two healthy babies born at our
hospital, whose only perceived difference was where they would
grow up. Assuming average life expectancy for their class and race,
one baby will survive to 2104 and the other will barely make it to
2090! Somewhere between Stevie Wonder's "Living for the City"
and Lady Gaga's "Born This Way" we have lost our way—especially
when it comes to health equity in our country.

It's grossly unfair that some people in our society get great healthcare and others don't. And the unfairness goes way beyond healthcare:
It starts with someone's living conditions and extends to how they're
educated, how much they earn, and their opportunities compared

with others who grew up in a different place. All of these factors are reflected in an individual's health status and life expectancy.

If healthcare leaders want to address these health disparities, they have to change how they look at their mission. Instead of saying, "I'm sorry you have asthma and you have mold in your house" to a patient who has visited your emergency department every month for the last six months, it may make more sense to hire someone to help the person get rid of that mold. Of course, all of that requires a sane approach to payment models, which we have discussed in previous chapters!

Right now, most health systems have no incentive to do that. If you're on Medicaid, you come to the emergency department, you're taken care of, and the hospital gets paid. The hospital website may say "We care about social determinants of health," but what is the organization doing about it? In a utopian world—or even a rational one, where a health system's CEO was incentivized to keep their population as healthy as possible—the organization would send someone to the patient's house and work with them to investigate their upstream health issues and how they could be solved.

For example, some north Philadelphia residents live in food deserts where there are no supermarkets, just a bodega that sells things like Fritos and Cheetos. Years ago, we couldn't do anything about that. Now we have Instacart and companies are investing in drone delivery. Government health policy could reward families willing to serve healthy food by giving them enhanced food assistance. Logical, creative, and forward-thinking moves like this would do more to combat childhood obesity and other long-standing public health issues than any drug or other healthcare intervention could. But our health systems' financial incentive is still to deliver more health services rather than more health.

Bottom line: America devotes 95 percent of its health spending to direct medical care, but as much as 80 percent of health outcomes are determined by other factors (Magnan 2017)—what we call social determinants of health (SDOH). These include behaviors, the environment, and most especially poverty, which influences jobs, education, and housing. Any organization that seeks to optimize population health needs to deal with these social determinants not just as an asterisk but as the core of its mission and operations.

One SDOH component, socioeconomic status, explains the nearly six-year difference in life expectancy between Americans aged 60 or older who are in the top and bottom halves of income distribution (Khullar and Chokshi 2019). Even more alarming, community studies indicate a 20-year gap in life expectancy between wealthy and poor communities in the United States (Johnson 2002). Meanwhile, US life expectancy has been declining overall. Some of this decline is due to the pandemic, but Americans' lives were growing shorter even before 2020, partly due to substance abuse, alcoholism, and suicide (Devitt 2018). Much of this decline can be traced to social determinants.

A PROVIDER'S VIEW OF SOCIAL NEEDS

Social determinants such as food, housing, and transportation are seen as being outside the control of physicians and health systems. Clinicians can work with community-based organizations (CBOs) to help patients who have these issues. But, while most doctors are aware these problems affect health, 80 percent of physicians say they're not confident in their capacity to deal with patients' social needs (Physician's Foundation 2022). And why should they be, when most medical education is rooted in a hospital-centric, twentieth-century view of the world in which healthcare and the payment structure revolve around hospital-based services?

Up to now, SDOHs have not been a major focus of most healthcare providers. There is some real optimism about changing this in areas of the country where payment shifts toward value are taking hold. Not surprisingly, payment model changes have had a lot to do with this shift. For example, when the Centers for Medicare & Medicaid Services (CMS) and other insurers started to penalize health systems for readmissions after hospitalization and the data made clear that many readmissions could be traced to patients' home circumstances, hospital CEOs took notice. To move the dial on engagement with patients' unmet social needs, however, health systems and physician groups will have to be at *real* financial risk, as proposed in chapter 6. When that happens, healthcare providers will have a strong incentive to work with CBOs to address social determinants.

With providers on board, technology could play a key role in integrating healthcare and social services. Applications for helping the two types of professionals collaborate have been developed, and some of them can be integrated into electronic health records (EHRs). But several challenges must still be overcome before this approach becomes commonplace.

Providers may be tempted to use this technology mainly to address the SDOH factors of high-risk, high-cost patients. But if the goal is to manage the health of the entire population, then SDOHs have to be dealt with at a population-wide level.

"Economically, focusing on the high-risk patients is probably going to give the highest [financial] return in the short run," says David Nash, MD, founding dean emeritus of the College of Population Health at Thomas Jefferson University. "But the underlying reason that they're at such high risk is driven by the social determinants." As one example, he cites homelessness: people who lack stable housing are "among the highest utilizers [of healthcare]. But the core problem is the fact that they're homeless. So, the answer to the riddle is to tackle the social determinants" (Terry 2020, 120–21).

A NEW APPROACH TO POPULATION HEALTH

In my current role as an executive in residence at General Catalyst and in my roles at Avia and Abundant Venture Partners, I have been looking at how technology, human effort, and new financial incentives can promote population health and health equity by addressing social determinants directly. With the right incentives, such an approach can be self-sustaining. For example, if we can create a company that significantly reduces the chance that anyone discharged from a hospital will be readmitted, that would greatly reduce health costs.

As we try to build such a company, we are realizing how many different elements it requires. In addition to technology such as artificial intelligence and predictive analytics, we will need a range of nonclinical employees (e.g., community health workers, digital educators, nutrition consultants) as well as food delivery services, hospital at home services, and other services that use currently available technologies. The technological components are all available as unrelated point solutions, but up to now we have not had the incentive or the mechanisms needed to put them all together.

Defining Social Determinants

The World Health Organization website defines SDOH as "the conditions in which people are born, grow, live, work and age, including the health systems." The Centers for Disease Control and Prevention (CDC) SDOH website defines the term as "conditions in the places where people live, learn, work, and play that affect a wide range of health and quality-of-life risks and outcomes" including social and community context, neighborhood and built environment, economic stability, education access and quality, and healthcare access and quality. So SDOHs encompass access to care and the kind of healthcare system a country has.

At an individual level, SDOHs include such factors as socioeconomic status, race, ethnicity, education, family structure, diet, food security, employment, working conditions, financial resources, housing, location, recreational resources, neighborhood crime, median neighborhood income, intimate partner violence, transportation, stress, social connections, social isolation, homelessness, and physical disabilities.

Numerous studies have established the correlation between socioeconomic status and health all over the world. A relationship also exists between education and diet: Better-educated people tend to have healthier diets than less-educated people do (Bleich et al. 2015). In addition, health is affected by a person's occupation, and working conditions in low-paid jobs—including low job control, high work demands, and long hours—are generally worse than those in higher-paid positions. One study found that individuals with more education and better-paying work have a longer life expectancy than those at the other end of the scale (Goh, Pfeffer, and Zenios 2015).

At a societal level, one way to understand how countries prioritize SDOH is to compare how much they spend on healthcare and social services. Data from 16 European countries shows they spend 24 percent of their GDPs on social services and 11 percent on healthcare, on average. In contrast, the United States spends 19 percent of its GDP on social services and 17 percent on healthcare—except in 2020, when we spent 19.7 percent on healthcare because of the pandemic (Gilfillan, Berwick, and Kronick 2022).

According to Gilfillan and colleagues, this difference in prioritization "is one reason why we're a sicker nation than others of equal wealth." Perhaps so, but the United States is not ready to shift its resources toward more social services. Increased social spending means either reducing payments to health systems and specialist physicians or raising taxes to help the less fortunate, which a large portion of the American electorate opposes.

Nevertheless, there are players that have an interest in addressing SDOH. Health plans and employers, for example, would like to reduce health costs, and they recognize how social determinants affect spending. Healthcare providers that hold value-based contracts have the same incentive. States want to cut Medicaid costs, which chew up a greater percentage of state budgets every year, and local communities have a natural interest in improving the health of residents and reducing the pressure on social services.

Therefore, the key to addressing SDOH is getting healthcare providers and payers to work together with states and communities to improve population health. It would take major societal changes to fully meet the SDOH challenges that affect population health, but we can ameliorate these problems in ways that make people healthier and less likely to get sick.

GOVERNMENT SDOH INITIATIVES

A few states have taken the lead on SDOH, mainly to contain surging Medicaid costs. North Carolina, Oregon, and Vermont have had varying degrees of success.

North Carolina

Community Care of North Carolina (CCNC), which launched in 2001, uses regional primary care networks to improve care for Medicaid patients. Physicians receive care management fees for coordinating care, as well as help from care managers, community health workers, pharmacists, and psychiatrists. They focus mostly on complex patients with multiple conditions (Livingston 2018).

Early on, CCNC's leaders recognized that they had to address the social determinants affecting Medicaid patients. The state helped the primary care networks create a shared infrastructure for this purpose and provided a registry of referral services for doctors and care managers. North Carolina providers are required to screen all Medicaid patients for SDOH, and clinicians are encouraged to use free software to refer patients to CBOs and follow up on them (Terry 2017).

Overall, CCNC has been a success. Over one four-year period, the program saved the state about $1 billion (North Carolina Health News 2015). CCNC has reduced emergency department visits by 13 percent, inpatient admissions by 27 percent, and readmissions by nearly 20 percent (Jackson, Boone, and Wroth 2020).

Oregon

Oregon has several coordinated care organizations (CCOs), which the state created with federal funding to lower its Medicare costs. In the early 2010s, the federal government gave Oregon almost $2 billion with the goal of cutting program spending by 2 percent within five years (Aney 2019). After that successful demonstration ended, Oregon continued the CCOs as part of the Oregon Health Plan (OHP).

The CCOs use OHP-certified community partners to help providers address SDOH. That network includes around 300 organizations that help connect people with resources such as food pantries, SNAP, rent assistance, energy assistance, unemployment benefits, and job resources.

During my healthcare leadership, I have seen many examples of the ways CCOs and community partners can make a difference in utilization rates and in people's lives, and other healthcare leaders have shared similar stories with me. For example, after visiting the emergency department at Oregon Health & Science University 15 times and being admitted to the hospital 11 times in a single year, a homeless man came to the attention of a local CCO. A care manager began to guide him through the healthcare system. She also provided him with the essentials to improve his health, starting with new shoes, a sleeping bag, and a temporary place to live. Due to the CCO's intervention, the man's ER visits and hospitalizations decreased substantially.

In another case I know of, a community partner team in another state visited a woman who had been to the ER more than 10 times in 6 months. She had diabetes, some developmental disorders, and a colostomy. When the community partner actually talked to her, it became clear that no one had ever taught her how to easily care for her ostomy, but she knew that if she went to the ER they would take care of it. A little education and some home visits kept her out of the ER for over a year. She was able to get a job and live more independently.

In a similar case, a woman had 12 ER visits in a year due to exacerbations of her asthma. Each time she was treated, and in some cases her medication was increased. A community partner team did a home visit and realized her home was infested with mold. A repairperson was able to remove the mold for less than $1,000. The woman had no asthma attacks for more than six months, saving the system over $100,000.

At Jefferson Health, we had similar results with a form of "hot-spotting," an approach that stresses holistic care for high-risk patients. We used teams of medical, nursing, public health, and other students to give such patients a sustained plan to prevent rehospitalizations and other intensive, expensive forms of care (Collins, Klasko, and Sicks 2020). It worked!

Vermont

The Vermont Blueprint for Health has also focused on SDOH to help cut costs, not only for Medicaid but also for Medicare and commercial payers, all of which fund the program. Built around the state's patient-centered medical homes (primary care practices that provide enhanced care coordination), the Vermont Blueprint gives these practices access to community health teams (CHTs) consisting of nurse coordinators, social workers, counselors, dietitians, health educators, and other professionals.

The CHTs augment the medical home care teams, driving better integration of medical and nonmedical services and improving coordination with other community providers. CHTs help physicians care for complex patients who have significant social issues. They also help patients address tobacco use, chronic pain, diabetes, and brain health issues.

One study showed that the practices supported by CHTs reduced spending per patient by $482 over two years when compared with a control group of nonparticipating practices. Most of the savings came from lower costs for inpatient and outpatient hospital utilization (Jones et al. 2016).

Other Government Strategies

CMS is working with California's Medi-Cal program to improve its ability to meet Medicaid recipients' social needs. The goal is to increase access to home and community-based services, integrate physical and brain health services, and build housing transition services. This is part of a larger program of the US Department of Health and Human Services to improve care in underserved communities and reduce race-based health disparities (De Lew and Sommers 2022).

CMS has authorized many states to launch and test a variety of pilot initiatives to address Medicare beneficiaries' social needs, including a health homes demonstration project that includes referrals to community and social support services. CMS is also piloting an Accountable Health Communities model to find out whether connecting Medicare and Medicaid recipients with community resources can improve health outcomes and reduce costs (Mahajan 2021).

Nearly 40 percent of states require Medicaid managed care plans to screen members for social needs (Mahajan 2021). Nevertheless, the rates of screening in hospitals and physician practices remain low, and many of them do no screening. A more fundamental problem with these efforts is that the social services in most areas lack sufficient resources to meet people's needs for basics such as food and housing. Given everything we know, it is administrative and health policy malpractice to not fully implement some of these community interventions to decrease overall health costs and reduce the health gaps that exist in underserved communities.

PRIVATE SECTOR INITIATIVES

Some payers have stepped up to the plate to help improve population health by subsidizing SDOH initiatives. Kaiser Permanente, for example, has a $400 million fund that invests in creating affordable housing (Abrams 2022). Kaiser has also launched a care network that helps its providers connect with CBOs to address social needs (Johnson 2019).

CVS and Aetna, its insurance subsidiary, have formed a similar network, and the pharmacy chain is also working with SDOH software developer Unite Us to connect Aetna members with social services. CVS has invested $100 million in affordable housing as well (Johnson 2019).

Humana (2021) launched its Bold Goal in 2015 under CEO Bruce Broussard's leadership, with a special focus on loneliness and social isolation. Six years into the program, Medicare Advantage members in affected communities were "experiencing fewer unhealthy days than those in non-Bold Goal communities."

UnitedHealthcare, the largest private insurer, has also made moves to address SDOH. Recently, United announced it would contribute an additional $100 million to housing initiatives, bringing the insurer's total housing investment to about $800 million (Lagasse 2022). United has also enabled providers in its Medicare Advantage plans to make referrals to social services and has distributed food to some of its members in partnership with Mom's Meals (Minemyer 2019).

The Geisinger Health Plan in Pennsylvania has found that providing fresh food to people with diabetes has a greater impact on their health than medications. After identifying people who are food insecure, Geisinger enrolls them in a diabetes self-management class, where they receive "prescriptions" to a food pantry at a Geisinger clinic. Each prescription gives them enough food to make 10 meals a week. Four years into the program, Geisinger has seen a significant drop in the participants' A1c level, medication use, and ER visits (eHealth Initiative 2019; Morse 2022).

One way to provide healthy food in food deserts is to deliver it by drone. While this may sound futuristic, drones are already being used to deliver food and health supplies. In 2021, Walmart started testing a drone service that delivered health products in northwest Arkansas in a partnership with a company called Zipline. Later, it expanded the service to thousands of items, including food. Walmart has about 3,000 stores that reach 70 percent of the US population (Browne 2021).

Digital food services, such as Amazon Fresh, Instacart, Uber Eats, and Walmart can now be accessed by 93 percent of the US population (George and Tomer 2022). This could be a game changer in food deserts. If the government also provided additional subsidies to low-income people for buying healthy foods, the positive health impact could be significant.

Some healthcare systems have also tackled SDOH. To help manage health costs under its risk contracts, for example, Montefiore Medical Center in Bronx, New York, hired about 600 care managers, including nurses, social workers, and community-based educators. High-risk patients are enrolled in educational programs and are linked with social services and other community organizations that can help them with their SDOH-related challenges (Terry 2017).

Norton Healthcare in Louisville, Kentucky, belongs to a community network of health, education, and social care providers that supply holistic services to area residents. Using the Unite Us platform, Norton providers can exchange electronic referrals with community resource partners to address these patients' health and social needs, says Karen Handmaker, a population health expert who is involved in the collaborative. People who need assistance with housing and utilities, food, substance abuse and brain health treatment, employment, transportation, or benefits navigation receive referrals to appropriate services.

Other health systems around the country have engaged in SDOH initiatives, but on the whole, the evidence shows that healthcare providers are spending fairly little on social determinants.

Not-for-profit hospitals, which make up nearly 80 percent of acute-care facilities, have always been required to supply community benefits in exchange for their tax exemptions. Under the Affordable Care Act (ACA), hospitals must now produce an annual community health needs assessment with an implementation strategy. But they don't have to spend a certain percentage of revenues on helping communities meet those needs (Terry 2020).

The Lown Institute (2022) documented just how little most not-for-profits devote to this goal. The researchers determined that 227 of the 275 health systems studied had "fair share deficits," meaning they spent less on charity care and community investment than the value of their tax exemption. Adding the fair share deficits of all hospital systems together revealed $18.4 billion in "stranded dollars" that could have been used to advance health equity and address housing, food, and other local needs.

Similarly, in a 2015 report to Congress, the US Treasury Department found that private tax-exempt hospitals provided less than 10 percent of their total expenses as community benefit, half of which represented charity care and unreimbursed care provided to Medicaid patients. Less than half a percent of the total went to "community health improvement services" (Terry 2020).

Defining Community Benefit

The main issue that needs to be addressed here is the definition of *community benefit*. As things stand today, hospitals can use the value of their charity care or the shortfalls in Medicaid payments as evidence of community benefit. In fact, some hospitals purposely set their charges very high—regardless of what insurance pays—so they can claim a higher community benefit!

Perhaps the IRS should tweak its definition of community benefit. For example, the government might require that every not-for-profit hospital add to its board of directors at least two patient advocates for the underserved. While most nonprofit health system and payer boards have health equity committees, health equity is rarely a key component in the compensation of senior leadership and in Tier 1 board activities. That might also change if the government required it. Or the IRS might say that a not-for-profit hospital or health system has to commission an annual analysis of the local SDOH by zip code and report on what the organization is doing to narrow the gaps between the affluent and the poor districts in its service area.

As mentioned previously, the ACA already requires a community needs assessment. But hospital reports about community needs tend to focus on social determinants they can't do much about, such as the lack of jobs or affordable housing. The reports I'm proposing would look at specific areas in which the hospital *can* make a difference and would show what they're actually doing to address each area. It might also make sense to include a section on the goals that determine the hospital CEO's compensation. If the hospital is serious about improving health equity, the CEO's salary should be based partly on that goal, not just on financial parameters such as patient census, net income, and the *U.S. News & World Report* rankings. "Paying the Cost to Be the Boss," in the words of B. B. King, needs to change if we are going to align health system and insurer incentives with real health.

TECHNOLOGY TO THE RESCUE

Providers can use information technology to address SDOH. In fact, some venture capitalists and company founders believe in "responsible innovation" that will help ensure that everyone has access to good healthcare and support in meeting their social needs. The one thing we don't want is for this technology to be designed mainly to make wealthy people healthier.

Some initiatives are using apps to connect healthcare providers with CBOs. For example, the Trenton Health Team (THT) is a collaboration of two New Jersey health systems, a community health center, and a public health agency. To deal with social determinants, THT has created partnerships between its member healthcare organizations and local CBOs. The organization has also built a health information exchange that integrates the SDOH software NowPow. The app can pull real-time data from partner EHRs and allows providers to view a patient's SDOH profile in their EHR (Raths 2019).

Rush University Medical Center in Chicago is also using NowPow to connect patients to community resources. Rush providers can refer patients to CBOs right from their EHR. When a provider enters a patient's social needs information, it flows to NowPow automatically. The software then recommends where to refer the patient. The social service agency can also send data back to the provider on whether a patient showed up and the outcome of the referral. However, these closed loops are not common yet, because many local CBOs haven't installed NowPow (Arndt 2019).

Community Collaboration

The community collaboration that includes Norton Healthcare, as noted earlier, is using the Unite Us platform, which is also being used by Kaiser Permanente and Intermountain Health. While Norton is mainly concerned about preventing readmissions, Handmaker, the executive administrator associated with the Norton collaboration, points out that the city and the school system are also helping to fund the Unite Us platform. "It's a community asset that we want all the payers and health systems to participate in," she says. The advantage of this approach, she notes, is that everyone can be on the same platform, simplifying the process of connecting providers with CBOs.

Unfortunately, this is not the case in communities where providers use a variety of SDOH applications, making it difficult for CBOs to connect with them. In addition to NowPow and Unite Us, these programs include Healthify, Aunt Bertha, Whole Person Care, and various homegrown solutions (Raths 2019).

Start-Ups That Target Disparities

Another kind of technology firm that specializes in caring for the underserved is Cityblock, which delivers primary, behavioral, and substance abuse care to Medicaid recipients and people who are covered by both Medicare and Medicaid. Cityblock has risk contracts with private health plans that insure these individuals using government money.

During the pandemic, Cityblock reached out to plan members who were at high risk of hospitalization for COVID-19. It screened these members for social needs related to the pandemic and used the information to send out teams to drop off food at members' homes. In addition, it has piloted a temporary housing program for people who face homelessness (Reuter 2021).

General Catalyst has invested in Cityblock and, as previously mentioned, in Eleanor Health, a start-up that focuses on substance use and abuse in the underserved population. While these seemingly intractable problems might not have looked like attractive investments in the past, we believe companies such as Eleanor and Cityblock will do good and do well as the industry moves from volume to value.

Eleanor uses a combination of software and health coaches, and it can be customized to emphasize the human touch when people lack access to the internet or computers. While federal funding is available to expand broadband access and bridge the digital divide, many people are still left out in the cold.

UnitedHealthcare's Optum subsidiary, which views telehealth as a method to better serve underserved communities, is dealing with this reality. The company recognizes that many patients can't afford broadband access or have old devices that don't support current telehealth platforms. So Optum has given some vulnerable patients with chronic conditions data-loaded devices, including a tablet connected to a cellular network. Currently, about 200,000 patients are benefiting from this program (Landi 2022).

In the future, combining new technologies with human efforts to provide healthcare at any address will enable our healthcare system to finally take advantage of all the research that has been done on population health to close care gaps and eliminate health inequities. But to achieve this goal, these initiatives must tackle SDOH on a comprehensive basis.

One holistic approach to SDOH is offered by the Blue Zones Project of Sharecare, a digital wellness company founded by WebMD founder Jeff Arnold. The project is based on the concept of "blue zones"—communities where people live measurably longer, healthier lives and are more likely to live to be 100 or older. In 2004, a project led by Dan Buettner and National Geographic investigated five of these blue zone communities: Okinawa, Japan; Sardinia, Italy; Nicoya, Costa Rica; Ikaria, Greece; and Loma Linda, California. Not surprisingly, they found that people who eat a plant-based diet, exercise regularly, drink moderate amounts of alcohol, get enough sleep, and have good spiritual, family, and social networks, among other factors, tend to live a longer and healthier life than the rest of us. The goal of Sharecare's digital-first tailored guidance is to create customized environmental and social changes that emulate the pro-health factors of blue zone cities.

TARGETING RACIAL HEALTH INEQUITIES

Despite the enormous sums we spend on healthcare, health inequities are as widespread in the United States as in some less developed countries that spend a fraction of what we do. Some of this disparity is caused by geography: People in rural areas simply have less access to healthcare than people in suburban and metropolitan areas because of where they live. But health inequity especially impacts minority populations, including African Americans, Hispanics, Native Americans, and Pacific Islanders, regardless of where they live.

In 2020, for example, COVID-19 reduced overall US life expectancy by 1.5 years, while Black and Hispanic people had their life expectancy lowered by more than 3 years. In Pittsburgh, Black patients with COVID-19 had higher hospitalization rates and were more likely to land in intensive care than white patients who had the disease. Death rates among Blacks were also significantly higher than among whites (Spolar 2021).

Another study revealed that age-adjusted, COVID-related deaths among Black and Hispanic Medicare patients were about double those among white Medicare beneficiaries. After adjusting for SDOH, however, the disparity was greatly reduced (Song et al. 2021).

Native Americans' hospital mortality rates from COVID-19 were two to three times higher than those of all other races. Among patients with the most comorbidities, nearly 70 percent of American Indian and Alaska Native patients admitted to the hospital with COVID-19 died before discharge, compared with less than 30 percent of Black or white patients (Devereaux 2022).

Racial and ethnic health disparities long predated the pandemic, especially for poor and uninsured populations. According to a report by the Agency for Healthcare Research and Quality (AHRQ 2020), some disparities decreased from 2000 to 2018, but other disparities persisted and even worsened. For about 40 percent of quality measures, for example, Blacks and Native Americans received worse care than whites did in a 2016–2018 study. For a third of quality measures, Hispanics/Latinos and Pacific Islanders received worse care than whites did.

Healthcare is also less safe for minorities than for whites. In a revealing study from the Urban Institute, Black patients had a higher rate of adverse safety events than did white patients when they were admitted to the same hospital, regardless of insurance coverage type or the percentage of hospitalized patients who were Black. The differences were especially great on surgery-related indicators (Terry 2021b).

Of everything we have discussed in this book and in my previous writings on what is right and wrong with American healthcare, this finding is among the hardest to explain (or swallow). In my long career in medicine, I've met very few doctors, nurses, residents, or students who expressed racist inclinations. Nevertheless, because of our segmentation of Medicaid and commercially insured patients, there is clearly an inherent bias that may subconsciously or unconsciously affect care. Another problem contributing to this unacceptable finding is that most US physicians who treat minorities do not belong to any of those groups.

Also, because of past race- and gender-based biases and outright abuses in clinical trials and healthcare, there is some mistrust of white male physicians among minority patients. When there is a disconnect of race and culture between physician and patient, trust needs to be earned—something that is difficult to accomplish in a single office or ER visit. Poor communication and a lack of trust between people who come from different backgrounds is hardly surprising, even in the best of circumstances, and that may contribute to the greater incidence of safety events among minority patients.

The Role of Systemic Racism

Clearly, racism has played and continues to play a major role in health inequity. To begin with, a large portion of health disparities are linked to social determinants shaped by historical racism. These adverse social determinants are the result of discriminatory policies that have produced unequal housing quality, job opportunities, education, justice, and healthcare (Braveman et al. 2022). The street-to-prison pipeline for poor young Black men is all about mental and physical health. So are substandard schools and a lack of information about birth control and reproductive health.

Social determinants are also implicated in some of the health conditions that people of color commonly develop. For example, kidney disease disproportionately affects communities of color. "Black or African Americans are almost four times more likely and Hispanics or Latinos are 1.3 times more likely to have kidney failure compared to White Americans," according to the website of the National Kidney Foundation (2021). Furthermore, "Black or African Americans make up more than 35% of dialysis patients." The foundation goes on to say that the major causes of kidney disease, including diabetes, hypertension, and cardiovascular disease, are all more prevalent among Black Americans than among whites.

The higher incidence of these chronic conditions among African Americans has much to do with the living conditions in Black communities. For example, differences in rapid infant weight gain and in socioeconomic status are correlated with the greater prevalence of obesity among Black children as compared to white children (Isong et al. 2018). Obesity is a well-known risk factor for diabetes, so it's not surprising that diabetes—one of the leading precursors of kidney disease—would afflict African Americans disproportionately.

The roles of racism and SDOH in health disparities are hard to disentangle. Zambrana and Williams (2022, 166) summarized the situation in *Health Affairs*:

> Research had long documented that socioeconomic status is inversely associated with multiple risk factors for disease (such as stress, poor living conditions, exposure to toxins, and unhealthy behaviors) and one of the strongest known determinants of variations in health status globally. Emerging research also demonstrated that race was strongly intertwined with socioeconomic status and that socioeconomic differences between the races accounted for a substantial part of the racial and ethnic differences in health. At the same time, race and socioeconomic status are two related but not interchangeable systems of social ordering that jointly contribute to health risks. Residual racial differences are present at every level of education and income, and attention should be given to the intersection of race- and class-based factors that undergird racial and ethnic health disparities.

Simply put, the conditions in which many people of color live—some of which are products of systemic racism—are major factors in health inequities, but they don't completely explain them.

Barriers to Healthcare Access

Access to healthcare, which is a social determinant, is another factor in health disparities. The reasons for poor healthcare access in marginalized communities include lack of transportation, limited availability of primary care, and the refusal of some specialists to see people who are uninsured or on Medicaid.

We ran into the latter problem when I was at Jefferson. Some of our most respected private physician groups refused to accept Medicaid, probably because of its low reimbursement rates. These groups often included the physicians who had the best reputations. They provided great clinical care, often in venues that were more cost-effective than our general acute-care facilities. But the net result was that the underserved, generally higher-risk people they declined to care for came instead to our hospital. In some cases, we had to recruit other physicians to take care of these clinically challenging patients. Thinking back to some of the payer solutions we espoused in previous chapters, anything that lowers barriers to insurance coverage for people living in poverty will help deal with these problematic situations. While these barriers are not directly race-related, they often contribute to the disparity in outcomes between people of different races and circumstances.

Biased outcomes in healthcare have deep and complex roots in our education system and in payment models that don't support population health. For example, we have done a poor job of accepting and training nurses and doctors who look like the people they're taking care of, but that's not because of racism in medical or nursing schools; it's largely because of an educational system that fundamentally disadvantages minority students. Moreover, by selecting students based on their ability to memorize complex scientific formulas (even though much of the related work is now done by machines), medical schools have created a tale of two cities: Students who can afford the specialized tutors needed to help them ace multiple-choice tests are admitted to medical schools; less affluent students, many of whom are people of color, don't receive the same level of formal education and can't afford the extra tutoring.

Here's another example: Most hospital systems haven't reached out to the underserved communities with an approach like "healthcare at any address" because that's not how they get paid. This lack of outreach is not systemic racism. The systemic piece is the messed-up incentives that determine what health systems do. Nevertheless, this has had an unfair, adverse effect on people of color.

CMS Health Equity Initiative

The government and the medical establishment have begun pushing back against health disparities related to race and ethnicity. In April 2022, CMS released a health equity plan that said the agency would address health disparities through stakeholder engagement and by making health equity a core function of CMS's activities. Among other things, CMS said, it will seek Medicare beneficiaries' perspectives on health equity, and it aims to integrate safety-net providers and CBOs into CMS programs.

Specifically, CMS (2022) plans to

- close gaps in healthcare access, quality, and outcomes for underserved populations;
- promote culturally and linguistically appropriate services;
- build on outreach to enroll eligible people in government programs;

- expand and standardize the collection and use of data necessary to achieve health equity in government programs;
- determine how CMS can better support safety-net providers and improve access to care; and
- screen for health-related social needs and promote broader access to meet those needs.

The challenge of providing "culturally and linguistically appropriate services" is underappreciated. In my obstetric practice, I realized that what I thought I was saying might be perceived differently by the patient from a different background. Also, where a language barrier exists, having to communicate complex medical advice through an interpreter can lead to all sorts of misinterpretations and quality issues. Physicians probably underestimate the number of people with limited English proficiency and, despite a spike in technological advances in many other areas of healthcare, language support still lags behind.

A start-up firm called Globo offers a rare combination of tech and unified language support with human interactions. Its language services include telephone, video, and on-demand text translation in 250 languages! The "Babel" Mumford & Sons sang about could be virtually erased with this type of technology.

CMS has made the six components just described a priority and is incorporating a new health equity index into star ratings for Medicare Advantage and Part D plans. It will also increase the number of graduate medical education slots to increase physician training in underserved areas. In addition, the agency will develop health equity-focused measures in all care settings; for example, a measure of the percentage of adults screened for SDOH and, of those, who have been screened positive for harmful social determinants. Further, CMS will make payment adjustments or enhance benefits to expand access to and improve the quality of care for underserved populations.

AMA's Efforts to Right Past Wrongs

The American Medical Association (AMA) has also made a concerted effort to improve its record on health equity. In 2021, the AMA released a three-year strategic plan to counter health inequities that hurt marginalized communities (Terry 2021a). The plan includes these goals:

- End segregated healthcare.
- Establish national healthcare equity and racial justice standards.
- End the use of race-based clinical decision models.
- Eliminate all forms of discrimination, exclusion, and oppression in medical and physician education, training, hiring, and promotion.
- Prevent exclusion of and ensure equal representation of Black, Indigenous, and Latino people in medical school admissions as well as medical school and hospital leadership ranks.
- Ensure equity in innovation, including design, development, and implementation, along with support for equitable innovation opportunities and entrepreneurship.
- Solidify connections and coordination between healthcare and public health.
- Acknowledge and repair past harms committed by institutions.

As the report acknowledges, the AMA has a long history of exclusion of and discrimination against Black physicians, for which the association apologized in 2008. In addition, the AMA has described racism as a public health crisis, stated that race has nothing to do with biology, said police brutality is a product of structural racism, and called on the federal government to collect and release COVID-19 race and ethnicity data.

Making a Difference

When I took the reins at Jefferson Health, I was struck by the disconnect between the mission of the academic medical center and the extreme poverty and health disparities in Philadelphia. The city had no less than five academic hospitals with advanced capabilities, yet Philadelphia was ranked in the bottom 10 percent among 50 metropolitan areas for the health statistics of minority residents.

In 2017, I decided to place health equity at the center of everything Jefferson did. To start, I linked 25 percent of my personal incentive compensation with reductions in health disparities. We then established the Philadelphia Collaborative for Health Equity (see chapter 5), partnered with Novartis to reduce disparities in cardiovascular disease, and partnered with Temple Health to lessen disparities in stroke outcomes.

Jefferson's Collaborative for Health Equity (https://p-che.org) is working closely with communities to improve their health and reduce health disparities. Using donated funds, including those raised by Jefferson's annual galas, the Collaborative is increasing access to healthcare, addressing hunger and food insecurity, training people for jobs, building new green spaces, helping residents achieve and maintain financial security, and addressing trauma in all its forms by providing support services for individuals and families.

Closing the Gap on Heart Disease

Another equity-focused program I helped launch is Closing the Gap, a $3 million collaboration with Novartis. This initiative focuses on five zip codes that are home to about 200,000 Philadelphians at high risk of cardiovascular disease. Novartis chose to work with Jefferson because we put our money and mission ("We improve lives") on the line to deal with the city's underperformance in population health. One key indicator of that underperformance was the enormous gaps in cardiovascular disease rates between Philadelphia's wealthiest and poorest residents.

Closing the Gap is expanding healthcare infrastructure in the affected areas and connecting people to the care they need. In addition, the program is addressing SDOH by providing financial assistance to local community organizations. Moreover, it has mounted a screening and community health worker program to ensure that individuals are assessed for cardiovascular risk factors, are connected with programs to reduce their risk, and receive the resources needed to optimize health, including nutritious meals, transportation, and specialty care (Cope et al. 2021).

When Andréa and Ken Frazier gave their $5 million gift to address stroke disparity in Philadelphia, they specified that we had to focus on the area where he was born. That neighborhood lay in Temple Health's service area, not ours, so I offered Temple half the donation, and our two health systems collaborated under the Philadelphia Collaborative for Health Equity umbrella.

Radical Moves to Increase Health Equity

The Jefferson-Temple partnership exemplifies one of the three main tenets of healthcare at any address: radical collaboration, radical communication, and radical concentration on health disparities.

Radical collaboration means that healthcare competitors should work together to meet the whole community's social needs. Instead of looking at Temple as a competitor, for example, we viewed them as a partner in reducing Philadelphia's health disparities. Such partnerships might be funded by taking some of the government money that academic medical centers get to research health inequities or population health management and putting it into action-oriented initiatives among several "competitors" willing to work together to eradicate the epidemic of health inequity.

The second tenet is radical communication. Instead of buying 30-second commercials or paying for billboards that tout their supposed excellence, hospitals should put that money into community outreach. In Jefferson's health equity programs, we went out to where the people were to learn about their problems and help improve their access to healthcare. That meant sending nurses and community health workers out to homes, churches, and nail salons. If you want to deal with cardiovascular disease in Black men, for instance, your team needs to meet with them where they are—at home, at work, and even in barbershops, which serve as discussion and teaching academies in many neighborhoods.

Radical communication also requires that health systems communicate with people in their own language, through representatives they can identify with, and in places where they normally get their information. When Jefferson rolled out COVID-19 vaccinations, for example, we didn't run commercials on Morning Joe or in the *Philadelphia Inquirer*. We had African American community health workers go to the Black churches, and Latino folks went to the Latino churches. For more than 100 straight weeks, I was on Sonny Hill's *In the Living Room* sports radio show with Robert Perkel, MD, (a premier Jefferson family physician) in a segment called "The Doctors Are in the House." In that two-year period, we had a major impact on vaccine hesitancy among that population. I remember one text from a listener: "We are not vaccinated because we usually don't trust people like you, but you seem sincere so I have decided to get my family vaccinated. It takes a lot for us to trust, so please keep it real!" Those Sunday mornings, we tried to live up to Beyoncé's lyrics in "Radio": "It never lets me down." The show's format gave me the opportunity to connect with the community, starting in their living rooms.

The final tenet, radical concentration on health disparities, means among other things that health system CEOs should be paid partly on the basis of what they are doing to attack those inequities. If it was part of their incentive, CEOs would be more likely to think of how their health system could help ensure that both of the babies featured in Platon's documentary project have the same chance to live a long, healthy life.

CONCLUSION

Health inequities have been with us for a long time, and they're not likely to disappear in the near future. To eliminate them, we must rebuild our society in ways that eliminate systemic racism and discrimination and that reduce the income inequality that is closely linked with health disparities. In the meantime, health systems are uniquely situated to work with community resources to minimize the impact of these disparities and produce better health for everybody.

This is not an easy problem to solve. The goal of this chapter is to have us live into Lady Gaga's challenge in "Born This Way." While "God makes no mistakes," we should all have an equal chance to live a healthy life. Our health should not be based on *Where You Live*. Tracy Chapman used that album to challenge us to "Change," asking "What chain reaction / What cause and effect / Makes you turn around"?

True healthcare transformation will not occur until we no longer are bound by Curtis Mayfield's "Choice of Colors." More than 50 years ago, the Impressions sang,

- A better day is coming, for you and for me
- With just a little bit more education
- And love for our nation
- Would make a better society

So, maybe at your next hospital board meeting, a medley of "Born This Way," "Change," and "Choice of Colors," with a smattering of "We Are Not Helpless" by Stephen Stills, might spark a different conversation around population health and equity!

The lack of health equity and the uneven quality of US healthcare are not the only factors that pose a danger to the health of many Americans. Another uncomfortable issue that periodically pops up on the radar of the healthcare community is the poor and uneven safety record of some providers and hospitals. Our next chapter explains why this perennial challenge hasn't gone away and what we can do about it.

REFERENCES

Abrams, M. 2022. "Kaiser Permanente Adds $200 Million to Its Affordable Housing Fund." *Modern Healthcare*, April 14. www.modernhealthcare.com/hospital-systems/kaiser-permanente-doubles-its-affordable-housing-fund.

AHRQ (US Agency for Healthcare Research and Quality). 2020. "2019 National Healthcare Quality and Disparities Report: Executive Summary." Published December. AHRQ Pub. No. 20(21)-0045-EF. www.ahrq.gov/sites/default/files/wysiwyg/research/findings/nhqrdr/2019qdr-final-es-cs061721.pdf.

Aney, K. 2019. "Former Oregon Governor Believes New Approach Needed on Health Care." *Blue Mountain Eagle*, September 23.

Arndt, R. Z. 2019. "Tending to Social Determinants of Health with Software." *Modern Healthcare*, January 26. www.modernhealthcare.com/article/20190126/TRANSFORMATION03/190129973/tending-to-social-determinants-of-health-with-software.

Bleich, S. N., J. Jones-Smith, J. A. Wolfson, X. Zhu, and M. Story. 2015. "The Complex Relationship Between Diet and Health." *Health Affairs* 34 (11): 1813–20. www.healthaffairs.org/doi/full/10.1377/hlthaff.2015.0606.

Braveman, P. A., E. Arkin, D. Proctor, T. Kauh, and N. Holm. 2022. "Systemic and Structural Racism: Definitions, Examples, Health Damages, and Approaches to Dismantling." *Health Affairs* 41 (2): 171–78. https://doi.org/10.1377/hlthaff.2021.01394.

Browne, M. 2021. "Walmart Launches Drone Deliveries with DroneUp." Supermarket News. Published November 22. www.supermarketnews.com/technology/walmart-launches-drone-deliveries-droneup.

CMS (Centers for Medicare & Medicaid Services). 2022. "Strategic Plan Pillar: Health Equity." Published April. www.cms.gov/sites /default/files/2022-04/Health%20Equity%20Pillar%20Fact %20Sheet_1.pdf.

Collins, L., S. K. Klasko, and S. Sicks. 2020. "Equipping the Work-force for Complex Care: How Jefferson University Trains Medical Students in Hotspotting." *NEJM Catalyst Innovations in Care Delivery* 1 (1). https://doi.org/10.1056/CAT.19.1087.

Cope, A. E., D. B. Nash, S. E. Brooks, and D. Platt. 2021. "Looking Upstream: Promoting Health Equity in Philadelphia through Novel Partnership Strategies." *Population Health Management* 24 (6): 635–37. https://doi.org/10.1089/pop.2021.0217.

De Lew, N., and B. D. Sommers. 2022. "Addressing Social Determinants of Health in Federal Programs." *JAMA Health Forum* 3 (3): e221064. https://doi.org/10.1001/jamahealthforum.2022 .1064.

Devereaux, M. 2022. "Native Americans' COVID-19 Hospital Mortality Rates Are Double Other Races." *Modern Healthcare*, March 30. www.modernhealthcare.com/safety-quality/hospital-covid -19-mortality-rates-double-native-americans.

Devitt, M. 2018. "CDC Data Show U.S. Life Expectancy Continues to Decline." *AAFP News*, December 10. www.aafp.org/news /health-of-the-public/20181210lifeexpectdrop.html.

eHealth Initiative. 2019. The Importance of Social Determinants of Health Data. Report. Published March 25. www.ehidc.org/sites /default/files/resources/files/Importance%20of%20SDOH %20Data%20March%202019.pdf.

George, C., and A. Tomer. 2022. "Delivering to Deserts: New Data Reveals the Geography of Digital Access to Food in the U.S." Brookings Institute. Published May 11. www.brookings.edu /essay/delivering-to-deserts-new-data-reveals-the-geography -of-digital-access-to-food-in-the-us/.

Gilfillan, R., D. M. Berwick, and R. Kronick. 2022. "How Medicare Advantage Plans Can Support the United States' Reinvestment in Health." Health Affairs Forefront. Published January 10. https://doi.org/10.1377/forefront.20220106.719333.

Goh, J., J. Pfeffer, and S. Zenios. 2015. "Exposure to Harmful Workplace Practices Could Account for Inequality in Life Spans Across Different Demographic Groups." *Health Affairs* 34 (10): 1761–68. www.healthaffairs.org/doi/10.1377/hlthaff.2015.0022.

Humana. 2021. "2021 Bold Goal Progress Report Shows Humana Medicare Advantage Members Maintained Their Overall Health In 2020, Throughout Pandemic" (press release). Humana News. Published May 18. https://press.humana.com/news/news-details/2021/2021-Bold-Goal-Progress-Report-Shows-Humana-Medicare-Advantage-Members-Maintained-Their-Overall-Health-In-2020-Throughout-Pandemic/default.aspx.

Isong, I. A., S. R. Rao, M.-A. Bind, M. Avendaño, I. Kawachi, and T. K. Richmond. 2018. "Racial and Ethnic Disparities in Early Childhood Obesity." *Pediatrics* 141 (1): e20170865. https://doi.org/10.1542/peds.2017-0865.

Jackson, C., A. Boone, and T. Wroth. 2020. "CCNC's Impactibility Approach: How 'Finding the Needle in a Haystack' Continues to Yield Savings from CCNC Care Management." CCNC Data Brief. Published January 30. www.communitycarenc.org/sites/default/files/2020-01/Data-Brief-12-Needle-in-a-Haystack.pdf.

Johnson, D. W. 2002. "Cracks in the Foundation (Part 3): Overcoming Healthcare's Services-Need Mismatch." *HFM Magazine*, April. https://mcusercontent.com/8a4bf5d1617f86a90e5a909f0/files/3bd3ea84-111d-48e8-2639-8195ccdff812/HFMA.Part3.DJohnson.ServicesNeedMismatch.Apr_2022.01.pdf.

Johnson, S. R. 2019. "Kaiser to Launch Social Care Network." *Modern Healthcare*, May 6. www.modernhealthcare.com/care-delivery/kaiser-launch-social-care-network.

Jones, C., K. Finison, K. McGraves-Lloyd, T. Tremblay, M. K. Mohlman, B. Tanzman, M. Hazard, S. Maier, and J. Samuelson. 2016. "Vermont's Community-Oriented All-Payer Medical Home Model Reduces Expenditures and Utilization While Delivering High-Quality Care." *Population Health Management* 19 (3): 196–205. Published online September 8, 2015. https://doi .org/10.1089/pop.2015.0055.

Khullar, D., and D. A. Chokshi. 2019. "Health, Income & Poverty: Where We Are & What Could Help." *Health Affairs* 38 (9): 1505–13. www.healthaffairs.org/do/10.1377/hpb20180817 .901935/full/.

Lagasse, J. 2022. "UnitedHealth Group Investing $100 Million in Affordable Housing Initiatives." *Healthcare Finance*, April 11. www.healthcarefinancenews.com/news/unitedhealth-group -investing-100-million-affordable-housing-initiatives.

Landi, H. 2022. "Here's Why UnitedHealth Group's CMO Says Virtual Care Is a 'Game Changer' to Reach Underserved Populations." *Fierce Healthcare*, January 25. www.fiercehealthcare .com/payer/how-unitedhealth-group-using-free-tablets-and -telehealth-visits-to-reach-underserved-patients.

Livingston, S. 2018. "Social Determinants Are Core of North Carolina's Medicaid Overhaul." *Modern Healthcare*, August 3. www.modernhealthcare.com/article/20180803 /TRANSFORMATION01/180809944/social-determinants-are -core-of-north-carolina-s-medicaid-overhaul.

Lown Institute. 2022. "Fair Share Spending: 2022 Results." Published April. https://lownhospitalsindex.org/2022-fair-share -spending/.

Magnan, S. 2017. "Social Determinants of Health 101 for Health Care: Five Plus Five." Discussion Paper. *NAM Perspectives*, October 9. Discussion Paper, National Academy of Medicine. https://doi.org/10.31478/201710c.

Mahajan, A. 2021. "Value in Medicaid, Part 2: Challenges Concerning Health-Related Social Needs." Health Affairs Forefront. Published December 16. www.healthaffairs.org/do/10.1377/forefront.20211214.703281/full/.

Minemyer, P. 2019. "Why UnitedHealthcare Wants to Expand Diagnostic Codes to the Social Determinants of Health." *Fierce Healthcare*, February 11. www.fiercehealthcare.com/payer/why-unitedhealthcare-wants-to-expand-diagnostic-codes-to-social-determinants-health.

Morse, S. 2022. "Geisinger Gets Type 2 Diabetes Costs Under Control." *Healthcare Finance*, April 1. www.healthcarefinancenews.com/news/geisinger-gets-type-2-diabetes-under-control.

National Kidney Foundation. 2021. "Health Disparities." Updated June 21. www.kidney.org/advocacy/legislative-priorities/health-disparities.

North Carolina Health News. 2015. "The Small-Town Doc with Big Ideas." Published April 14. www.northcarolinahealthnews.org/2015/04/14/the-small-town-doc-with-big-ideas/.

Physician's Foundation. 2022. *2022 Survey of America's Physicians: Part One of Three; Examining How the Social Drivers of Health Affect the Nation's Physicians and Their Patients*. Published March 22. https://physiciansfoundation.org/physician-and-patient-surveys/the-physicians-foundation-2022-physician-survey-part-1/.

Raths, D. 2019. "New Software Platforms Spring Up to Support Multi-Sector Partnerships." Healthcare Innovation. Published July 26. www.hcinnovationgroup.com/population-health-management/social-determinants-of-health/article/21089655/new-software-platforms-spring-up-to-support-multisector-partnerships.

Reuter, E. 2021. "CityBlock, a Primary Care Startup Focused on Underserved Communities, Passes $1 Billion Valuation."

MedCity News. Published December 10. https://medcitynews
.com/2020/12/cityblock-a-primary-care-startup-focused-on
-underserved-communities-passes-1-billion-valuation/.

Song, Z., X. Zhang, L. J. Patterson, L. Barnes, and D. A. Haas.
2021. "Racial and Ethnic Disparities in Hospitalization Outcomes Among Medicare Beneficiaries During the COVID-19
Pandemic." *JAMA Health Forum* 2 (12): e214223. https://doi
.org/10.1001/jamahealthforum.2021.4223.

Spolar, C. 2021. "Data Science Proved What Pittsburgh's Black
Leaders Knew: Racial Disparities Compound COVID Risk."
Kaiser Health News. Published December 7. www.medscape
.com/viewarticle/964282.

Terry, K. 2021a. "AMA Announces Major Commitment to Health
Equity." WebMD. Published May 13. www.webmd.com/a-to
-z-guides/news/20210513/ama-announces-major-commitment
-to-health-equity.

———. 2021b. "Study Identifies Racial Differences in Patient
Safety in Hospitals." WebMD. Published July 26. www.webmd
.com/a-to-z-guides/news/20210726/racial-differences-patient
-safety-hospitals.

———. 2020. *Physician-Led Healthcare Reform: A New Approach
to Medicare for All.* Washington, DC: American Association for
Physician Leadership.

———. 2017. "Why Physicians Must Step Up, Address Social
Determinants of Health." *Medical Economics*, February 25. www
.medicaleconomics.com/health-law-and-policy/why-physicians
-must-step-address-social-determinants-health.

Zambrana, R. E., and D. R. Williams. 2022. "The Intellectual Roots
of Current Knowledge on Racism and Health: Relevance to
Policy and The National Equity." *Health Affairs* 41 (2): 163–70.
https://doi.org/10.1377/hlthaff.2021.01439.

CHAPTER 9

"An Honest Mistake" by The Bravery

Don't look at me that way / It was an honest mistake.

THE GREAT MAJORITY of physicians regard every patient as if they were a family member. We want to ensure that mistakes don't happen. Obstetricians are especially attuned to this, because a mistake in our field affects three lives—the mother's, the baby's, and the doctor's. But "no room for error" is a maxim in diagnostics, treatment, and prevention in all aspects of medicine. We all went into healthcare intending to "do no harm," as we swear in the Hippocratic oath that we dutifully recite during graduation. If Hippocrates had been a DJ, he might have started his oath with Gladys Knight and the Pips' "I Don't Want to Do Wrong."

Yet the system is often byzantine, there is never enough time, and the processes have become way too "Complicated," as Avril Lavigne titled her 2002 song. In some cases, we don't even know how to define quality and safety; in others it's hard to determine whether the individual or the system is the main cause of error.

Patient safety, strictly defined, is "the absence of preventable harm to patients and the prevention of unnecessary harm by healthcare professionals" (Vaismoradi et al. 2020). If we use that definition, safety was improving significantly in the United States before the COVID-19 pandemic. In the last couple of years, this upward trend has been reversed in some respects. Safety will undoubtedly improve again after healthcare organizations recover from the sequelae of the pandemic, such as staff shortages and financial downturns. But experts say that the healthcare industry still has a long way to go to protect patients from harm with a "zero defect" goal.

In their national action plan, the National Steering Committee for Patient Safety (2020), a group of 27 organizations, stated, "Important progress has been made in the reduction of preventable harm" since the Institute of Medicine published *To Err Is Human* in 2000. "But the amount of patient harm is still unacceptably high."

To Err Is Human: Building a Safer Health System, the landmark report that launched the modern patient safety movement, estimated that up to 98,000 Americans were dying annually as the result of medical errors in hospitals (Institute of Medicine 2000). Subsequent estimates ranged up to four times that number. Relying on data from Johns Hopkins researchers, hospital rating firm the Leapfrog Group estimated there were 160,000 preventable deaths in US hospitals in 2018, compared to 205,000 in 2015 (Austin and Derk 2019).

Besides mistakes that lead to death, many other kinds of medical errors occur in acute-care hospitals. In 2006, for example, one wrong-site surgery occurred in every 113,000 procedures (Page 2021). While it's believed that these egregious mistakes are now rarer, they still occur. An estimated 400,000 preventable adverse drug events still happen in US hospitals each year, despite the advent of electronic drug checkers, and 1 in 31 hospitalized patients still contracts a hospital-acquired infection, according to the US Agency for Healthcare Research and Quality (AHRQ 2019).

In the view of Patricia McGaffigan, RN, vice president of patient safety programs at the Institute for Healthcare Improvement (IHI), progress on these issues has been limited by health systems' insufficient attention to systemic issues that contribute to patient harm. While the incidence of some widespread problems such as central line infections has declined, she told *HealthLeaders* that "the approach is relatively reactionary and focused on fixing the circumscribed things. Particularly at the point of care, it has ignored the systemic issues that continue to allow fault lines in healthcare to prevail" (Ward 2019).

THE EVOLUTION OF SYSTEMS THINKING

To Err Is Human argued that the bulk of medical errors were less the result of individual actions than of deficient safety systems in hospitals. Starting from that point, and spurred by a host of patient complaints, the industry began to embrace the systems approach starting in 2000, says Kedar Mate, MD, president and CEO of IHI.

"The health systems responded with diligent safety analyses and developed infrastructure that was capable of identifying where there were vulnerable care moments and putting in place fixes that responded to those things," he recalled when we spoke.

"Most hospitals now have quality and safety teams; we have patient safety officers that were developed during this time; we gave those individuals goals around certain kinds of harms such as infections, falls and pressure injuries. We also trained professionals to address those problems, and they did what they were trained to do. They brought high-reliability methods to the challenge at hand."

In addition, he noted, "The federal government eventually helped by adding incentives and disincentives to mobilize more support for these efforts." For example, the Centers for Medicare & Medicaid Services (CMS) imposed penalties on hospitals for excessive readmissions and hospital-acquired infections. "But that wasn't the originating point. The originating point for the work was when we realized harm was being systematically created in our health systems—not because anybody *intended* to create harm, but because we hadn't geared our *systems* to avoid harm."

IHI also contributed notably to this movement. Under the leadership of founder Donald Berwick, MD, who later served as administrator of CMS, IHI convened a series of hospital collaboratives that dealt with specific safety issues. Mate believes these efforts paid off. "When you get 20 or 50 organizations around a table, trading information about how best to avoid an infection, and how to prevent it in the future, the wisdom of the crowd is better than the wisdom of the individual. We learned much faster about how to improve safety than we would have ever learned in the absence of those kinds of collaboratives."

Radical collaboration between competing health systems can greatly improve safety. A collaboration among safety officers of Philadelphia health systems, for example, made it much easier for us to share those learnings when we were faced with the challenges brought on by the pandemic. Those ongoing quarterly meetings among safety leaders turned into weekly meetings among all the major players, including not only the safety officers but also the infectious disease leaders, chief nursing officers, chief medical officers, and CEOs.

The 2019 AHRQ report provided details on the strides that healthcare organizations had made in improving patient safety using this approach. From 2000 to 2017, the agency said, there had been gains in nearly two-thirds of patient safety measures in acute, post-acute, and ambulatory care. Hospital safety improved on nine metrics and was unchanged on three. The largest improvements in acute care were seen in four areas:

- Inpatient adverse events in adults receiving knee replacement.
- Hospital patients with certain adverse drug events.
- Inpatient adverse events in adults receiving hip joint replacement due to degenerative conditions.
- Adult surgery patients with postoperative pneumonia events.

Some other specific areas were singled out for notable improvement:

- In 2016, 4.9 percent of patients receiving a hip joint replacement experienced adverse events, versus nearly 8 percent in 2010.
- From 2014 to 2017, there was a 20 percent drop in some hospital-acquired conditions, including adverse drug events and *C. difficile* infections.

- The percentage of patients who contracted pneumonia after selected surgeries decreased from 1.8 percent in 2009 to 1.2 percent in 2016.

Despite the increased cooperation among health systems during the pandemic, COVID-19 reversed much of the progress in safety improvements because hospitals were overfilled, clinicians were overstressed, and some safety rules were ignored in the rush to treat very sick and dying patients.

Writing in the *New England Journal of Medicine* in February 2022, CMS officials said they had observed deterioration on multiple patient safety metrics since the start of the pandemic. For example, central line infections, which had dropped by 31 percent in the five years before the pandemic, jumped 28 percent in the second quarter of 2020, compared to the prior-year period. At the same time, skilled nursing facilities, which had also been slammed by COVID-19, saw rates of falls causing major injury increase by 17.4 percent and rates of pressure ulcers grow by 41.8 percent. Commenting on these developments, the authors said, "The fact that the pandemic degraded patient safety so quickly and severely suggests that our health care system lacks a sufficiently resilient safety culture and infrastructure" (Fleischer et al. 2022).

Mate concurs. "What happened during the pandemic indicates that, although we'd built those response mechanisms, we hadn't institutionalized them, we hadn't made them as highly reliable as we'd thought. That's the problem we need to address." The IHI president emphasizes the need to double down on "whole system safety. That starts with an effective quality and safety plan, based on the acceptable level of risk in a community. Healthcare, by definition, involves risk. We're dealing with highly vulnerable individuals and using powerful tools, including surgical procedures and medications. They can make people healthier but also entail great risk. So how we manage our healthcare systems and how we manage risk are really important."

In Mate's view, this means that "when something goes wrong, we might have to plan and operationalize a fix, but we won't always get it right. We need to learn proactively and take the lessons from that learning and feed them back into the design of the system to avoid future errors and harm to patients and families."

INDIVIDUAL RESPONSIBILITY

While systems thinking still holds sway in the patient safety movement, there has also been an increasing emphasis on the responsibility of individual clinicians in certain areas. About 10 years after *To Err Is Human*, Wachter and Pronovost (2009) published an influential paper titled "Balancing 'No Blame' with Accountability in Patient Safety" in the *New England Journal of Medicine*. The authors said that although system changes such as electronic drug interaction checking and surgical safety checklists had prevented a lot of errors, some healthcare leaders had begun to question the dominance of the "no blame" paradigm.

As an example of this shift, Wachter and Pronovost noted an emerging consensus that clinicians should be held accountable for a failure to wash their hands while providing patient care, which had caused countless infections. Many healthcare organizations, they said, had treated this as a systems problem, initiating hand hygiene campaigns and installing hand-gel dispensers all over their hospitals. "Despite these efforts, most hospitals continue to have hand-hygiene rates that range from 30 to 70%, and few have sustained rates over 80%." In their view, these poor results indicated that hand washing was no longer a systems problem and could be solved only by holding clinicians accountable.

The authors made a similar argument about other "common-sense" safety practices, such as using a checklist to reduce blood-stream infections, marking the surgical site to prevent wrong-site surgery, and performing a pre-op "time-out." These actions are recommended by most safety authorities and required by hospital accreditors, they noted, yet many physicians disregard, or even dismiss, such practices. They attributed much of hospitals' reluctance to discipline noncompliant doctors to the fact that most of them didn't work for the health system. In contrast, hospitals were able to deal with noncompliant nurses and pharmacists because they were employed by the organization.

In my view, the "individual versus system" issue in patient safety (as UB40 sang, "Don't Blame Me") goes much deeper. Much of my research over the past 20 years has concerned what makes physicians different from other people in regard to how we handle mandatory processes or changes. Because of how we select and educate physicians in the United States, our culture revolves around autonomy, competitiveness, and hierarchy (see chapter 10). This training has a direct impact on patient safety.

No Delta or American Airlines pilot would ever say, "I have this corporate preflight checklist, but I'm going to use my own." If pilots had to wash their hands within 10 minutes before every flight, they would do just that. As physicians, we have been told that we are "captains of the ship" for so long that we often reject and even resent anyone else telling us what we have to do. Anecdotally, however, I have noticed some positive signs among younger physicians who have seen the results of this kind of behavior among their teachers and its effects on patients and providers.

Today, hospitals employ nearly half of US physicians (Terry 2019), but it's unclear whether any more of them are being disciplined for infractions of safety rules. If they are, it's probably less because of their employment status than because of changes in payment rules. For example, let's say a patient had surgery and was readmitted for a wound revision. In the past, both the hospital and the physician were able to charge for that wound revision. Then payers began refusing to pay for that kind of readmission, and CMS imposed fines for excessive readmissions and hospital-acquired infections. As a result, hospital managers realized that the sloppiness of some surgeons was costing them money. So, some hospitals started to tell physicians, "That's going to affect whether I want to continue to employ you."

THE RISE OF "JUST CULTURE"

In general, says Mate, IHI has adopted a "just culture" rather than a "no blame" approach to individual responsibility. Just culture, he explains, "is a tool that allows us to share responsibility for safety across all parties that are part of the accident, error, or event. It's not about blaming and shaming. Rather, we're seeking to understand the relative contribution of human and system dynamics and then to understand the motivations of the individual and the way in which that error took place: Is this at-risk behavior, reckless behavior? Is it intentional harm? These are very different situations, and they call for very different actions."

The just culture classification of safety events, he says, "includes inadvertent human errors—at-risk behavior, where people make choices without recognizing the risk or believing it's real—and conscious disregard of risks that are very apparent. That's unreasonable or reckless risk. If it's at-risk behavior, there's coaching to help people recognize the risk and why their position is unjustified. If they consciously reject an approach that can reduce the risk of harm, the next level may be to discipline the individual."

I view the situation similarly, but with a slight difference. I see three different aspects of safety that require different solutions. The first consists of safety issues where there's something wrong with the process. In that case, you have to change the system or change the process. Second, some doctors don't follow evidence-based practice and need counseling. And third, there are some irresponsible doctors who may have to be disciplined.

When I was in practice 15 years ago, systems issues predominated. That part has improved because health systems created a safety infrastructure. The combination of folks either not following protocols or saying "that's not how I do it" or "that's not how I trained," especially among senior physicians, is probably the bigger issue today. If you've been practicing for 30–40 years, chances are you're not going to change.

What makes this worse is that, by virtue of their seniority, those physicians are often in leadership and teaching roles. It made me proud when I trained a resident who was not afraid to stand up to an attending when they didn't follow safety protocols. When I was an ob-gyn department chair, and also when I was dean of two different medical schools, I always supported those younger physicians as long as they made their stand privately and respectfully!

There's a Process for That

My esteemed colleague Jonathan Gleason, who used to be chief clinical officer at Jefferson and now holds an expanded post at Prisma, believes that medical errors caused by a doctor's refusal to follow safety protocols are rare, and that this scenario forms a very small portion of the opportunity to improve patient safety. When a physician does violate safety rules, he notes, hospitals have a process for dealing with the situation.

"There is a peer review process in every hospital that is outlined by The Joint Commission and CMS, whereby a physician's practice has to be monitored on an ongoing basis," he explains. "If there are issues identified, they have to go into a separate process called a focused practice—a professional practice evaluation. That happens regardless of whether the doctor is employed or independent.

"That process is a function of the medical staff, which is independent of the hospital. That's how it's designed by The Joint Commission. Certainly, hospitals could have influence. But I'd argue that hospitals are committed to having great doctors and practicing safely. Everyone is aware of the famous 'Dr. Death' case in Texas. Nobody wants that to happen at their facility."

The key to safety improvement, Gleason stresses, is strong physician leadership. "Whether they're employed by hospitals or not, the way to lead physicians is through transparency around quality and safety. At Jefferson, we won the National Patient Safety award, and I did not focus at all on" finding rogue physicians. "It was all about building safety systems."

High-Reliability Systems

Other high-risk industries such as nuclear power and aviation have long applied the concept of the high-reliability organization (HRO) to reduce the chance of errors to near zero. While this idea was introduced in healthcare about 15 years ago, it has been slow to spread (Butcher 2021).

The organizational elements required to become an HRO, according to IHI, include leadership, psychological safety, accountability, teamwork and communication, negotiation, transparency, reliability, improvement and measurement, and continuous learning (Frankel et al. 2017). At the level of the individual physician, an HRO requires absolute compliance with evidence-based best-practice interventions, such as the five components of care needed to prevent ventilator-associated pneumonia (VAP). Many hospitals have virtually eliminated VAP through the consistent use of this safety bundle, yet VAP continues to be one of the infections that patients most frequently acquire in intensive care units (Butcher 2021).

Healthcare organizations are the only organizations that require high reliability that never test the competence of their practitioners. When you take a flight, you can be certain that your pilot is technically qualified, as I pointed out in chapter 7; but when you have surgery, you don't know whether your surgeon is technically competent by objective and tested parameters. Surgeons used to be board certified for a specified time, after which they had to pass a recertification exam to renew their certificates. Now the American Board of Surgery lets many surgeons assess their own cognitive competence in an online process that has no technical competence component, and their board certification is permanent.

THE SAFETY CHALLENGES OF NURSING

While doctors make diagnostic and treatment decisions, they may spend only 30–45 minutes a day with even a critically ill hospitalized patient (Phillips, Malliaris, and Bakerjian 2021). In contrast, nurses are frequently at the patient's bedside and regularly interact with physicians, pharmacists, families, and other care team members. They are responsible for observing the patient's condition and communicating that to other members of the care team. They monitor patients for clinical deterioration and detect safety errors and near misses.

For all these reasons, it's vital to have enough nurses caring for hospitalized patients. "Nurses' vigilance at the bedside is essential to their ability to ensure patient safety," Phillips and colleagues noted. "It is logical, therefore, that assigning increasing numbers of patients eventually compromises a nurse's ability to provide safe care. There are many key factors that influence nurse staffing such as patient acuity, admissions numbers, transfers, discharges, staff skill mix and expertise, physical layout of the nursing unit, and availability of technology and other resources."

Studies have shown that as the number of patients per nurse rises, the risk of patient safety events, morbidity, and mortality also rises. As of March 2021, however, only 16 states had passed legislation regulating nurse staffing; most states did not specify nurse-to-patient ratios. The sole exception was California. CMS requires hospitals to ensure adequate numbers of registered nurses (RNs), licensed vocational nurses, and other clinical staff, but doesn't require specific ratios. Nursing homes typically have far fewer RNs to patients, despite the many benefits of a high staffing ratio for patients, nurses, and the facility (Phillips, Malliaris, and Bakerjian 2021).

While the statistics and importance of nurse staffing are impressive in themselves, one of the tenets that has connected the private practice phase of my career and my leadership roles at Drexel, USF, and Jefferson is the importance of nurse leadership and radical communication with the nursing staff. I still tell pregnant friends who are moving to a new city that the best way to find an obstetrician is to ask the charge nurse in labor and delivery.

One of the best decisions my team and I made during the pandemic was the decision not to furlough or lay off staff despite the financial tsunami overwhelming our hospitals. While that was a huge financial cost and ran counter to the rest of the industry, our quality results during that difficult time were some of the best in the nation. So, lesson #1 for aspiring health system CEOs who want a long, successful career: Your nursing staff is the heart of your system—take care of your heart!

Labor-Management Relations

Much has been written about the increased workload of nurses during the pandemic, but many hospitals have long been plagued by inadequate staffing. That is understandable in rural areas that have a shortage of healthcare professionals. But the RN workforce in the United States grew from about 1 million RNs in 1982 to 3.2 million in 2020—roughly 100 RNs per 1,000 residents nationwide (Auerbach et al. 2022). In 2017, the US Department of Health and Human Services said there would be enough RNs to meet the nation's health needs until 2030 (Terry 2021).

However, growth in the RN workforce plateaued in the first 15 months of the pandemic. For all of 2021, the total supply of RNs decreased by more than 100,000—the largest drop in at least four decades. Increasingly, younger nurses and nurses in training are leaving the profession. This is not a good sign for the future or for patient safety (Auerbach et al. 2022).

From the viewpoint of nurse unions, insufficient nurse staffing in hospitals is largely the fault of the facility owners. For example, National Nurses United, a California-based union with 175,000 members, said in September 2021 that hospitals were to blame for the nursing shortage that arose during the pandemic. The inadequate supply of nurses, the union said, was the direct result of hospitals' tendencies, long before COVID, to understaff units and shifts to maximize profits or, in the case of not-for-profits, "excessive revenue." Then, when the pandemic struck, hospitals cut staff from units that had a temporarily low patient census because people were avoiding hospitals.

Responding to the union's charges, Robyn Begley, DNP, RN, chief nursing officer and senior vice president of workforce for the American Hospital Association, told Medscape Medical News, "Shortages of critical healthcare workers were projected long before the pandemic began . . . . Hospital and health system leaders have used a variety of approaches to recruit, retain, and support their workforce" (Terry 2021).

One of those methods has been to offer very high reimbursement to travel nurses. In 2021, travel nurses were being paid $3,500 per week or more, almost triple nurses' median pay of $63,000 per year. Not surprisingly, many nurses left hospitals to work for travel nurse agencies (Terry 2021).

Unfortunately, this development has not been conducive to patient safety. Between travel nurses and nurses leaving the profession we've had a turnover tsunami, and the people who are exiting are often the older, more experienced nurses. High-quality nursing relies on instinct, intelligence, and experience, and numbers do not tell the whole story. There are new nurses, but during the pandemic some nurses just one year out of school were leading shifts. Moreover, nurses who take time-limited assignments in a particular hospital don't understand the safety systems of that facility as well as nurses who have worked there for years.

Nursing turnover is also complicated because, as mentioned in previous chapters, hospitals are dealing with high administrative overload, high fixed costs, and decreased margins, all of which have been exacerbated by the pandemic. Paying full-time nurses higher wages would increase labor costs and make it difficult for hospitals to stay financially viable.

Technology and strategic partnerships can have both an immediate and a long-term effect on these challenges. Strongline, which was originally conceived at Jefferson, was a response to the national crisis of workplace violence against nurses and frontline healthcare workers that escalated during the pandemic. Nurses, clinicians, security teams, and IT leaders collaborated with Strongline to build a tool that allows staff to discreetly alert hospital security and nearby staff when they are under duress or need help with de-escalation. During the pandemic, our ability to use technology *and* value-driven human resources policies was an important factor in maintaining nurse and employee morale at Jefferson.

Error Reports as a Safety Tool

Transparency is one of the basic tenets of the systems approach to patient safety. To prevent repeated errors, clinicians are encouraged to report the mistakes they see to hospital safety committees or at the morbidity and mortality (M&M) conferences in which physicians discuss serious safety incidents within the confines of the peer review process. But not everybody in the hospital reports what they see.

A 2008 study by the US Department of Health and Human Services found, for example, that surgical staffers failed to report 86 percent of adverse safety events to their hospitals. This was not too surprising, considering that when The Joint Commission released its universal protocol to prevent wrong-site surgeries in 2004, surgeons and their teams didn't usually report adverse events (Page 2021).

Hospitals are required to report "sentinel events"—serious medical errors or unexpected outcomes—to The Joint Commission, and the number reported has increased markedly. In 2020, The Joint Commission received reports of 794 sentinel events across all care settings, versus 597 in 2005 (The Joint Commission 2021). Still, considering there are about 5,000 hospitals in the United States, the 2020 number may strike some observers as an undercount.

Even within the constraints of peer review, where mistakes are not publicly revealed, the likelihood of hospital staff routinely reporting medical errors depends largely on the type of institution where they work. In my experience at a few academic medical centers, mistakes were generally reported at M&M conferences. Interns and residents were expected to bring these episodes to the attention of their superiors. The better community hospitals probably operate the same way. But in some hospitals the medical staff bylaws are designed to protect the doctors, so if a physician has two or three bad cases in a row, and they're reported, the most likely proctor is the doctor's best friend on the medical staff. In some cases, the incidents are never even reported.

Peer review needs to be a full and closed-loop process. Every sentinel or negative event must be reviewed; systems must be redesigned based on what has been learned; and the rare cases of repeated individual recklessness must be dealt with in a transparent and objective manner. As a leader of several healthcare organizations, my criterion was that if I would not trust a physician on the medical staff to treat a member of my own family, I needed to reeducate, retrain, or remove that clinician. (Of course, that is before attorneys get involved, which is another "complicated" aspect of the physician responsibility story.)

Reporting and Accountability

As noted earlier, transparency about medical errors has been improving slowly but can be severely affected when there's any chance of a safety incident leading to a malpractice suit or a criminal charge. That reality was brought home to many clinicians in 2022 when RaDonda Vaught, a former nurse at Vanderbilt University Medical Center, was convicted of negligent homicide and abuse of an impaired adult after making a medication error that caused the death of a 75-year-old patient in 2017. She was sentenced to three years of probation and stripped of her nursing license (Bean and Carbajal 2022; DePeau-Wilson 2022).

Vaught's conviction sent a tremor through the healthcare industry. IHI said it had damaged the progress made in patient safety because it would reduce transparency and accountability. "We know from decades of work in hospitals and other care settings that most medical errors result from flawed systems, not reckless practitioners. We also know that systems can learn from errors and improve, but only when those systems encourage reporting, transparently acknowledge their mistakes, and are held accountable for those errors" (Bean 2022).

Elaborating on this statement, Mate says, "If the doctor or nurse no longer feels comfortable about reporting the error because they face criminal prosecution, or even if they feel their supervisor might punish them or they might be fired, then we lose all of the opportunity as a system to understand what happened and to take the steps necessary to prevent the harm from occurring again. In situations like the one at Vanderbilt, we're losing the ability to prevent future errors." The correct paradigm to follow, he says, is what the Federal Aviation Administration does after an air accident. "It sets up an investigation, and whatever it finds, it distributes that information widely, and everybody adopts the change in practice across their systems."

In the Vanderbilt case, Mate adds, the nurse made her mistake partly because of the design of the medication cabinet she used. She entered two letters of the medication's generic name into the machine and it came up with something else that she mistakenly drew out. Safety advocates have long called for requiring nurses to type in at least five letters of a drug's name when using electronic medication cabinets—a feature their manufacturers have belatedly introduced.

"If this was an FAA investigation, that finding would become universal across all airlines immediately when a conclusion like that was reached. We don't have a mechanism like that in healthcare," Mate notes.

OUTPATIENT SAFETY ISSUES

There are plenty of medical errors in ambulatory settings, where most medical care occurs, but less research has been done on this than on inpatient safety issues. The National Academy of Medicine has postulated that adverse safety events may be more common in ambulatory than in acute-care settings (Shekelle et al. 2016).

In most cases, mistakes in ambulatory care are of a different type than the errors in hospitals, says Mate. Whereas hospital safety incidents usually stem from patient treatment, those on the outpatient side most often involve diagnostic errors, failure to diagnose, or miscommunication.

Studies of closed malpractice claims by The Doctors Company, a leading liability insurance carrier, support this observation. The Closed Claims Studies on the company's website, which highlight reoccurring patient risks and avoidance strategies for clinicians, include studies of "missed or delayed diagnoses" of prostate cancer and heart attacks. Among the contributing factors for the missed heart attacks were false "assumptions, lack of a thorough history and physical, communication failures, and failure to recognize atypical signs and symptoms."

The traditional visit-based model of ambulatory care has potential safety gaps (Shekelle et al. 2016). Weeks or months may separate visits or referrals or diagnostic studies, which can affect patient safety. Also, physicians are under pressure to see a lot of patients, and smaller practices lack resources for effective coordination of care.

Most of the time, ambulatory patients manage their own care. They decide when to seek care from physicians and whether to follow doctors' recommendations. For people with chronic diseases, this advice might involve an extensive regimen of medications, diet, and exercise. When patients have difficulty with self-management, they are at risk for adverse events. Safety issues frequently arise because providers or health systems fail to provide patients or caregivers with the knowledge or skills they need to safely manage their conditions. For example, patients may err in self-administering medications or in interpreting their symptoms.

Shekelle and colleagues (2016) found that there were few validated safety measures in ambulatory care. Even if there were, ambulatory care is decentralized, making it difficult to measure what providers are doing. Experts they interviewed identified five major safety issues in ambulatory care settings: medication safety, diagnosis, transitions among providers in ambulatory settings, referrals from one provider to another, and management of test results. There was agreement that each of these issues is complex, multifaceted, and important for patient safety. Improving communication with patients and families could reduce adverse outcomes related to diagnoses and medication safety, they said.

One other factor is partly responsible for the uneven safety record of ambulatory care, Gleason says: the relative lack of safety regulations. He believes this has led to complacency and poor transparency about safety issues in outpatient practices. "Hospitals are required to have a safety event reporting platform, but that's not a requirement in the ambulatory space. I've built safety management systems for three health systems, and in all of them, I've established safety systems in the ambulatory environment for the first time. Some of these clinics are 100 years old, and they never had a safety system."

Other Outpatient Settings

There isn't enough space in this chapter to discuss safety in other outpatient settings such as skilled nursing facilities, ambulatory surgery centers, and home healthcare. A few observations will have to suffice: First, safety regulations and the scrutiny of providers vary by care setting. Hospitals are the most regulated, followed by ambulatory surgery centers, nursing homes, and outpatient clinics.

Second, skilled nursing facilities continue to have serious quality issues. In 2015, deficiencies in federal regulatory compliance were found an average of 8.6 times per facility—a rate similar to those documented in 2005 and 2010. More than one in five nursing homes received notices for serious quality violations in 2015. "These deficiencies include causing harm or jeopardy, or the potential for harm or jeopardy" (Harrington et al. 2017, 3).

As previously noted, higher nurse staff levels are associated with better care quality. But state laws do not require what experts consider to be minimum clinical staffing of nursing homes (Consumer Voice 2021). In 2022, the Biden administration proposed a national minimum staff requirement for skilled nursing facilities funded through Medicare and Medicaid (Hsu 2022).

HEALTH IT SAFETY

Digitization in the healthcare industry since 2010 has had a huge impact on patient safety. Some of the changes have been beneficial, while others have been less helpful or even harmful. The shift to electronic health records (EHRs) and other health IT systems, above all, has underlined the need for human factors engineering to minimize the risk of patient harm resulting from dysfunctional interactions between humans and computers.

One of the greatest benefits of EHRs has been the instant availability of patient records, says Dean Sittig, PhD, a professor at the University of Texas Health Science Center in Houston. Paper records were sometimes missing when a patient showed up in a doctor's office. Now providers are always sure they can find the records—as long as the power and internet are working and the system hasn't been hacked.

Drug interaction checkers are another EHR component that many people—myself included—have regarded as beneficial to safety. But research has shown that these features have significant holes. EHR systems used in hospitals failed to fire alerts for up to one-third of potentially harmful drug interactions and other medication errors simulated in one study (Terry 2020). Not that alerts have made patients much safer. While it's true that EHRs will stop physicians from ordering, say, a medication at 10 times the normal dose, physicians and other licensed prescribers can still prescribe the wrong medication, the wrong dose, or the wrong duration without triggering an alert, depending on how their EHR is set up.

This "EHR-ization" of healthcare, while doing much to prevent human errors, can also lead to an increased reliance on computers to override any mistakes. In some cases, the default itself is a problem. For example, the EHR at Jefferson had a default setting that prompted physicians to prescribe oxycodone, a powerful opioid, for seven days after hip replacement procedures. The system didn't recognize that some patients had addiction issues and that a week's worth of oxycodone could readdict them. Physicians could override that prompt, but they had to make a conscious decision to do it. So we changed the default in the EHR to three days or no days.

Gleason, who was involved in that episode when he was at Jefferson, cites other errors that might be averted by proper EHR configuration. "Let's say it was possible for an adult dose of insulin to be erroneously ordered in the neonatal ICU, and that if the drug showed up in the NICU, the nurse might miss the error and deliver the wrong dose to the baby. Before that could happen, I'd make it impossible for someone in the NICU to order that concentration of the drug."

Savvy health IT directors and chief clinical officers know how to reconfigure EHRs to match the parameters they consider safe, but the default settings in EHRs are designed by their manufacturers. The vendors leave it up to the providers to change those settings, says Gleason. "In effect, the EHR maker says, 'You've got a medical license and can order anything you want. So, we're going to make every option available to you, and the responsibility is yours.'"

Physicians can be sued or can even lose their medical license if they cause serious harm to a patient. But EHR developers may have little to worry about if patients are injured due to defects in their products. EHR safety is not effectively regulated, Gleason says. In fact, "health care information technology (HIT) vendors enjoy a contractual and legal structure that renders them virtually liability free" because of "hold harmless" clauses in their contracts with providers (Koppel and Kreda 2009). The 21st Century Cures Act requires, as a condition of government certification, that "health IT developers do not prohibit or restrict communications about certain aspects of the performance of health IT," including safety (US Department of Health and Human Services 2020, 21), but it's unclear whether that makes it illegal for EHR vendors to include "hold harmless" clauses in contracts.

Alert Fatigue as a Cause of Errors

Even when a drug interaction checker triggers an appropriate alarm, the physician might not pay attention to it. In fact, it's unusual if a physician does pay attention. Drug alerts in clinical decision support "appear to result in almost no benefit" (Bates et al. 2022). In one study, physicians responded to none of 5,000 warnings about renal dosing, and in another, drug-drug interaction alerts were regularly overridden. Sittig explains why.

> The EHR issues a huge number of alerts. They're true alerts, but they don't necessary relate to the patient they're supposed to be for. For instance, if I tried to order Ativan for a 30-year-old, an alert might pop up saying, 'Ativan shouldn't be given in the elderly.' That's true. But the system didn't take the patient's age into account before putting out the alert. So the next thing that comes up says this patient is allergic to this medication. But the doctor has already gotten one alert that was wrong, so he or she ignores that one too. The first override was appropriate, the second wasn't. We're putting up so many alerts that we've lost the trust of physicians.

In hospitals, electronic monitoring systems emit a variety of beeps and other sounds that warn nurses and doctors about concerning vital signs in patients. Partly because of alarm fatigue, the clinicians ignore many of these alerts. As a result, this kind of telemetry monitoring made ECRI's top 10 patient safety hazards list for 2022 (Terry 2022).

Electronic monitoring can also create another problem: If nurses and doctors wait for an alarm to tell them something has gone wrong, safety can be compromised. When I used to deliver babies on a regular basis, I'd go into every room and spend time with the patient, and I knew the state of that patient. When clinicians depend on machines or centralized monitoring to tell them that, it's a negative safety factor.

Sittig points to another drawback of interconnected systems within hospitals and across healthcare organizations: A mistake in one component, such as computerized physician order entry, can be quickly replicated across the system and affect a lot of patients before anyone notices it. "The computer makes it easy and efficient to do things. And if a computer makes an error happen, you can make a lot of errors very fast. If you get a bad order set with a bad default value in it, you can make a lot of errors very quickly. Because a lot of people will accept the default value and not notice it."

HUMAN FACTORS ENGINEERING

The situations just described are examples of faulty health IT systems that put patients at risk. Some other faulty systems in hospitals have easy and foolproof fixes. When I was a practicing obstetrician, for example, one of the great risks in delivering infants was mixing up the anesthesia tube with the oxygen tube. It was widely believed that some mothers were dying because they were getting too much oxygen during delivery. It turned out, however, that the anesthetic agent was responsible. Anesthetists were mixing up the two agents because the hose connectors looked similar. Hospitals began using circular connectors for oxygen and square connectors for anesthetics, so it was impossible to make a mistake—which should be the goal of all safety systems.

This change is an example of human factors engineering. Gleason believes this discipline could solve many of the safety problems in healthcare. "Are pilots who crash planes bad pilots? That's not how the airline industry transformed safety. They just made it impossible to crash a plane. So, we need a better airplane." Many of the systems used in hospitals today, he says, "facilitate harm. They're passive systems, and they need to be active." Ultimately, the problem is that "we haven't designed systems that are geared to human capabilities and human limitations and that facilitate them doing the right thing and prevent them from making errors."

Sittig agrees with this approach. For example, he believes many medication errors could be prevented if health systems adopted "indication-based" prescribing. "Instead of physicians starting with a medication name in the prescribing process, they'd start with what they wanted to treat—say, hypertension. If they typed 'hypertension' first, the computer could help them. It could say, 'here's the best medication for hypertension.'" The list wouldn't include dangerous drugs the physician might order accidentally.

Human factors engineering of this kind could make healthcare much safer, Gleason says. But it's not enough to require EHR developers to include human factors in product design. "Every hospital and health system is unique and different in how they do things. They have to be able to customize things on their end as well. So, the expertise should be in both the hospitals and the EHR companies."

CONCLUSION

While we sometimes get caught up in discussions about measurement, patient safety and healthcare quality are literally life-and-death issues, and both should be included in the ratings of physician groups and hospitals that were discussed in chapter 6. As with quality scores, safety ratings should be expressed in simple, easy-to-understand terms: for example, the term "bed sores" should be used instead of "pressure ulcers," so that patients and caregivers can make decisions based on terms they understand.

My guess is that by now you have come to the same conclusion we did about safety in doctors' offices: More validated safety measures are needed in ambulatory care. Gleason points out that the biggest safety issue in healthcare is diagnostic errors, including missed diagnoses, and those most often occur in physician offices. We should get the National Quality Forum and other measure-making bodies to start doing the hard work it will take to measure the prevalence of diagnostic errors.

While individual physicians are not responsible for most patient harms, physician culture needs to be held accountable for certain kinds of errors. For instance, Sittig points out, most physicians would not favor his idea of indication-based prescribing because they'd think it was a waste of time to pick out a diagnosis before ordering a medication. "I am the captain of the ship" and "this is how I have always done it" are a major part of the cultural problem preventing greater progress in patient safety.

So, in DJ terms, every physician and nurse starts out with the "I Don't Want to Do Wrong" mindset. Despite that, we are all human and we may always be prone to "An Honest Mistake." The key is to not make it "Complicated" (Avril Lavigne, 2002) to do the right thing and avoid errors. You can "Make It Easy on Yourself" (Jerry Butler, 1962) to strive toward a zero-defect mentality. And while I would not depend on the Ramones for healthcare advice, "Learn to Listen" to teammates and let them advise you if something seems wrong. When the physician listens to the team and recognizes that, as Taking Back Sunday sang in 2002, "There's No 'I' in Team," the patient gets the best care possible, which, after all, is why we went to medical school. As soon as you don a white coat, you are looked up to, and patients give you great latitude and respect when they say "Make Me Feel Better" (Alex Adair, 2014). Now let's all do "The Safety Dance" (Men Without Hats, 1982)!

The next chapter will examine aspects of physician culture that affect our views on healthcare reform and technological change. In addition, I'll discuss how medical education needs to change to prepare doctors for the healthcare system of the future.

REFERENCES

AHRQ (Agency for Healthcare Research and Quality). 2019. National Healthcare Quality and Disparities Report Chartbook on Patient Safety. Published October. AHRQ Pub. No. 19(20)-0070-2-EF. www.ahrq.gov/sites/default/files/wysiwyg/research/findings/nhqrdr/chartbooks/patientsafety/2018qdr-patsaf-chartbook.pdf.

Auerbach, D. I., P. I. Buerhaus, K. Donelan, and D. O. Staiger. 2022. "A Worrisome Drop in the Number of New Nurses." Health Affairs Forefront. Published April 13. www.healthaffairs.org/do/10.1377/forefront.20220412.311784.

Austin, M., and J. Derk. 2019. "Lives Lost, Lives Saved: An Updated Comparative Analysis of Avoidable Deaths at Hospitals Graded by The Leapfrog Group." Armstrong Institute for Patient Safety and Quality at Johns Hopkins Medicine. Published May 2019. www.hospitalsafetygrade.org/media/file/Lives-Saved-White-Paper-FINAL.pdf.

Bates, D. W., H.-Y. Cheng, N. T. Cheung, R. Jew, F. Mir, R. Tamblyn, and Y.-C. Li. 2022. "'Improving Smart Medication Management': An Online Expert Discussion." *BMJ Health & Care Informatics* 29 (1): e100540. https://pubmed.ncbi.nlm.nih.gov/35477691/.

Bean, M. 2022. "Nurse's Conviction Should Be Wake-Up Call for Health System Leaders, IHI Says." *Becker's Hospital Review*, March 31. www.beckershospitalreview.com/patient-safety-outcomes/nurse-s-conviction-should-be-wake-up-call-for-health-system-leaders-ihi-says.html.

Bean, M., and E. Carbajal. 2022. "'We Can't Punish Our Way to Safer Medical Practices': 2 Experts on Criminalization of Medical Errors." *Becker's Hospital Review*, March 1. www.beckershospitalreview.com/patient-safety-outcomes/we-can-t-punish-our-way-to-safer-medical-practices-2-experts-on-criminalization-of-medical-errors.html.

Butcher, L. 2021. "What Physician Leaders Need to Know About High Reliability." American Association for Physician Leadership. Published December 23. www.physicianleaders.org/news /what-physician-leaders-need-to-know-about-high-reliability.

Consumer Voice. 2021. *State Nursing Home Staffing Standards Summary Report*. Published December. https://theconsumervoice .org/uploads/files/issues/CV_StaffingReport.pdf.

DePeau-Wilson, M. 2022. "Nurse Vaught Sentenced for Deadly Medical Error." Medpage Today. Published May 13. www .medpagetoday.com/special-reports/exclusives/98706.

Fleischer, L. A., M. Schreiber, D. Cardo, and A. Srinivasan. 2022. "Health Care Safety During the Pandemic and Beyond—Building a System That Ensures Resilience." *New England Journal of Medicine* 386: 609–11. https://doi.org/10.1056/NEJMp2118285.

Frankel, A., C. Haraden, F. Federico, and J. Lenoci-Edwards. 2017. *A Framework for Safe, Reliable, and Effective Care* (white paper). Institute for Healthcare Improvement. www.ihi.org/resources /Pages/IHIWhitePapers/Framework-Safe-Reliable-Effective -Care.aspx.

Harrington, C., J. M. Weiner, L. Ross, and M. Musumeci. 2017. "Key Issues in Long-Term Services and Supports Quality" (Issue Brief). October 2017. Kaiser Family Foundation. https://files.kff .org/attachment/Issue-Brief-Key-Issues-in-Long-Term-Services -and-Supports-Quality.

Hsu, A. 2022. "Nursing Home Residents Suffer from Staffing Shortages, but the Jobs Are Hard to Fill." *NPR*, April 6. www .npr.org/2022/04/06/1088660155/nursing-home-minimum -staffing-labor-shortage-medicare-medicaid-nurses.

Institute of Medicine. 2000. *To Err Is Human: Building a Safer Health System*. Washington, DC: National Academies Press. https://doi.org/10.17226/9728.

Koppel, R., and D. Kreda. 2009. "Health Care Information Technology Vendors' 'Hold Harmless' Clause." *Journal of the American Medical Association* 301 (12): 1276–78. https://doi.org/10.1001/jama.2009.398.

National Steering Committee for Patient Safety. 2020. *Safer Together: A National Action Plan to Advance Patient Safety.* Institute for Healthcare Improvement. www.ihi.org/SafetyActionPlan.

Page, L. 2021. "Doctors Doing Wrong-Site Surgery: Why Is It Still Happening?" WebMD Health News. Published September 30. www.webmd.com/a-to-z-guides/news/20210930/doctors-wrong-site-surgery.

Phillips, J., A. P. Malliaris, and D. Bakerjian. 2021. "Nursing and Patient Safety" (updated). Patient Safety Network. Agency for Healthcare Research and Quality. Updated April 21. https://psnet.ahrq.gov/primer/nursing-and-patient-safety.

Shekelle, P. G., U. Sarkar, K. Shojania, R. M. Wachter, K. McDonald, A. Motala, P. Smith, L. Zipperer, and R. Shanman. 2016. "Patient Safety in Ambulatory Settings." Technical Briefs, No. 27. Report No. 16(17)-EHC033-EF. Published October. Agency for Healthcare Research and Quality. https://europepmc.org/article/NBK/nbk396055.

Terry, K. 2022. "Staffing Shortages Are Top Patient Safety Concern: Report." *Medscape Medical News*, March 14. www.medscape.com/viewarticle/970187.

———. 2021. "Are Hospitals to Blame for Pandemic Nursing Shortage? It's Complicated." *Medscape Medical News*, September 2. www.medscape.com/viewarticle/958097.

———. 2020. "Hospital EHRs Miss Many Potential Medication Errors: Study." *Medscape Medical News*, May 29. www.medscape.com/viewarticle/931417.

———. 2019. "Hospitals Continue to Acquire More Physician Practices." *Medscape Medical News*, February 22. www.medscape.com/viewarticle/909411.

The Joint Commission. 2021. "Summary Data of Sentinel Events Reviewed by the Joint Commission." Published January 27. www.jointcommission.org/-/media/tjc/documents/resources/patient-safety-topics/sentinel-event/summary-se-report-2020.pdf.

US Department of Health and Human Services. 2020. "21st Century Cures Act: Interoperability, Information Blocking, and the ONC Health IT Certification Program; Final Rule." 45 CFR Parts 170 and 171. RIN 0955-AA01, 21. www.healthit.gov/sites/default/files/cures/2020-03/ONC_Cures_Act_Final_Rule_03092020.pdf.

Vaismoradi M., S. Tella, P. A. Logan, J. Khakurel, and F. Vizcaya-Moreno. 2020. "Nurses' Adherence to Patient Safety Principles: A Systematic Review." *International Journal of Environmental Research and Public Health* 17 (6): 2028. https://doi.org/10.3390/ijerph17062028.

Wachter, R. M., and P. J. Pronovost. 2009. "Balancing 'No Blame' with Accountability in Patient Safety." *New England Journal of Medicine* 361 (14): 1401–6. https://med.fsu.edu/sites/default/files/userFiles/file/NEJMHandwashing.pdf.

Ward, B. 2019. "Q&A: Patient Safety Impact of 'To Err Is Human' at 20th Anniversary." *HealthLeaders*, December 3. www.healthleadersmedia.com/clinical-care/qa-patient-safety-impact-err-human-20th-anniversary.

CHAPTER 10

"You Don't Learn That in School" by The King Cole Trio

You can put away your lessons / Throw away your
books / 'Cause I'm gonna tell you what cooks.

LET ME START by saying I am not advocating for the physicians
of the future to throw away their books. Nor am I saying that traditional science aptitude should not be a major criterion for becoming
a physician. I do believe, though, that we need more than incremental change in how we select and educate physicians and other
healthcare professionals.

With some exceptions, medical schools still choose physicians
based on science GPA, MCAT scores (a multiple-choice test that
assesses your memorization skills), and organic chemistry grades;
yet we are amazed that physicians are not more empathetic, com-
municative, and creative. The competition for a limited number
of medical school slots also determines who becomes a doctor. At
Jefferson, we had over 10,000 people applying for 300 slots, and the
need to win this competition permeates many of the undergraduate
premed schools in the country. It's no wonder that physicians often
find it hard to collaborate in high-powered teams. In contrast, when
I pursued my MBA at Wharton Business School in 1994, we were
told on the first day of class that one of the most important decisions

we would make is who would be in our study group, because many of our grades would be based on the team's output.

In chapter 8, I noted that healthcare inequity for people of color exists partly because there are not enough doctors who look like them and share their culture. Some parents invest $100,000 to get Johnny or Mary three tutors and a Princeton review so that they can "ace the MCATs," while another student of equal ability lacks those resources. In the words of Lily Allen, it's "Not Fair."

The resulting inequity was understandable—though still unfair—when I went to medical school in the 1970s: If I could memorize 19 reasons why you had a headache and another physician could only memorize 15, I was the better doctor. But now every aspect of the differential diagnosis is available in my electronic health record (EHR), my smartphone, or even on Google. It's more important that I'm able to communicate with a patient in a culturally competent manner—a skill that is minimally appreciated as a selection or an advancement parameter in most medical colleges.

In research I did with Wharton professor G. Richard Shell, we found that the way physicians are selected and educated reflects four biases: autonomy, competition, hierarchy, and "non-creativity" (Shell and Klasko 1996). The non-creativity piece is the most interesting. Physicians are as creative as anyone else, but this characteristic is less important to them than strategy, focus, or discipline, according to a survey we did.

Why does that matter? Because the robot that will be standing next to me in a few years will be able to memorize better than I can, but will never be able to understand the human sitting across from us.

This point was driven home to me by a speech by Jack Ma, cofounder of Alibaba, at a World Economic Forum meeting in Davos. Talking about the relationship between people and computers, he said, in essence, that when we created cars, we didn't try to get humans to run faster. When we created planes, we didn't try to get humans to fly. We used machines to expand human capabilities without giving up human control of the machines.

Computers will always be smarter than people, he noted, but will never be as wise.

We took that insight to the next level when I was the dean of the medical college at University of South Florida. In 2011, a cohort of our medical class was enrolled in a program we called SELECT (Scholarly Excellence. Leadership Experiences. Collaborative Training.), which we developed in concert with the Lehigh Valley Health Network in Pennsylvania. This program de-emphasized the traditional parameters of medical training, although there were minimum requirements. We chose students based on self-awareness, empathy, communication skills, and cultural competence.

In a previous survey of young physicians who had graduated from residency in the past three years we had asked, "Did we teach you in medical school what you most needed in your practice?" The answer was a pretty resounding no. They had learned a lot of microbiology, anatomy, and physiology, and how to ace multiple-choice tests, but these young doctors didn't feel they'd learned enough about health equity, public health, healthcare financing, communication, new technologies, and the cost of healthcare.

So we developed the SELECT program, which emphasized some of those skill sets while minimizing (within accreditation standards) some of the pure science multiple-choice skills. That program has endured and has created some excellent, empathetic physicians.

CHANGING MEDICAL EDUCATION AND PHYSICIAN CULTURE

To reform healthcare along the lines proposed in this book, both medical education and physician culture need to change. Today's method of physician training focuses on episodes of acute care rather than on the chronic diseases and social determinants that affect most people's long-term health. In addition, the current model doesn't teach physicians how to manage population health, which will become increasingly important as the industry transitions to value-based care. And, as technology advances and routine care becomes more automated, doctors trained in the current way won't be ready for the new model of care.

The century-old approach to medical education in the United States has produced a physician culture that doesn't meet the needs of twenty-first century healthcare. Instead of physicians who are autonomous, competitive, hierarchical, and noncreative, we need doctors who are creative, flexible, and collaborative, so they can fit into holistic care teams of health and social work professionals. Training must emphasize not only science but also the business and social aspects of healthcare, with a heavy dose of cultural diversity and compassion.

The inadequacies of the current model are painfully evident in US healthcare. "Modern medicine's defining paradigm is evidenced-based diagnosis and treatment of disease and injury," said David W. Johnson and David Nash, MD (2022a) in a series of articles on medical education. "This singular focus blinds orthodox medicine to the compelling national need for population-based healthcare."

To make the leap to the physician culture that population health management requires, argue Johnson and Nash (2022c), "America's clinicians must overcome deeply-ingrained beliefs, behaviors and processes that shape organizational cultures and the practice patterns. They must retool to deliver healthcare services that are effective, efficient, comprehensive, accessible, equitable, integrative, holistic, preventive and promotive."

Medical schools must begin preparing for the future, rather than holding onto a past that is rapidly slipping away. We're building a world where 90 percent of what doctors do now will be worthless—data collection, dosing calculations, and selecting the right drug or clinical trial, and so on—because robots will be able do much of that work. Eventually, robots may even be able to make recommendations for diagnosis and treatment. The doctors of the future will have to be more human than the robots, not better robots than the robots.

Therefore, we need new, creative methods of selecting and training doctors—methods that emphasize emotional intelligence, self-awareness, and empathy instead of rote learning and memorization. As Jack Ma colorfully illustrated in his Davos talk, computers can scour the medical literature and provide most of the biomedical knowledge that physicians require at the point of care. Software that uses AI to analyze remote monitoring data can supply the latest updates on a patient's health status and how it has changed over time; lab and imaging tests interpreted by AI can help fill in the picture. Only human doctors can glean insights into individuals and their environment while providing the care and the self-management advice essential to maintaining health and managing chronic diseases.

The robot supporting an ob-gyn a few years from now will be better than any human at analyzing the phenotypic traits of a baby born with congenital anomalies. That robot will be able to spot the key chromosomal anomaly, but will never understand that patients ask what this means, they are not interested in a scientific explanation or a list of potential medical complications. The doctor understands that "What does this mean?" signifies "What does this mean to my image of a perfect baby?" That discussion will require the human side of medical training.

SELECTION AND TRAINING OF PHYSICIANS

I'm not suggesting that we eliminate the MCAT or that medical schools disregard applicants' grades. But other qualities should be weighted more heavily than they are now. Once applicants have demonstrated a minimum degree of proficiency in science and didactic knowledge, their ability to understand other people, communicate with them, and work in teams should be prime considerations in their selection for medical school.

Today, admission committees choose applicants mostly based on their qualifications for being a good physician-scientist at an institution like Yale. That's why there's such a strong emphasis on biochemistry and other scientific courses. Their aptitude is measured by the MCAT, which is a multiple-choice test; then, after studying more science for the first two years of medical school, they take step one of the United States Medical Licensing Examination (USMLE), another multiple-choice test. At no point do we say, "In order to get to the next level, we don't just want to check your ability to reason and to memorize; we also want to find out whether you can talk to people and have other doctoring skills."

According to the Association of American Medical Colleges (AAMC 2022b), applicants' grades and test scores are not the only criteria for medical school admission. For example, the University of Michigan Medical School (2022, 1) "holistically" screens applicant files in several categories, including "academic excellence, exposure to medicine, service to others, teamwork/leadership, inquisitiveness/research, cultural humility, and life experience/resilience." Still, unless an applicant has very high grades and test scores, they're not likely to make the cut at this school or most others.

So why should medical schools pay as much attention to qualities like emotional intelligence and empathy as they do to MCAT scores? First, as I suggested in chapter 1, the nature of the clinical encounter and the patient-doctor relationship will change when technology helps transform healthcare into a continuous, home-centered process. Instead of spending most of the office visit investigating the person's physical condition and documenting it in an EHR, the physician will ask questions about recent trends in the individual's health habits, find out more about their personal situation, and jointly prepare or adjust a treatment plan with the person. The physician will already know the key facts about the patient's health status before the visit starts, but often the "between the lines" aspects of a person's life—social, spiritual, and emotional—will be gleaned only through a human-to-human interaction.

When I was in private practice seeing a new patient for an annual exam, I would always ask her a few questions about her life. "My son Ryan is going off to college." "My husband John has decided to run a marathon." "My mom is going through chemotherapy for cancer." During the next exam, before talking about her medical issues, I asked about Ryan, John, and her mom. That sent a strong signal that any part of her life was open for discussion, should she choose. I believe that willingness to allow patients to open up to us as humans was a key to my group's successful word-of-mouth practice growth.

The other reason medical schools should screen for emotional skills is that the new emphasis on social determinants of health will require a comprehensive, team-based approach. This approach is totally different from what is taught in medical school and residency today. The healthcare provider will have to take into account the resources that the person has at home, for example. Looking at health from this perspective also forces consideration of the patient's family situation and their neighborhood. Do they have adequate access to good food, can they afford a medication, can they get a ride to the doctor's office, do they have internet access?

Just being able to see a patient's home in a telemedicine visit can be eye-opening, my former colleague Michael Hoad points out. "You're at home, and I can see that your refrigerator doesn't work, that you don't have AC. If you don't have AC, can you sleep, and if not, does that mean you're anxious all the time? Maybe you don't feel safe in the neighborhood. We have people saying they sleep on the top floor. They don't want to sleep on the first floor because they're afraid of a bullet coming through the wall. The top floor in an unairconditioned row house in Philadelphia is the hottest floor, so they're not sleeping."

Kevin Mahoney, the CEO of Penn Medicine, made a similar point during the pandemic. He reminded some of our public health officials that asking people to stay in separate rooms in the house during COVID-19 surges is fine for people with five-bedroom houses, but is not helpful to a family of seven or eight living in a small apartment.

This thought process is very different from the one doctors are trained to use in a tightly focused 10- or 15-minute office visit. To gain the requisite insights and apply them to patient care, physicians need a different kind of personality than the competitive, rational, scientific type that medical schools are currently seeking. So yes, it's important to excel in science and math, but it takes more to make an excellent physician today.

Training Doctors for a Vanished World

The current paradigm of medical education has its roots in the famous Flexner report of 1910, which led to the closing of most US medical schools because of their low standards. The Johns Hopkins University training model, which replaced the old curriculum, included two years of science education and two years of clinical training, followed by residencies at teaching hospitals. This model still dominates medical education (Johnson and Nash 2022a).

The Johns Hopkins model's focus on hospital-based training is one reason there are far more specialists than primary care doctors in America. Other factors include the huge educational debts accrued by medical students ($200,000 or more) and the higher average incomes of specialists relative to generalist doctors. If we want to improve quality and lower costs, we need to make it easier for students who choose primary care to pay off their debt (perhaps by increasing the salary of primary care residents) and decrease the gap between specialist and primary care incomes.

Meanwhile, medical schools offer very little training in the areas of the fourth Industrial Revolution—such as genomics, AI, drones, and robotics—that will become part of mainstream medicine in the next decade. The main reason is that few faculty members are versed in those subjects. There's also hardly any training in health equity, although medical schools claim they are increasingly adding aspects of population health and care gaps to an already overloaded curriculum.

The ingrained beliefs and behaviors of traditional medical schools have shaped their cultures and the kinds of doctors they turn out, as Johnson and Nash (2022c) observe:

> Old Medicine has created a "superstar" physician marketplace that rewards individual achievement and discourages

team-oriented behaviors. It lacks standardization, avoids accountability and delivers suboptimal care outcomes. It grants enormous autonomy to physicians, supports hierarchical command-and-control management systems and discourages innovation.

As a result, fragmentation in care delivery occurs, communication suffers, workarounds abound, and status-quo practices predominate. These archaic and counterproductive behaviors are endemic. Their perpetuation compromises patient safety and care outcomes.

Medical schools have little reason to change, Nash told me when we spoke. They all have large numbers of applicants, so they suffer no penalty for maintaining the status quo. Nevertheless, he argues, those schools that do try to change will eventually benefit when the industry adopts financial risk and population health management.

Today, Nash says, "The medical education continuum is corrupted by the care delivery system, which is not designed to improve health. The two are closely entwined, and it's difficult to disconnect one from the other because of the inflow of dollars. It's very sad. The average American has no idea of this. If the goal of medical education is to improve health, you have to design a curriculum to improve health."

Appearance and Reality in New Courses

The medical school establishment would argue that schools are changing their curricula to keep up with the times. According to the AAMC (2022a), the bulk of medical schools offer, either as requirements or electives, courses in biomedical and clinical informatics, communication skills, community health, continuity of care, costs of care, counseling for behavior change, cultural competence, healthcare financing, quality improvement, healthcare systems, health disparities, health systems science, population health, population-based medicine, public health issues, social determinants of health, systemic racism, and value-based care.

Nash, a former dean and academic attending physician, was not impressed when I shared this list. First, he pointed out that, before the COVID-19 pandemic, medical error was the third leading cause of death in the United States. "There's not a single allopathic medical school with mandatory course work in quality and safety in America."

Second, he says, the AAMC checklist consists mostly of elective courses that medical students tend to take in their fourth year as they prepare to graduate. "Sure, there's a senior elective on population health. 'Box checked; we teach it.' But it's not culturally supported, it's not trumpeted, it doesn't have prestige. The prestige factor comes in year 3 or 4, when students see in the hospital wards which doctors get the rewards and the prestige: It's the super subspecialists. And this is learned behavior; it's cultural modeling of the first degree."

The same psychology prevails when medical school graduates apply to residency programs, he says. Unless they are screening for a joint degree program such as an MD-MPH or an MD-MBA, residency selection committees don't care about any nonclinical courses their applicants took in medical school.

"All admission committees have one critical fault: they reproduce in their own image," Nash says. "And who is on most residency selection committees? People who haven't had the kind of experiences we're talking about. So, it seems unimportant to them."

I agree, and I'd take his argument further. In my experience, many of the physicians who train residents are aged 50 or older. This attending has developed certain habits and ways of thinking that are inculcated into residents. The residents imbibe all the bad habits, such as the overordering of tests, that the attendings have drummed into them. That's a major reason why physician culture is so hard to change.

We often call this the "hidden curriculum." Medical colleges often do a great job of emphasizing teamwork, patient-centered approaches, and ethics at the beginning of a medical student's career, but during their clinical rotations students frequently spend time with mid- or late-career physicians who imprint the "real facts," according to them. I remember being in the hospital at night listening to a faculty member tell a student interested in OB-GYN that she should not take a residency in that specialty because she would never have an "academic career." I felt compelled to interrupt and tell the student, "Be careful of nevers. I did my residency in a small community program, and I'm his boss!"

THE MEDICAL SCHOOL OF THE FUTURE

Johnson and Nash (2022b) cite four schools that they say have gone far beyond traditional methods of teaching medicine: the Kaiser Permanente Bernard J. Tyson School of Medicine, the Geisinger Commonwealth School of Medicine, the University of Houston College of Medicine, and the Whole Health School of Medicine and Health Sciences. I decided to find out more about the Kaiser Permanente school to see what's happening on the frontier of medical education.

Kaiser Permanente launched its medical school in 2015, and the school enrolled its first class of 50 students in July 2020. That class will graduate in 2024.

As the largest group-model HMO in the United States, Kaiser hires many new physicians and recognizes that many have not learned the practice of integrated, team-based care. That was one of the reasons Kaiser created the medical school, says Mark Schuster, MD, PhD, its founding dean and CEO. While the organization attracted very talented physicians, "they hadn't always learned about person-centered care, population health, team-based care, quality improvement, and health equity. These are important skills for students to learn. So KP saw a national need they wanted to help fill. They view it as an extension of their commitment to the health of individuals and communities."

However, Schuster adds, his school does not offer any incentives to students to apply for residencies at Kaiser Permanente or to go to work there afterward. "We support them in going into any field and doing residencies and practicing wherever their heart takes them. Some of them will fall in love with integrated care and team-based care and how KP works and will want to practice here. But there are no incentives to do that."

Applicants who are accepted to the Kaiser school have fairly high MCAT scores, on average, he says, but neither MCATs nor grades are the determining factor in admission. He describes the admissions process as "holistic," considering "life experiences, activities beyond the classroom, beyond the workplace. The committee also looks at 'distance traveled.' Maybe somebody came from a community where it's unusual to go to college, let alone be in a position to apply to medical school. The hurdles of all kinds that people face, their passions—all of these are looked at in addition to their academic metrics."

The need for greater diversity in the physician workforce is also a key factor in selecting students, he adds. "Forty-one percent of our students are from groups that are underrepresented in medicine. *U.S. News & World Report* had us tied for the sixth most diverse medical school."

A Different Kind of Curriculum

The training offered by the KP school differs in many significant respects from the traditional model. To start with, "it's not a lecture-based curriculum," Schuster notes. "It's group-based learning, in which groups of eight or nine students are facilitated by a biomedical scientist and a physician faculty member. We have biomedical science, clinical science, and health systems science. We've elevated the latter to be one of our three pillars; it's not an elective or an extra course. It's part of every week."

Even in their classroom training, the students engage in "active learning." They read and watch videos about the didactic content before they go to class. "At that point, they're problem-solving as a group, they're learning to work in teams. They're actively learning in the classroom. Likewise, in doctoring, they're learning how to work with standardized patients—actors who are simulating patients. The whole curriculum is based around active learning, rather than passively listening to lectures."

Students get their first exposure to clinical practice in the third week of school. "They spend half a day a week for the first year in a family or internal medicine clinic with the same physician preceptor all year," Schuster says. "So that physician gets to know them." If they've never seen a patient with asthma and they're taking the pulmonary course, he notes, the doctor makes sure they see a patient with asthma.

In the second year, while continuing their family/internal medicine training, the students devote a second half day a week to clinical work in five or more specialties, including emergency medicine, OB-GYN, pediatrics, psychiatry, and surgery. "They're still in the classroom a day and a half a week, but they're now heavily involved in clinical care," Schuster says. In years three and four, most of their training is in clinical settings.

The Kaiser school doesn't emphasize primary care as a career choice; students are encouraged to pursue whatever specialty they find most interesting. In contrast, he says sometimes schools can unintentionally discourage students from becoming primary care physicians. Professors may even tell students they're "too smart" to go into primary care and urge them to go into a more challenging field. Another example of the hidden curriculum!

"That's not the message our students get here," Schuster says. "KP respects and values primary care, and supports primary care physicians in practicing at the highest level. So, the students see primary care doctors being respected and supported and doing great work."

Integrated Learning Approach

Another distinguishing characteristic of the Kaiser school is how it organizes the subject matter.

> We don't have a biochemistry course for a semester and an anatomy class for a semester. It's all integrated, based on organs. If we're teaching you about the cardiovascular system, you'll learn the physiology, the anatomy, and the histology of the heart. At the same time, you're learning about prevention, diagnosis, and treatment of cardiovascular disease.
>
> Students also learn that men tend to receive better care for myocardial infarction than women, and that white people tend to receive better care for MI than do people of color. If students figure out the right antihypertensive medication to give, that's fantastic. But they are also expected to remember that when they write or refill the prescription, they need to talk to patients about whether they have the copay, ask them if they're stretching out the medication to save money, and explain that that could harm their health.

The KP school uses advanced technologies in innovative ways, he says. For example, instead of traditional cadavers, the school uses plastinated ones in which donated bodies and organs are replaced by silicon. In addition,

> we 3D scan all our plastinated bodies and organs, so students on their phones can have a 3D scan of every plastinated body and organ that they've learned from, and they can view it and spin it. They can look at the heart from all angles on their phones. We also use point-of-care ultrasound in our anatomy lab.

In our simulation center, we have advanced mannequins that can simulate a heart attack. We have a man-
nequin that delivers a baby, and then the baby moves and
blinks. These mannequins are very sophisticated. We can
change the heart rate, the blood pressure, the oxygen
saturation. The students are learning on mannequins
and what we call "task trainers" before they actually work
with patients. They can develop their skills and get quite
comfortable.

More surgical residencies should adopt this approach. Instead of
the outdated "see one, do one, teach one" model that still prevails
in some places (which is fine unless you are the one at the other end
of the scalpel), trainee surgeons—and experienced surgeons who
have never done a particular procedure before—should work in
mentored simulation centers to gain the skill and confidence needed
to perform each procedure. The ability to develop these capabilities
in a simulated environment rather than in the heat and stress of an
operating room would increase surgical competence and patient
safety. No resident physician in training should be performing any
difficult operation on a real human until they have proven that they
have the requisite technical skills and confidence to perform that
procedure on an inanimate object.

When we opened our simulation center at the University of
South Florida, the speaker that day was Jeffrey Skiles, the copilot
on the "Miracle on the Hudson" flight. He lauded the simulator
approach and noted its similarity to how aviation views training and
new technology. Medicine's "see one, do one, teach one" mentality,
he noted, would be like him seeing a new Airbus that he had never
flown and saying, "Let's see how this thing flies with 600 people on
board!" Obviously, that would never happen in commercial aviation, and it shouldn't happen in healthcare or in any other activity
where someone's life may hang in the balance.

Transferable Training

Schuster sees a connection between his school's emphasis on population health management and the concentration on the care of individual patients in traditional healthcare. "Giving good individual care involves understanding population health. You can keep treating your patient for asthma, but if you see an uptick in patients coming to the ER with asthma exacerbations, you run the data and you see there's a concentration in a certain zip code. Perhaps there's a new factory in that area that didn't put in emission filters. Maybe you can help that patient by persuading the factory to install those filters. Providing good individual care often involves understanding their community."

If graduates of the Kaiser school eventually work in a traditional health system where they have 10–15 minutes with each patient and population health isn't supported, how will their unique training help them?

"I don't think you need to work in a system that supports population health to give population-health-informed care to patients," Schuster says. "You can ask your patients questions about their community, understand the importance of social determinants of health, and still give outstanding care. I think more healthcare is moving toward valuing community and population health, anyway."

The students who don't end up working in an organization such as KP, he adds, can evangelize for and help lead the change to the values it represents. "We hope our students will take the skills that are part of being outstanding physicians and take them wherever they go, and help others learn things they didn't learn in med school. We hope our students will find kindred spirits wherever they go, and even if they don't, we think they'll have the leadership and communication skills to teach others what they've learned."

Reverse Mentoring with Patient Feedback

I like what the Kaiser medical school is doing, especially its emphasis on hands-on learning. Rather than being an anomaly, this should be the model in most medical schools. Not everybody needs 16 weeks of microbiology and 16 weeks of biochemistry. Students would be better off studying health systems science and population health from the beginning.

The concept of "segmenting" your medical school class is one I've become progressively more interested in. The Wharton Business School went through a similar change when I matriculated in the executive MBA program. They knew they could always get the top finance students and emerging leaders who had graduated from Yale, Penn, and Harvard, but they recognized they needed to "segment" their class and bring in folks from the nonprofit sector, entrepreneurs, and others with a different background. They also removed some of the more onerous "quantitative" parts of the curriculum and added more time on global health, public health, and social and leadership skills. We should be doing the same thing in medical colleges. Some of the students should be potential physician scientists, selected the traditional way. But we should leave openings for applicants with high emotional intelligence and empathy scores, as well as applicants who are interested in getting their MD degree and then going out and creating new companies.

I'd also recommend an approach known as "reverse mentoring." Pioneered by Sheba Medical Center and the Israel Center for Medical Simulation, this teaching method involves having patients evaluate medical students. These people can either be standardized patients, such as the actors used by Kaiser, or real patients that medical students encounter during clinical rotations. Reverse mentoring could help prevent students from picking up their attendings' bad habits by giving them valuable feedback from another source.

When medical students have an encounter with a standardized patient today, the evaluation of their interaction with that person focuses on whether they asked the right questions and did the right things in the physical exam. In the Sheba simulation center, by contrast, the standardized patients are asked whether the student made eye contact and expressed genuine interest, or interrupted them and seemed rushed. The student watches a video of the encounter afterward.

Amitai Ziv, MD, medical education director of that center and a consultant on the simulation center we developed in Tampa, believes that virtual reality and metaverse technology, combined with human interaction to hone listening and empathy skills, will eventually be as important as learning cardiology or internal medicine. In fact, Sheba Medical Center is starting a medical school in Israel with Reichman University that is based on these principles.

The same approach might be taken with a real patient in an office visit. After the doctor introduces the patient to a student in the exam room, the patient is told the student is going to take their history and do their physical. In addition, the physician asks the patient whether they would mind answering a few questions about the student after the exam. Among the questions would be this: "If this student were your doctor, how would you feel?"

While reverse mentoring doesn't prove anything about the competence of the medical student, it measures a key skill that every doctor must have and that will be even more important in the future: the ability to communicate with and convey empathy to patients.

On a personal level, my son has started a company called Artly Working. As an actor, he spent some time learning improv and recognized that in medicine (as well as some other professional fields), the art of improv can improve listening skills. It can also force you to think before you give a quick answer and hones your skill of understanding the second and third order consequences of what you are saying.

CME THAT MAKES A DIFFERENCE

Our goal should be to move 70 percent of the medical schools in the United States to the kind of models exemplified by Kaiser Permanente, Geisinger, University of Houston, Boston University School of Medicine, and a few others. But if we feel good about ourselves in 10 years because 10 percent of the schools are more than incrementally changing their selection criteria and curriculum, we'll have failed. And failure is very likely, because, as David Nash notes, the other schools will continue to turn out physicians for the current care delivery system until the financial incentives change.

If we want physicians to be prepared for the transformative changes occurring in healthcare, we have to find ways to upgrade the skills and alter the attitudes of the doctors who are now in practice. And that means, first and foremost, changing physician culture.

As one would expect, the training physicians receive in medical school and residency carries over into their professional careers. Thus, as Johnson and Nash (2022d) write, physicians tend to be autonomous, following the "heroic model of physician leadership" that reflects a time when most doctors worked independently. Teamwork is discouraged, and there are large variations in the care that patients get.

In contrast, the model they propose "relies on continuous performance improvement supported by massive data sets and incisive analytics" (Johnson and Nash 2022d). Physicians will learn how to function as care team leaders, rather than captains of the ship. These collaborative teams, they say, will prioritize patient needs, rather than the needs of physicians, and team members will hold one another accountable for outcomes.

Continuing medical education (CME) can facilitate this cultural change—but not the traditional CME that most doctors still use to maintain their licensure and board certification. That kind of CME usually consists of taking online courses or attending conferences that are often supported by pharmaceutical companies. "CME programming is largely pro forma, ad hoc, user led, process driven and disconnected from operations. Granting certificates satisfies a professional development requirement but doesn't translate into better clinical-care outcomes or customer experience" (Johnson and Nash 2022c).

According to Johnson and Nash (and I heartily agree with them), traditional CME credits "perpetuate an unwinnable and exhausting knowledge chase" as doctors try to keep up with the geometric increase in the medical literature. Moreover, this endeavor doesn't teach doctors the key pieces of nonclinical knowledge that they didn't learn in medical school. "As an industry, healthcare must move beyond certification programs to encompass broader simulation and virtual reality training, online courses, team-based training, coaching and experiential learning. From the beginning of a career to retirement, programs must teach, coach and cultivate core skills all clinicians need in the digitally enabled, highly complex, consumer-focused, collaborative and information-saturated care delivery environments. Clinicians need these core skills to deliver compassionate, effective and efficient care" (Johnson and Nash 2022d).

In my view, CME ought to be divided into three parts. The first part would be similar to what it is today, including lectures and courses. The second part would be the assessment of a doctor's technical competence. The third part would be in-person conferences that focus on self-awareness, empathy, and the other social skills that physicians didn't learn in medical school. Maybe doctors would go to four conferences a year that teach these skills, plus training in community and population health.

CME for Value-Based Care

To fundamentally change physician culture, though, doctors' financial incentives must change. When that happens, physicians will have to learn how to practice differently and to function differently in their organizations than they do in the fee-for-service world. To understand how this might work, I spoke with Ken Cohen, MD, senior medical director of Optum Care and executive director of clinical research for UnitedHealth Group.

Optum Care, part of UnitedHealthcare subsidiary Optum, is focused on helping physicians make the transition from volume to value-based care. The 30 large groups that make up Optum Care employ or have contractual relationships with tens of thousands of physicians across the country.

Cohen was formerly the president and CEO of New West Physicians, a 130-doctor primary care group based in Denver. When his group was sold to Optum in 2017, the company asked Cohen to infuse the ideas behind New West's Bench to Bedside program, which taught doctors evidence-based medicine, into the other groups in Optum's fold.

Renamed Optimal Care, this evidence-based program requires physicians to follow clinical guidelines based on high-grade evidence for most medical decisions. The goal is to eliminate low-value care and the consequent patient harm and waste of resources. In addition, Optum tries to persuade physicians to incorporate important new evidence-based-medicine findings into their practices sooner rather than later. In community practices, it takes many physicians 5 to 10 years to do that; with the help of Optimal Care, Optum's physicians can do it in just 12 weeks.

Optimal Care starts by educating clinicians about the value of evidence-based-medicine, with experts delivering CME-accredited lectures in each specialty area. Recent, high-quality studies are distilled into easily deployed recommendations, and infographics serve as point-of-care reminders to avoid low-value care. EHR tools show specialists their outcomes, quality scores, and total cost of care for specific procedures and diagnoses. Both primary care doctors and specialists get regular reports on quality and utilization comparing their performance to their previous data and to that of other physicians in their specialty.

Cohen agrees with Johnson and Nash that CME should be continuous and rooted in clinical work, but he doesn't think that didactic CME is less important than other kinds of training. "We've created a whole CME curriculum for Optimal Care that promulgates high-level evidence-based medicine and focuses on the elimination of waste and harmful care. So CME can be the tool to educate physicians about value-based care. But standard CME that's printed at the end of a journal might not meet the need. It's not CME that's the problem, it's the content of that CME."

Cohen suggests that physicians should also be trained in two other areas: the use of "highly effective shared decision-making with patients" and "routine measurement of patient-reported outcomes, so we have real-world evidence on the outcomes of day-to-day interventions. With those two caveats, I agree with the framework" provided by Johnson and Nash, "but the content of the CME is still important. You could design the type of CME they describe, but if the content fosters filling ERs and hospital beds and ORs, as opposed to using evidence to determine clinical decision-making, it still might not meet the need."

JOLTing Current Medical Staff

All this talk about physicians of the future elicits an obvious question: What about our current physicians? At the University of South Florida medical school, we created a Center for Transformation and Innovation (CTI) and brought in a transformational leader from GE Healthcare to help us make our talented but way too self-satisfied faculty ready for the future. CTI now works with healthcare systems throughout the United States.

When I arrived at Jefferson, I also noticed that faculty preferred the status quo, so we started a program called Jefferson Onboarding and Leadership Transformation (JOLT). My experience with CTI taught me that 20 percent of any given medical staff really get it and will follow a transformative path. Fifteen percent will never get it and will fight everything you want to do to change the old model. The other 65 percent are in the middle, the ones listening rather than talking in the medical staff lounge.

As leaders, we spend 40 percent of our time with the folks who get it, because it feels comfortable. We spend 45 percent of our time banging our head against the wall with the docs who will never get it because they are loud, and we think we can fix them. We spend the least amount of time with the folks in the middle, even though they have the best chance of changing the culture of the institution. At JOLT, we turned the "converted" into mentors and ignored the docs who would never get it. We called that "administrative hospice"—we hoped those doctors would move to a competitor. We took Passenger's 2012 advice ("Let Her Go") and concentrated on that vast middle.

In eight years, we were able to show a significant difference between JOLT alumni and controls—a 325 percent improvement in dealing with difficult issues and situations, a 133 percent increase in commitment to and engaging in ensuring the organization's success, a 250 percent increase in loyalty to the organization, and an 80 percent increase in willingness to serve in a leadership capacity. A significant part of Jefferson's resounding growth and success from 2013 to 2021 is attributable to this group of emerging leaders.

Beyond leadership institutes, one of the key factors in employee recruitment and retention is the provision of learning and development opportunities through mentoring, feedback, coaching, and customized approaches to "upskilling." In the past, in most organizations, these programs were created institution by institution, with variable results. To survive the workforce transformation crisis, health systems will have to do more. Healthcare employees are increasingly citing education benefits as a reason to stay in an organization, and an increasing number of employees are willing to stay in their institution longer if they believe that their leadership cares about their development. Guild is an example of a technology/human interface that was very successful at developing talent brand, mobility, and retention strategies in other employment sectors and is now taking their customized upskilling approach to healthcare.

Aligning Culture and Incentives with Value

Successful healthcare start-ups are recognizing and meeting the need for reeducation in the future value-based healthcare systems. The foundation of the Optum Care group's ability to deliver high-quality care efficiently is a physician culture that embraces value-based care and population health management, Cohen says. For groups that were predominantly fee-for-service or had just a small amount of financial risk before joining Optum Care, this requires a major attitudinal shift among their doctors. For example, they have to start regarding the provision of low-value care as wasteful rather than as a source of revenue.

Optum Care has been mostly successful in getting physicians to make this cultural change, partly because they were prepared for it. "People join Optum Care because they want to learn how to do two-sided risk contracting" Cohen says. "If the group has no interest in moving down the value-based-care continuum, there's no reason for them to join."

The second challenge is to make it easy for Optum physicians to practice evidence-based medicine, he says. This is harder in some groups than in others. Optum Care consists of primary care groups, multispecialty groups, and independent practice associations (IPAs) that the company manages. Many of the specialists are still being paid fee-for-service, so it's difficult to realign their reimbursement with value-based care. In the contracted IPAs, the doctors want to learn how to practice in the new way, and they appreciate the analytics and other tools they've been given. But some IPAs have up to 50 different EHRs, and it's challenging to convey the key elements of the clinical guidelines through an "easy button" in their EHRs.

The Malpractice Threat

Regardless of how much a physician may want to make this transformative change, there's still a preoccupation with something that has shadowed that doctor since residency: the threat of being sued for malpractice. No matter what an evidence-based medicine guideline tells doctors to do, they are likely to practice defensive medicine to avoid a potential error that could result in a lawsuit.

The actual costs of malpractice suits and defensive suits add up to only 2.4 percent of health costs, according to a widely cited study (Mello et al. 2010). But the toll of defensive medicine may be far higher, perhaps as much as 10–15 percent, because many of its ramifications are hidden from view.

For example, the United States does far more breast biopsies than any other country. We also have the highest rate of noncancer results from those biopsies, and according to the World Cancer Research Fund International (2022) we have no more breast cancer per capita, on average, than do most other European nations.

Why is this the case? When I was a practicing gynecologist and a patient came in for her annual breast exam, I was sort of a family doctor of the breast. In other words, we would do the screening breast exam and potentially order a mammogram, but general surgeons actually do the diagnostic procedures. From a malpractice point of view, I was responsible for that patient's breast health once I did the initial exam. Next to lawsuits related to obstetrics, breast cancer is one of the leading areas of malpractice suits for ob-gyns. So, I probably referred 20 percent of my patients to general surgeons. I did this for two reasons: I didn't always trust mammograms, and if I sent the patient to the surgeon, then my malpractice risk was mitigated or eliminated.

The surgeon, in turn, would see the patient and say to themselves, "I'm not sure there's anything here, but the ob-gyn or family doctor was concerned enough to send her to me, so I'd better do a biopsy. If I don't do it and she turns out to have breast cancer, I'll get sued." That's the real cost of malpractice suits, and the reason we have more negative biopsies than any other country.

The C-Section Dilemma

As is well known in the trade, obstetricians get sued more than most other kinds of specialists. It just comes with the territory, because babies are so precious and because so much can go wrong in labor and delivery. Nevertheless, this fact makes us especially careful about how we protect ourselves and our reputations. It also increases the odds of women receiving cesarean sections.

According to the US National Center for Birth Statistics (2022), the rate of C-sections in the United States in 2020 was 32 percent—four points higher than the average for other wealthy countries (OECD 2019). But in Philadelphia, the rate was probably around 50 percent, based on my experience. While there are several reasons for this, the biggest factor is the high likelihood of being sued in Philadelphia.

C-sections are medically indicated in only certain situations, such as fetal distress, infection of the placenta, failure to progress, and life-threatening complications of pregnancy (Mylonas and Friese 2015). But C-sections are done in many other circumstances, partly because these procedures are very safe and have relatively few complications compared to vaginal births, especially for the baby. Today's OB-GYN residents are taught that "you never get sued for doing a C-section." On the other hand, if a physician lets the patient go into labor and anything goes wrong, somebody (probably a plaintiff's lawyer or a jury) is going to say "You should have done a C-section."

Then there's payment and convenience. When I was in practice, I got paid 2.5 times more to do a C-section than to do a vaginal delivery. I was in the hospital for maybe half an hour, and generally both mom and partner were thrilled that they got to see their bouncing baby. The alternative was following the patient in labor for up to 26 hours. In many cases, that meant I'd have to spend part of my weekend in the hospital instead of with my family, and sometimes have to perform an emergency C-section for one of the previously listed indications.

Early in my academic career, I wrote an article for the *American Journal of Obstetrics & Gynecology* titled "The Impact of Mandated In-Hospital Coverage on Primary Cesarean Delivery Rates in a Large Non-University Teaching Hospital" (Klasko 1995). This study compared C-section rates of obstetricians who were on call in the hospital and those of physicians who were called in from home. The C-section rates were four times higher when the obstetrician came in from home.

A doctor coming in from home would often tell the patient, "Things aren't progressing as well as I'd like. We can give you some medication to increase the contractions, but it might take quite a while, or you could see the baby in an hour." If the obstetrician was on in-house call, or what we now call a laborist, they'd be more likely to say, "Things aren't progressing as well as I'd like. But you're here and I'm here, so let's give it some more time and see if we can get your labor to progress." When I asked the physicians whether they took a different approach with patients whether they were on in-house call or coming in from home, they said, "Of course not, that would be unethical." But it appears that convenience did play a role (conscious or otherwise) in their decisions.

Then of course there is patient choice. Toward the end of my private practice career, patients started telling me, "I just want a C-section. My friend was in labor for 24 hours, and I don't want to go through that." When I heard that, I was in a bind. While there was no medical reason to do a C-section, if I did not accede to the patient's request and something went wrong, the patient would be more likely to sue me and to say, "I told him I wanted a C-section."

Cohen rejects the idea that following evidence-based guidelines, even if that means not practicing defensive medicine, results in a higher level of liability risk. "If you're using level 1 and level 2 evidence to guide clinical decision-making, you are practicing what I'd consider totally defensible medicine. What could be better than practicing based on the best available evidence?" Also, "patients sue when they're angry, as we've known for decades. And they're angry when they don't have a transparent relationship with their physician. There's nothing about a value-based care model that prevents a physician from meaningfully engaging with patients, so that relationship would make a malpractice suit highly unlikely."

Perhaps he's right about the liability risk of doctors who follow evidence-based guidelines. But in the current practice environment, the incentives to earn more and protect yourself from liability are hard to resist. We all start our careers wanting to do the right thing and take care of patients, but external factors, administrative overload, and perverse incentives turn those lofty intentions inside out. Between malpractice risk and the way doctors get paid, the incentives turn idealistic, quality-driven, patient-driven physicians into defensive, revenue-maximizing physicians. They still want to do the right thing, but they do it under the guise of the incentives that are driving them. And then they perpetuate the cycle by teaching young, idealistic students the hidden curriculum.

CONCLUSION

Medical education and physician culture are mirror images of each other. When the payment system changes, so will medical education; then, I hope, the next generation of physicians will be much better prepared to deliver optimal healthcare than the current generation is. I am excited and optimistic about the "new medical schools" that are willing to ignite a debate around what skill sets doctors of the future must have. I am pleased to be a faculty member at Reichman University in Israel, which is building a next-generation, first of its kind medical school. Many of the concepts discussed in this chapter—such as true interprofessional and interdisciplinary education, communication skills, cultural competence, population health, and fourth Industrial Revolution competencies—will be core to the curriculum. The physicians graduating from Reichman (much like those graduating from the SELECT program and the Kaiser program in the United States) will be better prepared for the technology and human healthcare future they will face.

But we can't wait for that to happen. People need higher quality, safer care now, at a price they can afford. Therefore, it's incumbent on physician leaders to revamp their organizations so they can provide the continuous, practice-based learning doctors need to deliver efficient, high-quality care.

Physicians will also have to learn how to partner with AI-based software that will make their clinical work much easier, freeing them to spend more time with patients. It took us 50 years to get doctors and nurses to work together using interprofessional education; now we will have to add intersentient education, as doctors and robots will need to get along! Humans will also need better communication skills in order to engage their patients, ask them about their social determinants and health behaviors, and guide them wisely on their journey to better health.

If all this sounds like a tall order, it is. I am passionate about moving population health, social determinants, health equity, and predictive analytics from philosophic and academic exercises into the mainstream of clinical care, payment models, and medical education. As Pink Floyd famously declared in "Another Brick in the Wall," education should expand our creativity, not suppress it—"no dark sarcasm in the classroom"! We need teachers who are willing to present an optimistic view of the future that combines the best of both worlds—personalized medicine and population health.

I'm not minimizing the challenges of altering physician culture or of preparing doctors for a world that is changing at warp speed. But, like climate change, this is an issue we cannot ignore. We owe it to our patients, our families, and our society to build a health system based on value and the intrinsic worth of every individual.

REFERENCES

AAMC (Association of American Medical Colleges). 2022a. "Curriculum Topics in Required and Elective Courses at Medical School Programs" Data & Reports: Curriculum Reports (online database). www.aamc.org/data-reports/curriculum-reports/interactive-data/curriculum-topics-required-and-elective-courses-medical-school-programs.

————. 2022b. "How Medical Schools Review Applications." Students & Residents ("Aspiring Docs"). https://students-residents.aamc.org/applying-medical-school/how-medical-schools-review-applications.

Johnson, D. W., and D. Nash. 2022a. "Overcoming Medical Orthodoxy (Part 1): The Origins of Dysfunction." 4sightHealth. Published March 17. www.4sighthealth.com/overcoming-medical-orthodoxy-part-1-the-origins-of-dysfunction/.

————. 2022b. "Overcoming Medical Orthodoxy (Part 2): Reinventing Medical Education." 4sightHealth. Published March 24. www.4sighthealth.com/reinventing-medical-education/.

————. 2022c. "Overcoming Medical Orthodoxy (Part 3): Forces Disrupting 'Old Medicine.'" 4sightHealth. Published May 12. www.4sighthealth.com/overcoming-medical-orthodoxy-part-3-forces-disrupting-old-medicine/.

————. 2022d. "Overcoming Medical Orthodoxy (Part 4): Retooling Clinicians for 'New Medicine.'" 4sightHealth. Published May 19. www.4sighthealth.com/overcoming-medical-orthodoxy-part-4-retooling-clinicians-for-new-medicine/.

Klasko, S. 1995. "The Impact of Mandated In-Hospital Coverage on Primary Cesarean Delivery Rates in a Large Non-University Teaching Hospital." *American Journal of Obstetrics & Gynecology* 172: 637–42.

Mello, M. M., A. Chandra, A. A. Gawande, and D. M. Studdert. 2010. "National Costs of the Medical Liability System." *Health Affairs* 29 (9): 1569–77. https://doi.org/10.1377/hlthaff.2009 .0807.

Mylonas, I., and K. Friese. 2015. "Indications for and Risks of Elective Cesarean Section." *Deutsches Ärzteblatt International* (112): 489–95. https://doi.org/10.3238/arztebl.2015.0489.

OECD (Organisation for Economic Co-operation and Development). 2019. "Caesarean Sections." Health at a Glance 2019: OECD Indicators. www.oecd-ilibrary.org/sites/fa1f7281-en /index.html?itemId=/content/component/fa1f7281-en.

Shell, G. R., and S. K. Klasko. 1996. "Negotiating. Biases Physicians Bring to the Table." *Physician Executive* 22 (12): 4–7.

University of Michigan Medical School. 2022. "Office of Admissions Process for the Evaluation of M.D. Applicants." Updated June 30. https://medicine.umich.edu/medschool/education /md-program/md-admissions/timeline at "Please review our process . . ."

US National Center for Health Statistics. 2022. "Births—Method of Delivery." FastStats. Last reviewed May 16. www.cdc.gov /nchs/fastats/delivery.htm.

World Cancer Research Fund International. 2022. "Breast Cancer Statistics." www.wcrf.org/cancer-trends/breast-cancer -statistics/.

Epilogue

"Don't Stop Believin'" by Journey

IT'S JANUARY 2, 2035. A mutant strain of an RNA encapsulated virus has been afflicting people in Australia. Of course, people who remember the COVID-19 crisis of the early 2020s panicked briefly. Then they relaxed and smiled, because they knew healthcare had evolved from a broken, fragmented, expensive, inequitable "sick care" system to a "health assurance" system where most of their care happens at home.

Most healthcare information is now continuously streamed to the cloud and AI "bots" are constantly analyzing the data for any changes, so the early symptoms of this new virus were immediately identified. Anyone exhibiting those early symptoms was immediately notified and asked to socially isolate. If necessary, their employer was notified and asked for an excused absence. Software was immediately sent through the Internet of You (what we used to call the Internet of Things) so that your home 3D printer could begin creating masks for your family. People struggling with anxiety and panic could immediately communicate with their bot psychiatrist and, if necessary, receive drone-delivered medications.

Within a month, new bioprocessing techniques had identified the virus and researchers had developed and tested vaccines through rapid prototyping. The United States had finally attained universal broadband access in 2025, so instruction for K-12 students continued seamlessly. Just as "healthcare at home" is now mainstream, so are creative ways of teaching in a variety of venues.

This was a far cry from what we'd witnessed throughout the country during the COVID-19 crisis. Back then, healthcare data was siloed in different hospitals and other care settings, and there was no coordinated analysis. There were different strategies in different states, and sometimes in different counties of the same state. Jefferson Health, which I had the honor to lead at the time, went from 50 telehealth visits a day to 3,000, but many health systems did not have the bandwidth to provide widescale virtual care. And speaking of bandwidth, most public schools shut down for months, because in cities such as Philadelphia, a large percentage of the population lacked broadband or computers at home.

The "war on the underserved"—which is what historians called the reaction to the 2020 COVID crisis—forced a change in payment models so that every healthcare provider was adequately compensated for keeping populations healthy. Payers and providers aligned their efforts to improve health, resulting in higher income for providers. Healthcare and insurer CEOs are now paid based partly on how healthy their communities are. That change coincided with the Comprehensive Health Ethics and Equity Reform Act (CHEER Act) of 2025, which created a payment model that narrowed the gap between primary providers and specialists. Family physicians, general internists, and pediatricians were fairly compensated for the first time in several decades.

It was not an easy road. The dirty not-so-secret secret of healthcare in the 2020s was that almost everybody made more money when more people were sick. It was hard to get big institutions excited about changing something when their revenue depended on them not changing it. So, the healthcare industry didn't transform until it had no other choice.

As they watched hospitals fail and insurers reap record profits during the COVID crisis, consumers, business owners, and all rational people recognized that healthcare had escaped the consumer revolution. They watched the underserved and minority population get sicker because we had failed to address social determinants of health (SDOH). The failure of health IT entrepreneurs and the traditional healthcare ecosystem to work together to disrupt the healthcare industry became undeniable. Most providers were not ready to increase their telehealth bandwidth, most physicians and nurses had not been trained in virtual visits, electronic health records (EHRs) and other technology systems were fragmented, and there was no national repository for data or mutually agreed-upon population health analytics. The new system changed all that.

The arrival of health assurance was a long overdue change. Think about how the 2020 pandemic would have been different if we'd had continuous data coming in from patients through their wearables and other sources about their temperature, respiratory rate, and so on, or if 3D printers had been as ubiquitous as cell phones. It's hard to believe that only 10 years ago people were going to a physician's office once a year for a static physical. Today, your T-shirt sends continuous data to your physician, with AI filtering and human interaction when necessary.

HOW IT ALL TURNED AROUND

The players in the healthcare system had long blamed each other for its serious flaws. This finger-pointing got even worse in the aftermath of the pandemic. Insurers, providers, and payers tried to make up for lost income and took the easy path by doubling down on the sick care payment system. Thankfully, consumers said "enough is enough." They demanded and were eventually offered the government-mandated transition to our current healthcare model.

At the same time, digital medicine allowed healthcare providers to address SDOH and democratize access to the best healthcare in the nation. In 2022, many underserved patients were not taking advantage of available resources like clinic visits because they didn't have time off or childcare. That was part of why the underserved population had a greater complication rate during the COVID crisis. Thanks to poor healthcare access and SDOH, they already had much higher prevalence rates of diabetes, asthma, hypertension, and heart disease—all risk factors for COVID-19 morbidity and all due to social factors, not medical or genetic differences.

When we reinvented the system, "alternative" delivery models such as community health centers and midwifery became mainstream; global health and wellness such as Ayurvedic medicine, yoga, and mindfulness became prescribed more often than opioids; and nutritional science became a major part of the curriculum for all medical and nursing students. Meanwhile, the Zip Code Discrepancy Act of 2025 mandated that at least 25 percent of the salary of any health system or insurance CEO must depend on the health equity evident in the community the system serves.

I speak to you now as the chief digital officer for President Taylor Swift, who swept to power with a simple healthcare message: "Make healthcare tailored to the individual and the community and make it swift," neither of which was true in the early 2020s.

All in all, great progress has been made in the delivery of healthcare, and the transformation would not have been as dramatic if not for the COVID crisis. The pandemic of 2020–2022 was the lightning strike needed for American healthcare to get an extreme makeover and for the sick system to finally get well!

THE MESSAGE IN THE MUSIC

In my 40 years as Stevie K the DJ, I've learned a lot through the message in the music. As Stephen K. Klasko, MD, MBA, I continue to learn every day about the long journey to a healthier America. So, I'll leave you with six songs that exemplify what I've learned from my somewhat unusual path in life.

The Myth of Trust (Billy Bragg)

Trust is more important than technology. Regenerative medic
precision medicine, -omics, and other trends are fine, but healthcare
must start with values, and the core of values is ethics.

Ethics is not a list of rules. It is a process of asking the big
questions first, before we create programs and products that could
injure people even inadvertently. Complex failure starts at the top,
with misplaced values and with hubris. As history shows repeatedly,
the failure of experts is much more damaging than the failure of
incompetents. We weed out incompetence quickly, but we allow
"experts" to lead whole systems into danger.

Our health assurance transformation may have side effects, like
every other transformation, and we have to be resolute in pursuing
the goal of "responsible innovation." Just look at the great revolu-
tions of the past: If we'd known that the oil-based Industrial Revolution would have led to a century of wars to control oil and then to
catastrophic climate change, could we have changed course? If we'd
known that the corn-based agricultural revolution would spur obesity, could we have prevented the rise in obesity and its concomitant
diseases? If we'd known that the social media revolution would not
just give us pictures of grandchildren, but could also spew hate and
affect elections, would we have erected guardrails?

Being involved in over 2,000 births during my career as an
obstetrician taught me the importance of total trust between the
patient and the physician. Third-year students at every medical
school participate in a "white coat" ceremony symbolizing the trust
and faith that patients will confer on them when they don that coat.
Technology and administrative burdens have diluted that unique
doctor-patient relationship for a time, but because we put ethics
in at the beginning of this creative construction we have achieved
transformation, and trust is no longer a myth.

Take the Long Way Home (Supertramp)

We've come a "long way" to recognize that advancing technology alone will not transform healthcare and that reform also requires us to move to "healthcare at any address."

At the peak of the industry's consolidation into giant conglomerates of brick-and-mortar facilities, it suddenly became clear that this was not the wave of the future. In fact, it was the backwash of the past. Burdened by their high fixed costs, these dinosaurs could not keep up with the nimbler mammals that were eating their lunch, ranging from pharmacy retail clinics and urgent care centers to revolutionary start-ups creating new points of care. These new options stripped away some of the health systems' most lucrative business outside of acute care. Even within their traditional sphere, procedures were moving to outpatient clinics and ambulatory surgery centers that the hospitals didn't own. To top things off, it turned out that patients didn't love receiving their care in hospitals. This became stunningly obvious during the COVID-19 pandemic, when an increasing number of health systems began to provide hospital-at-home care with the support of telehealth and remote patient monitoring (RPM).

At some point, "healthcare at any address," once viewed as a wild fantasy, was embraced by most health systems. Realizing that if they wanted to stay within budget they had to provide care in the least costly settings, health systems started providing as much care as possible in people's homes. We saw sudden growth in telehealth visits for ambulatory care, in hospital at home, and in post-acute care that was provided at home rather than in rehab and skilled nursing facilities. Consumers with minor acute problems who had to be seen in person were encouraged to go to retail clinics and urgent care centers, which contracted with their basic care groups and were connected online to their personal physicians. We took the long way to home care, but we finally got there.

Invisible Connections (Vangelis)

Because of the new incentives to coordinate care, interoperability between disparate EHRs finally became a reality. Information blocking stopped when the government started fining providers and EHR vendors that engaged in this practice. Networks based on Fast Healthcare Interoperability Resources (FHIR) were designed to overcome the issues that caused semantic interoperability, and the Centers for Medicare & Medicaid Services (CMS) persuaded EHR suppliers to allow write-back from outside apps and systems by threatening to remove their product certification.

AI voice assistants were eventually replaced by virtual scribes that could handle most clinical documentation duties for doctors, and EHRs became much more accurate. This meant that AI algorithms now had the clean data they needed to be useful in many new ways.

The next step was to develop AI-assisted clinical decision support that was nearly always accurate. Only since the late 2020s has this proved feasible, and it's still a work in progress. But we've reached the point where a physician can see a patient and feel confident that most of the heavy lifting of diagnosis and treatment can be done in the background by algorithms that have the entire medical literature at their disposal and that know how similar patients with the same condition have been treated most successfully in the past.

Naturally, the physician insists on making the final decision, and sometimes the clinician looks at the evidence the algorithm has used to reach its conclusion. But with this tool, and thanks to our invisible connections, a physician can now spend most of the encounter finding out more about the patient and what matters most to that person.

Into the Groove (Madonna)

Older physicians are still having a hard time wrapping their heads around these new approaches, because it's so different from the way they practiced years ago. A good amount of new-style continuing medical education and on-the-job training was required to get them into the groove. But younger doctors who went to medical school in the late 2020s have had no difficulty adapting. Those clinicians learned from the start how to partner skillfully with the robots and algorithms designed to make their work easier. In addition, they were selected for their ability to communicate easily with patients and trained to improve that skill so they could elicit the underlying complaints and the obstacles encountered in self-care. This focus on personal communication and personalized health has resulted in improved health behavior, better drug selection and dosing, and more effective use of the health apps that now help patients manage their chronic conditions.

Patient data analysis is handled by algorithms that can learn and continuously improve. Their capabilities have improved to the point where doctors who usually follow the algorithm's recommendation are able to diagnose patients more accurately than physicians who usually ignore it. Of course, some patients are unusual, and some doctors have more diagnostic skill than others. But studies have shown that the machine-recommended diagnoses are mostly accurate. We expect to see a drop in wrong and missed diagnoses as more doctors learn to trust the algorithms. In ambulatory care, that will lead to improved patient safety and a decrease in malpractice suits.

Safety improvement in hospitals depends mainly on creating better systems, but AI could help here as well. Back in the 2010s, algorithms were already beginning to predict the onset of sepsis, for instance. Now we have many more and better predictive algorithms.

There's no question that physicians are delivering higher quality care in 2035, mainly because they're following evidence-based guidelines that reside in the AI cloud. Physicians still make the final decision, of course, and they can diverge from the recommendations when they know something unique about a patient. It was a bit of a struggle at first, but as physicians began taking risk and managing population health, they realized that evidence-based medicine wasn't just better care; it also saved money by reducing waste. One by one, they are getting into the groove.

Breaking Free (Zac Efron)

So how did we break free of the iron triangle of cost, access, and quality? In several ways. First, people are simply healthier, on average, and fewer of them end up in the ER or the hospital in 2035. That has led to lower spending. Rising longevity could raise long-term costs, but we don't think it will. People generally stay healthier longer, the yearslong slow decline seen in previous generations is becoming less common, and the final year of life involves radical communication between the patient and physician and is no longer a financial nightmare.

Second, continuous healthcare means that people are alerted when they have health problems and told what to do about them. If they're relatively healthy, this usually takes the form of automated alerts, online information, and robot "doctors" who advise them on preventive care. For people who have chronic diseases, there's more human intervention when their condition is exacerbated, along with online coaching. People with serious chronic illnesses receive periodic calls from nurse care managers who visit them at home if necessary. When their condition warrants it, patients can make an appointment with their doctor or be prompted to book one. This combination of online and human interventions reduces the number of visits required while supporting patients so they can avoid unnecessary trips to the hospital.

Third, the infrastructure of the healthcare system is less costly than it used to be. Much less care is provided in the most expensive care settings, such as hospitals and specialists' offices. Primary care physicians are the workhorses of the system, seeing patients for most nonemergent complaints and referring people to specialists only for problems that they can't handle. The specialists, who are selected by basic care groups for their quality and efficiency, provide appropriate care. Tests are performed only when indicated, and results are shared among all treating providers so they don't have to be repeated in the same time frame. Health assurance means breaking free of the old system to enjoy healthcare at any address.

Change the World (Eric Clapton)

In 2009, I had the opportunity to lead one of the first "digital health" conferences in the country with Apple Computer. All of us have had "aha" moments, and one of mine was the recognition that when industries go through more than incremental change, the black swans don't rely on 100-page strategic plans. When Steve Jobs recognized that the computer industry was getting stale and commoditized, his three- to five-year plan for Apple was simple: Year 1: We Change. Year 2: We Change the Industry. Year 3: We Change the World.

Have we solved all the problems of healthcare in America? Of course not. Our system still has shortcomings, and we could learn many things from other countries. Yet we have broken the back of the out-of-control spending that was bankrupting our country and making healthcare inaccessible for many people. Guided by the vision of our healthcare, technology, and government leaders, we'll continue to perfect the system we have and to integrate new technologies and possibilities as they come along.

And so I leave you with the core message of this book: To borrow words from Stevie Wonder's landmark album, songs are the key to life! Becoming a physician, delivering thousands of babies, and leading healthcare institutions and universities have defined my professional life. I am proud of the strategy, focus, and discipline that I learned through medical school, residency, and business school. But my love of music and the DJ world has added a whopping dose of creativity, passion, and flexibility, allowing me to reimagine an optimistic future in my personal life and in my professional dream of every American having an opportunity to thrive without healthcare or health getting in the way.

There's no better way to end this book than the words of fellow Philadelphians Daryl Hall and John Oates in their song "So Close."

So close, yet so far away
We believe in tomorrow, maybe more than today!

Index

AAFP. *See* American Academy of Family Physicians

AAMC. *See* Association of American Medical Colleges

ACA. *See* Affordable Care Act

Academic medical centers (AMCs), 159

Accenture, 55, 59

Accountability, reporting and, 243–44

Accountable care organizations (ACOs), 24, 38, 84–85, 136–37, 179

ACOs. *See* Accountable care organizations

Adair, Alex, 252

Administrative hospice, 279

Administrative streamlining, 29–30

Adult BMI (body mass index) and follow-up, 181

Advisory Board Company, 37

Aetna, 205

Affordable Care Act (ACA), 133, 135–36, 141, 143, 144, 155, 207, 208

African Americans: biases and abuses in clinical trials and healthcare, 213; cardiovascular disease among, 214; COVID-related deaths among, 212; diabetes among, 214; health disparities among, 212; hypertension among, 214; kidney failure among, 213–14

Agency for Healthcare Research and Quality (AHRQ), 212, 230, 232

AHRQ. *See* Agency for Healthcare Research and Quality

Airbnb, 1, 105, 123, 189

AirPod, 64

Akasa, 30

Alcohol use, 77, 185, 186, 197, 211

Alert fatigue, 249–50

Alexa, 65

Algorithms: inequities in development of, 66–67; supervised *vs.* unsupervised, 57–58

Alibaba, 258

Alignment Healthcare, 14

AliveCor, 50, 63, 64

Allen, Lily, 258

All.health, 65

All-payer rates, 137, 149, 150, 156–57

Allscripts, 89

AMA. *See* American Medical Association

Amazon, 1, 6, 8, 9, 14, 39, 64–65

Amazon Care, 14, 27, 176

Amazon Fresh, 206

Ambient computing, 90

Ambient intelligence, 54, 76, 94, 126

CMS (*continued*)
Initiative, 216–17; hospital price transparency rule, 138–39; incentives for moderating spending growth, 156; Maryland's rate-setting experiment and, 149–50, 151, 157; Medicare Advantage, 140; Medicare beneficiaries' social needs, 204; Medicare Shared Savings Program, 136–37, 140; nurse staffing regulations, 239; patient safety metrics since COVID-19, 233; peer review process, 237; Quality Payment Program, 135, 179–80; readmission penalties, 116, 136, 197–98, 231, 235; reimbursements for RPM, 47–48, 126; RTI International report, 151–52; Total Cost of Care Model, 153, 157

Cerner, 52, 87, 89

Cerrato, Paul, 50, 66–67

"Change" (Tracy Chapman), 222

Change Healthcare, 7–8, 170

"Changes" (David Bowie), 19

"Change the World" (Eric Clapton), 298–99

Chapman, Tracy, 222

CHEER Act, 143–49, 159, 160, 290; basic care groups, classification of, 146; claims processing simplified and subcontracted, 148–49; competition between provider groups, 145–46; independent physicians, 147–48; redefining insurance, 144–45

ChenMed, 14, 39, 104, 146

"Choice of Colors" (The Impressions (Curtis Mayfield)), xxiii, xxvi, xxxiii, 222

Christiana Care, 30

Chronic conditions, 7, 14, 23, 25, 26; among African Americans, 214, 296; behavior change for, 29, 185–86; managing through telehealth, 10, 210; outcome measures and, 170; quality scores/patient experience ratings and, 179–80; remote patient monitoring of, 46, 47–48, 51, 52–53, 59–60; social determinants of health and, 62–63

Chronic obstructive pulmonary disease. *See* COPD

CHTs. *See* Community health teams

Cigna, 9–10, 13, 48, 108

Clapton, Eric, 298–99

The Clash, 53

Cleveland Clinic, 28, 34, 46, 94

Clinical decision support (CDS), 91–96

Closed Claims Studies, 245

Clover Health, 14

CME. *See* Continuing medical education

CMS. *See* Centers for Medicare & Medicaid Services

Coca-Cola, xvi

Cohen, Ken, 277–78, 280, 283

Coldplay, 104

Cole, Keyshia, 61

Collateral Opportunities, 32

College of Health Information Management Executives (CHIME), 81–82

Comcast, 34

Common-sense safety practices, 234–35

Commonwealth Fund study, 190

CommonWell Health Alliance, 80

Community-based organizations (CBOs), 197–98, 201, 205, 208–9, 216

"Ironic" (Alanis Morissette), 95
Iron triangle, 135–36, 160, 297
Israel Center for Medical Simulation, 273
"It's All Wrong but It's Alright" (Percy Sledge), 169
"It's Impossible" (Perry Como), xli
"It's Time" (Imagine Dragons), 36
"I've Changed" (Jaheim, feat. Keyshia Cole), 61
"I Want to Take You Higher" (Sly and the Family Stone), 134

Jaheim, 61
Jamiroquai, xli
Jawbone, 65
JCPenney, 9, 39
JeffConnect, 139–40
Jefferson College of Population Health, 119, 198
Jefferson Health System, xv, xvii, xxii, xxv, xxvi, xxxvi, 1, 4–5, 18, 28, 37, 63–64, 105–6, 139, 175, 190–91, 195, 203, 219, 290; building, 107–11; "healthcare at any address" model, 7, 45, 60, 61, 104, 109, 111, 126, 211, 216, 220, 294, 298; health plan, 108–10; improving health equity, 110–11; shifting priorities at, 32–33
Jefferson Medical College, 106
Jefferson Onboarding and Leadership Transformation (JOLT), 278–80
Jeffrey, Thomas, 15
Jethro Tull, xxxiii, 84
Jobs, Steve, xviii–xix, 298
Joel, Billy, 139
Johns Hopkins University training model, 264–65
Johnson, David W., 153, 260, 264–65, 267, 275, 276, 277–78

Johnson, Jack, 93
The Joint Commission, 237, 242
JOLT. *See* Jefferson Onboarding and Leadership Transformation
Journey, 289
"Jump into the Fire" (Harry Nilsson), 41
Just culture, 236–38

Kaiser Family Foundation, 125
Kaiser Permanente, 16, 36, 47, 112, 142, 146, 205, 209
Kaiser Permanente Bernard J. Tyson School of Medicine, 267–70, 272, 273, 275, 285
"Keep the Customer Satisfied" (Simon & Garfunkel), 23
Kidney failure, 213–14
King, B.B., 208
King, Martin Luther, Jr., 5
The King Cole Trio, 257
KLAS Research, 81–82
Kvedar, Joseph, 48, 50, 53, 65–66

Laborist, 283
Labor-management relations, 240–42
Lady Gaga, 195, 222
Laguna Health, 125, 126
"Land of Confusion" (Genesis), 86
Lansky, David, 168, 171, 173, 174, 175, 177
Larsen, Eric, 37–38
Latinos. *See* Hispanics/Latinos
Lauper, Cyndi, 131, 160–61
Lavigne, Avril, 229, 252
Leapfrog Group, 230
"Learn to Listen" (Ramones), 252
Lehigh Valley Health Network, 112
"Let Her Go" (Passenger), 279
LifeXT, 28
Lipa, Dua, xl

About the Authors

STEPHEN K. KLASKO, MD, MBA

Dr. Klasko has been a university president, a dean, a CEO, and an obstetrician, and now pursues his vision for the creative reconstruction of American healthcare by bridging traditional academic centers with entrepreneurs and innovators. His passion is using technology to eliminate health disparities and offer everyone the promise of health assurance. Dr. Klasko is also a lifelong DJ who believes that the message in the music can give us the courage to tackle a broken, fragmented, unfriendly, expensive, and inequitable healthcare system.

He currently serves as an executive in residence at General Catalyst, as North American ambassador for Sheba Medical Center in Israel, and as CMO of Abundant Partners. He also serves on the board of directors at Teleflex, a global NYSE medical device company. In 2022, President Biden appointed him to the National Board of Education Sciences.

As president of Thomas Jefferson University and CEO of Jefferson Health from 2013 to 2021, he led one of the nation's fastest growing academic health institutions based on his vision of reimagining healthcare and higher education. Over the past few years, his track record of success has earned him *Modern Healthcare*'s #2 among the "100 Most Influential People in Healthcare," #21 in *Fast Company*'s "100 Most Creative People in Business," Ernst & Young's "Greater Philadelphia Entrepreneur of the Year," a consistent spot on the *Becker's Hospital Review* list of "100 Great Leaders in Healthcare," and a designation as a distinguished fellow of the World Economic Forum.

Dr. Klasko is internationally recognized as an advocate for transformation. His previous books are *UnHealthcare: A Manifesto for Health Assurance*, with Hemant Taneja; *Patient No Longer*, with Ryan Donahue; *Bless This Mess: A Picture Story of Healthcare in America*; and *We CAN Fix Healthcare* and *The Phantom Stethoscope*, both with Gregory P. Shea.

He is married to Colleen Wyse, a fashion leader and former ad director at *Vogue*, and has three children—Lynne, David, and Jill—as well as five perfect grandchildren!

KEN TERRY

Ken Terry has been writing about the healthcare field for 30 years and has won several journalism awards. He has also written four books: three about healthcare reform and one on population health management.

Praise for *Feelin' Alright*

Steve Klasko is one of the most remarkable leaders in healthcare and in general. He has the uncommon ability to combine a great vision, perspective, and intellectual power with great skills at building and executing the vision. Dr. Klasko sees across areas in a way that very few people can. He is incredible in his ability to see solutions and inspire and build teams to bring those solutions to the most complex of challenges. We highly recommend his latest book.

Scott Becker
Publisher and founder, Becker's Healthcare

You will read in this book that Steve shares the soul, the music, and the passion for making a change in people's lives; he does it from the healthcare side with a dash of music, and I do it from the music side, hopefully making people healthier and happier in the process.

Jerry Blavat, DJ
"The Geator with the Heater,"
"The Big Boss with the Hot Sauce"

As a fellow obstetrician, I can say definitively that Steve delivers with *Feelin' Alright*. Steve helps identify a path to deliver us, as he would say, from "the dirty not-so-secret secrets" of healthcare—the inequities, the misalignments, the waste, and the prosophobia. What makes this book uniquely Steve is a radical understanding of healthcare and the human experience that delivers a profound message while being insanely fun.

Rebekah Gee, MD
CEO of Nest Health

True to his reputation, Steve Klasko is once again raising our line of sight in *Feelin' Alright*, with a vision toward accelerating health equity. This inspiring sequel to *UnHealthcare: A Manifesto for Health Assurance* lyrically weaves a blueprint for the future of health with optimistic realism, laying out common-sense, practical strategies to improve lives. In humming along to *Feelin' Alright*, I couldn't help but think that it is time to transition from the Talking Heads to the Smiths—let's stop asking, "How did I get here?" and start asking, "How soon is now?"

Karen E. Knudsen, MBA, PhD
CEO of the American Cancer Society

Steve Klasko has done it again. He has harnessed his irrepressible energy and love of music to provide us with a healthcare road map to the future. The truth is, Steve is already in 2032 and has been there for a while. He is not just a futurist; he has been an inhabitant of the future and can therefore give us excellent advice about the directions for that road map so that we can successfully join him on the journey. To me, Steve is George Harrison circa 1975 belting out "Can't Stop Thinking About the Future." We should all be listening to the beat, stomping our feet, and clapping our hands as Steve Klasko once again leads us all to a more optimistic world. Count me in!

David Nash, MD
Founding dean, College of Population Health, Sidney Kimmel Medi-
cal College
Author of How Covid Crashed the System

Like Steve Jobs, Steve Klasko is a visionary—a health industry leader who believes in using smart teams, adaptable culture, flexibility, and creative problem solving to shift perceptions in and of the industry. *Feelin' Alright* explains how healthcare leaders can help create a consumer-centric healthcare experience focused on health assurance, allowing more people to enjoy healthy lives as they age.

John Sculley
Tech entrepreneur, former CEO of Apple

Steve Klasko's new book had me "feelin' all right" about the future of healthcare and is a must-read for anyone aspiring to a leadership role or desiring a road map for the necessary changes that must occur to have an equitable, sustainable system of health. He is, in the words of Elvis Costello, "a man on a mission in two or three editions," as this is a great sequel to his other books, including *UnHealthcare: A Manifesto for Health Assurance.* Thank you, Steve, as you (and Fleetwood Mac) "don't stop thinking about tomorrow."

Lee Shapiro
7wireVentures